Social Studies Excursions, K-3

Book Two: Powerful Units on Communication, Transportation, and Family Living

JANET ALLEMAN AND JERE BROPHY

With Contributions by Barbara Knighton

HEINEMANN
Portsmouth, NH

Heinemann
A division of Reed Elsevier Inc.
361 Hanover Street
Portsmouth, NH 03801–3912
www.heinemann.com

Offices and agents throughout the world

Library of Congress Cataloging-in-Publication Data
Alleman, Janet.
     Social studies excursions, K–3 / Janet Alleman and Jere Brophy with contributions by Barbara Knighton.
          p.   cm.
     Includes bibliography references.
     Contents: Bk. 2. Powerful units on communication, transportation, and family living.
     Book 1: ISBN 0-325-00315-7 (pbk.)
     Book 2: ISBN 0-325-00316-5 (pbk.)
     1. Social sciences—Study and teaching (Primary). I. Brophy, Jere E.
  II. Knighton, Barbara. III. Title.

LB1530 .A44 2001
372.83'044—dc21   00-054121

Editors: William Varner and Danny Miller
Production: Lynne Reed
Cover Design: Darci Mehall, Aureo Design
Cover Illustrations: Mark E. Speier and Nate Fowler
Typesetter: Drawing Board Studios
Manufacturing: Steve Bernier

Printed in the United States of America on acid-free paper
06   05   04   03   02   VP   1   2   3   4   5

We dedicate this volume to June Benson, who for many years now has contributed immeasurably to our work by providing us with fast and accurate tape transcriptions, reliable text processing, and many other forms of assisstance with our professional activities. Thank you, June, for all you have done for us.

Contents

. . . .

Contents

Series Preface

. . . .

This series contains three volumes, each of which includes detailed plans for social studies units intended for
use in the primary grades. The unit plans provide a substantive content
base and learning and assessment activities designed to help primary-
grade teachers provide their students with a powerful introduction to
social education. Like the major primary-grade social studies textbook
series, these units focus on cultural universals—basic human needs and
social experiences found in all societies, past and present (food, clothing,
shelter, family living, communication, transportation, government,
money, and childhood). However, unlike the units found in the major
textbook series, the units in this series are structured around powerful
ideas and designed to develop those ideas in depth and with attention to
their applications to life outside of school. Consequently, they are suitable
for use as substitutes for, or elaborations of, material on the same topics
found in the textbook series.

Such elaboration is needed because the textbooks produced for use in
the early grades are primarily picture books that do not provide sufficient
content to support a powerful social studies program. Concerning transportation, for example, textbooks typically include just a few pages on the
topic in units on neighborhoods or communities. A few pages on the
manufacture of a school bus might be located within a unit on work in
the community, or a few pages describing and illustrating transportation
types might be found in a unit on communities around the world. Or, the
topics of transportation and communication might be combined within a
few pages describing how technological innovations in these areas have
changed the world and brought people closer.

These short textbook segments often contain good pictures but usually do not explain how different forms of transportation were developed and why different forms are used even today in different parts of the world. Furthermore, the manuals that accompany the texts do not provide guidance to teachers about how they might develop such understandings with their students.

In contrast, our transportation unit explores multiple facets of this cultural universal in depth, including consideration of geographic, economic, and cultural factors that led various past and present societies to develop their characteristic transportation modes. Students emerge from the unit with connected understanding about how and why humans in different times and places developed contrasting responses to their transportation needs, along with enhanced knowledge about cultural, economic, ecological, and technological aspects of transportation in today's world.

The series has been developed primarily for preservice and inservice primary-grade teachers who want a more substantive and powerful social studies program than the major textbook series can support. Each volume contains plans for three instructional units intended to support instruction for forty to sixty minutes per day for three to four weeks. Units are divided into lessons that elaborate the content base in detail and include plans for suggested learning activities, assessment tasks, and follow-up home assignments. The home assignments are not conventional worksheets but instead are activities calling for students and their parents to engage in conversations or other enjoyable activities connected to the unit topic. Along with the unit plans as such, each volume includes information about how and why the units were developed, suggestions about how teachers might adapt them to their students and local communities, and tips about planning and implementing the units from the authors and from Barbara Knighton, the teacher who has had the most experience teaching the units to her students.

Besides teachers who will use the units directly with their own students in their own classrooms, the volumes in this series should be useful to several other audiences. State- and district-level staff developers and social studies curriculum coordinators should find the volumes useful as bases for workshops and presentations on making primary-grade social studies more powerful and more in line with national and state standards. Each unit develops a network of powerful ideas (basic social understandings) about the topic and provides opportunities for students to apply these ideas in their lives outside of school. The instructional content and processes reflect the guidelines of the National Council for the Social Studies and related professional organizations.

Finally, the volumes should be useful to professors and others conducting preservice and inservice teacher education relating to social studies in the primary grades. Using materials from this series, instructors can show teachers how the cultural universals addressed in the early social studies curriculum can be developed with a focus on powerful ideas and their applications, so as to create a social studies program that reflects reform standards. Also, by assigning preservice teachers to teach one or more lessons from these units, instructors can provide opportunities for their students to experience what it is like to develop big ideas in depth and to begin to build habits of good professional practice.

Since the 1930s, there has been widespread agreement among primary-grade curriculum makers and teachers that cultural universals are appropriate topics for introducing students to social studies concepts and principles. Given this "wisdom of practice," we believe that instructors will find that the approach taken in this series (i.e., retaining the cultural universals as unit topics but developing them much more coherently and powerfully) makes more sense as a response to criticisms of the contemporary primary-grade social studies textbooks than commonly suggested alternatives that call for shifting to something else entirely (e.g., a primary focus on history or on social issues). We elaborate this point at the end of the first chapter in each volume.

Acknowledgments

The units presented in this series could not have been developed without the assistance of a great many people. Most prominent among them is Barbara Knighton, the teacher who first makes our unit plans come to life in her classroom and provides us with many suggestions for improving them. We also wish to acknowledge and thank Gina Henig, Barbara's colleague, who also has provided us with useful feedback and suggestions; the principal, parents, and students associated with the school at which Barbara teaches; Carolyn O'Mahony and Tracy Reynolds, who interviewed students before and after they experienced the units; and June Benson, who transcribed the audiotapes of the class sessions and the interviews. We also wish to acknowledge and thank the College of Education at Michigan State University for its support of the research and development that led to these units and the Spencer Foundation for its support of a related line of research on what K–3 students know (or think they know) about topics commonly addressed in early elementary social studies.

1

Background
How and Why We Developed the Units

This is the second in a series of three volumes in which we present plans for instructional units on cultural universals—basic human needs and social experiences found in all societies, past and present—designed to be taught in the primary grades (K–3). The units primarily reflect the purposes and goals of social studies, but they do include some science content. They also integrate language arts by including writing assignments and reading and discussion of children's literature. The units may be used as supplements to (or substitutes for) the primary-grade textbooks in the major elementary social studies series.

This second volume includes plans for units on communication, transportation, and family living. Volume 1 contains plans for units on food, clothing, and shelter. Volume 3 will contain plans for units on government, economics/money, and childhood throughout history and across cultures. Each unit has been developed to stand on its own as an independent module, so there is no inherent order in which they need to be taught.

The units have been taught successfully to first and second graders, and they can be adapted for use in kindergarten and third grade. This is because all students, even kindergarteners, have had a variety of personal experiences with cultural universals and are ready to learn more. At the same time, however, what primary-grade students know (or think they know) about these topics is spotty, mostly tacit, and frequently distorted by misconceptions, so even third graders can benefit from opportunities to learn most of what is included in these units. In schools where the complete set of units is taught, the primary-grade teachers will need to coordinate their planning to determine which units will be taught at which grade level.

The Need for a Powerful Content Base in Early Social Studies

In most American elementary schools, the primary-grade social studies curriculum addresses three major goals: (1) socializing students concerning prosocial attitudes and behavior as members of the classroom community, (2) introducing them to map concepts and skills, and (3) introducing them to basic social knowledge drawn mostly from history, geography, and the social sciences. Even though all three of these instructional goals and related content emphases are featured in state and district curriculum guides for elementary social studies, they are not equally well addressed in the resource materials commonly made available to elementary teachers. The major textbook series generally do a good job of providing appropriate content and learning activities for developing students' map concepts and skills. They are more variable in what they offer as a basis for socializing students as citizens of the classroom community (and subsequently, successively broader communities).

A good selection of ancillary resources is available to support primary-grade teachers' planning of experiences designed to help their students learn to interact respectfully, collaborate in learning efforts, resolve conflicts productively, and in general, display prosocial attitudes and democratic values in their behavior as members of the classroom community. Unfortunately, good instructional resources are not readily available to support primary-grade teachers' efforts to help their students develop basic knowledge about society and the human condition. There is widespread agreement among critics of the major elementary social studies series that the content presented in their primary-grade texts is thin, trite, and otherwise inadequate as a foundation for developing basic social understandings. (These criticisms are reviewed in detail in Brophy & Alleman, 1996, and in Larkins, Hawkins, & Gilmore, 1987).

The social studies curriculum for the elementary grades is usually organized within the expanding communities sequence that begins with a focus on the self in kindergarten and gradually expands to address families in Grade 1, neighborhoods in Grade 2, communities in Grade 3, states and geographic regions in Grade 4, the United States in Grade 5, and the world in Grade 6. However, the categories in the expanding communities sequence refer primarily to the levels of analysis at which content is addressed, not to the content itself. That is, although there is some material on families in first grade, on neighborhoods in second grade, and on communities in third grade, the topics of most instructional units are the human social activities that are carried on within families, neighborhoods, and communities. These activities tend to be structured around cultural universals (food, clothing, shelter, communication, transportation, government, etc.).

Despite problems with the textbook series, we believe that the cultural universals traditionally addressed in the primary grades provide a sound basis for developing fundamental social understandings. First, they are basic to the human condition. Human activities relating to these cultural universals account for a considerable proportion of everyday life and are the focus of much of our social organization and communal activity. Furthermore, children begin accumulating direct personal experiences with most cultural universals right from birth, so that by the time they begin school, they have developed considerable funds of knowledge and experience that they can draw upon in constructing understandings of social education concepts and principles.

If cultural universals are taught with appropriate focus on powerful ideas and their potential life applications, students should develop basic sets of connected understandings about how the social system works, how and why it got to be that way over time, how and why it varies across locations and cultures, and what all of this might mean for personal, social, and civic decision making. The units in this series provide a content base capable of supporting this kind of powerful social studies teaching.

As we've noted, such a content base is needed because it is not provided in the major publishers' elementary social studies textbook series. The primary-grade texts in these series (especially the K–2 texts) are better described as picture books than textbooks. Their pages often contain rich collages of color photos relating to the unit topic, but these photos are accompanied by little or no text—a sentence or two at most. The photos are potentially useful as instructional resources if students are induced to process them with reference to powerful ideas, but the texts typically do not convey such ideas to students. Nor do the accompanying manuals convey them to teachers or provide guidance concerning how the photos might be used as bases for powerful social studies teaching.

For example, a lesson on communication might contain several collages of photos showing a variety of ways that people communicate (e.g., talking, drawing, writing). However, the text on these pages might do little or nothing more than name these modes of communication and state that people today have many more ways to communicate than people in the past. Students will not learn much from exposure to such collages unless they are helped to process what they are seeing with reference to powerful ideas (in this case, ideas that will help them understand how various communication methods have evolved over time from grunting, wall paintings, and smoke signals, to electronic media). For example, with the use of a time line, students might learn that communication long, long ago was limited to primitive forms of language and art, and as a result, only very limited records remain that allow us to know something about early cultures. As time passed, however, people began developing languages with larger vocabularies and pictographic forms of writing. Still later, the invention of written language led to printing and books, and the invention of electronics led to telephones, radio, television, and computer networks. People could communicate across distances more and more quickly (culminating in today's real-time conversations), and related technology made it possible to preserve certain communications much more completely and accurately. With exposure to ideas such as these, students can begin to appreciate photo collages on communication as illustrations of developments over time in responses to humans' need to acquire information and interact with one another. In contrast, students exposed only to the collages and limited narrative are likely to develop only superficial understandings of communication modes and to view some of the modes used in the past merely as primitive instead of appreciating them as ingenious inventions for their times.

Teaching Cultural Universals for Understanding, Appreciation, and Life Application

Our development of instructional units on cultural universals has been guided by several sets of principles. One set reflects an emerging consensus about what is involved in teaching school subjects for understanding, appreciation, and life application. Reviews of research on such teaching (e.g., Good & Brophy, 2000) suggest that it reflects the following ten principles:

1. The curriculum is designed to equip students with knowledge, skills, values, and dispositions that they will find useful both inside and outside of school.
2. Instructional goals emphasize developing student expertise within an application context and with emphasis on conceptual understanding of knowledge and self-regulated application of skills.
3. The curriculum balances breadth with depth by addressing limited content but developing this content sufficiently to foster conceptual understanding.
4. The content is organized around a limited set of powerful ideas (basic understandings and principles).
5. The teacher's role is not just to present information but also to scaffold and respond to students' learning efforts.

6. The students' role is not just to absorb or copy input but also to actively make sense and construct meaning.

7. Students' prior knowledge about the topic is elicited and used as a starting place for instruction, which builds on accurate prior knowledge but also stimulates conceptual change if necessary.

8. Activities and assignments feature tasks that call for critical thinking or problem solving, not just memory or reproduction.

9. Higher-order thinking skills are not taught as a separate skills curriculum. Instead, they are developed in the process of teaching subject-matter knowledge within application contexts that call for students to relate what they are learning to their lives outside of school by thinking critically or creatively about it or by using it to solve problems or make decisions.

10. The teacher creates a social environment in the classroom that could be described as a learning community featuring discourse or dialogue designed to promote understanding.

These principles emphasize focusing instruction on big ideas that are developed in depth and with attention to their applications. In identifying big ideas to feature in our units, we sought an appropriate balance among the three traditional sources of curriculum: (1) knowledge of enduring value (including but not limited to disciplinary knowledge), (2) the students (their needs, interests, and current readiness), and (3) the needs of society (the knowledge, skills, values, and dispositions that our society would like to see developed in future generations of its citizens).

Teaching for Conceptual Change

Related principles come from research on teaching for conceptual change. Students' prior knowledge about topics sometimes includes naive ideas or even outright misconceptions that can cause the students to ignore, distort, or miss the implications of new information that conflicts with their existing ideas. Teachers who are aware of common misconceptions can plan instruction to address these directly. This involves helping students to recognize differences between their current beliefs and the target understandings, and to see the need to shift from the former to the latter. Such instruction is often called *conceptual change teaching*.

Kathleen Roth (1996) developed an approach to conceptual change teaching that she applied to science and social studies. She embedded the conceptual change emphasis within a more comprehensive "learning community" model of teaching school subjects for understanding. This approach emphasizes eliciting valid prior knowledge that instruction can connect with and build upon, not just identifying misconceptions that will need to be addressed. Our instructional units have been designed accordingly.

These efforts also were informed by a series of studies that we have conducted on K–3 students' knowledge and thinking about cultural universals. These studies yielded a great deal of information about accurate prior knowledge that most students are likely to possess as they begin each unit, as well as about important knowledge gaps and common naive ideas or misconceptions that will need to be addressed during the instruction. These findings are noteworthy because some proponents of alternative curricula have claimed that there is no need to teach about cultural universals in the primary grades because children learn all that they need to know about them through everyday experiences. This claim was made in the absence of relevant research. Our studies speak directly to this issue.

We have found that the knowledge about cultural universals that children accumulate through everyday experiences is limited, disconnected, and mostly tacit rather than well articulated. Also, it frequently is distorted by naive ideas or outright misconceptions. We do not find this surprising, because most of children's experiences relating to cultural universals are informal and do not include sustained discourse structured around key ideas. In any case, it is now clear that primary-grade students stand to benefit from systematic instruction about these topics. A summary of our key findings concerning each of the cultural universals is included in the introduction to its corresponding instructional unit.

NCSS Standards

Our unit development efforts also were informed by two definitive standards statements released by the National Council for the Social Studies (NCSS) during the 1990s: one on curriculum standards and one on powerful teaching and learning. The curriculum standards are built around ten themes that form a framework for social studies (see Figure 1). The publication that spells out these standards elaborates on each theme in separate chapters for the early grades, the middle grades, and the secondary grades, listing performance expectations and potential classroom activities that might be used to develop the theme (National Council for the Social Studies, 1994). The NCSS subsequently sponsored publication of a collection of readings illustrating how the ten themes might be addressed in elementary social studies teaching (Haas & Laughlin, 1997) and a survey of children's literature published in the 1990s that relates to these themes (Krey, 1998).

Along with its curriculum standards, the NCSS released a position statement identifying five key features of powerful social studies teaching and learning (see Figure 2). The publication that elaborates on these five key features frames them by stating that social studies teaching is viewed as powerful when it helps students develop social understanding and civic efficacy (National Council for the Social Studies, 1993). Social understanding is

Ten themes serve as organizing strands for the social studies curriculum at every school level (early, middle, and high school); they are interrelated and draw from all of the social science disciplines and other related disciplines and fields of scholarly study to build a framework for social studies curriculum.

I. Culture

Human beings create, learn, and adapt culture. Human cultures are dynamic systems of beliefs, values, and traditions that exhibit both commonalities and differences. Understanding culture helps us understand ourselves and others.

II. Time, Continuity, and Change

Human beings seek to understand their historic roots and to locate themselves in time. Such understanding involves knowing what things were like in the past and how things change and develop—allowing us to develop historic perspective and answer important questions about our current condition.

III. People, Places, and Environment

Technical advancements have ensured that students are aware of the world beyond their personal locations. As students study content related to this theme, they create their spatial views and geographical perspectives of the world; social, cultural, economic, and civic demands mean that students will need such knowledge, skills, and understandings to make informed and critical decisions about the relationship between human beings and their environment.

IV. Individual Development and Identity

Personal identity is shaped by one's culture, by groups, and by institutional influences. Examination of various forms of human behavior enhances understandings of the relationship between social norms and emerging personal identities, the social processes that influence identity formation, and the ethical principles underlying individual action.

V. Individuals, Groups, and Institutions

Institutions exert enormous influence over us. Institutions are organizational embodiments to further the core social values of those who comprise them. It is important for students to know how institutions are formed, what controls and influences them, how they control and influence individuals and culture, and how institutions can be maintained or changed.

VI. Power, Authority, and Governance

Understanding of the historic development of structures of power, authority, and governance and their evolving functions in contemporary society is essential for emergence of civic competence.

VII. Production, Distribution, and Consumption

Decisions about exchange, trade, and economic policy and well-being are global in scope, and the role of government in policy making varies over time and from place to place. The systematic study of an interdependent world economy and the role of technology in economic decision making is essential.

VIII. Science, Technology, and Society

Technology is as old as the first crude tool invented by prehistoric humans, and modern life as we know it would be impossible without technology and the science that supports it. Today's technology forms the basis for some of our most difficult social choices.

IX. Global Connections

The realities of global interdependence require understanding of the increasingly important and diverse global connections among world societies before there can be analysis leading to the development of possible solutions to persisting and emerging global issues.

X. Civic Ideals and Practices

All people have a stake in examining civic ideals and practices across time, in diverse societies, as well as in determining how to close the gap between present practices and the ideals upon which our democracy is based. An understanding of civic ideals and practices of citizenship is critical to full participation in society.

Source: National Council for the Social Studies. (1994). *Curriculum Standards for Social Studies: Expectations of Excellence* (Bulletin No. 89). Washington, DC: Author.

FIGURE 1   Ten Thematic Strands

Meaningful

The content selected for emphasis is worth learning because it promotes progress toward important social understanding and civic efficacy goals, and it is taught in ways that help students to see how it is related to these goals. As a result, students' learning efforts are motivated by appreciation and interest, not just by accountability and grading systems. Instruction emphasizes depth of development of important ideas within appropriate breadth of content coverage.

Integrative

Powerful social studies cuts across discipline boundaries, spans time and space, and integrates knowledge, beliefs, values, and dispositions to action. It also provides opportunities for students to connect to the arts and sciences through inquiry and reflection.

Value-Based

Powerful social studies teaching considers the ethical dimensions of topics, so that it provides an arena for reflective development of concern for the common good and application of social values. The teacher includes diverse points of view, demonstrates respect for well-supported positions, and shows sensitivity and commitment to social responsibility and action.

Challenging

Students are encouraged to function as a learning community, using reflective discussion to work collaboratively to deepen understandings of the meanings and implications of content. They also are expected to come to grips with controversial issues, to participate assertively but respectfully in group discussions, and to work productively with peers in cooperative learning activities.

Active

Powerful social studies is rewarding but demanding. It demands thoughtful preparation and instruction by the teacher, and sustained effort by the students to make sense of and apply what they are learning. Teachers do not mechanically follow rigid guidelines in planning, implementing, and assessing instruction. Instead, they work with the national standards and with state and local guidelines, adapting and supplementing these guidelines and their instructional materials in ways that support their students' social education needs.

The teacher uses a variety of instructional materials, plans field trips and visits by resource people, develops current or local examples to relate to students' lives, plans reflective discussions, and scaffolds students' work in ways that encourage them to gradually take on more responsibility for managing their own learning independently and with their peers. Accountability and grading systems are compatible with these goals and methods.

Students develop new understandings through a process of active construction. They develop a network of connections that link the new content to preexisting knowledge and beliefs anchored in their prior experience. The construction of meaning required to develop important social understanding takes time and is facilitated by interactive discourse. Clear explanations and modeling from the teacher are important, but so are opportunities to answer questions, discuss or debate the meaning and implications of content, or use the content in activities that call for tackling problems or making decisions.

Source: National Council for the Social Studies. (1993). A Vision of Powerful Teaching and Learning in the Social Studies: Building Social Understanding and Civic Efficacy. *Social Education*, 57, 213–223.

FIGURE 2   Five Key Features of Powerful Social Studies Learning

integrated knowledge of the social aspects of the human condition: how these aspects have evolved over time, the variations that occur in different physical environments and cultural settings, and emerging trends that appear likely to shape the future. Civic efficacy is readiness and willingness to assume citizenship responsibilities. It is rooted in social studies knowledge and skills, along with related values (such as concern for the common good) and dispositions (such as an orientation toward confident participation in civic affairs).

Along with publishing the statement on powerful teaching, the NCSS has made available a multimedia teacher education resource. It is a professional development program that includes print materials and videotapes for use by district-level staff developers working with teachers to revitalize local social studies programs (Harris & Yocum, 1999).

In developing our units, we did not begin with these NCSS standards. Instead, we began with lists of powerful ideas that might anchor networks of social knowledge about the cultural universal under study. As unit development proceeded, however, we used the NCSS content and teaching standards as guidelines for assessing the degree to which the unit was sufficiently complete and well balanced. No individual lesson includes all of the ten content themes and the five features of powerful teaching, but all of these content and process standards are well represented in the plans for the unit as a whole.

We have found that units planned to develop connected understandings of powerful ideas consistently meet the NCSS standards (as well as state standards). Our units include embedded strands that address history, geography, economics, culture, government, and decision making. However, the units were developed as pandisciplinary (or perhaps we should say, predisciplinary), integrated treatments of the topic, not as collections of lessons organized around the academic disciplines treated separately.

Key Characteristics of the Units

In summary, we emphasize teaching for understanding (and where necessary, conceptual change) by building on students' prior knowledge and developing key ideas in depth and with attention to their applications to life outside of school. The unit plans provide a basis for three to four weeks of instruction, depending on the topic and the degree to which the teacher includes optional extensions. All of the units feature six common components:

1. The units begin with focus on the cultural universal as experienced in contemporary American society, especially in the students' homes and neighborhoods (this includes eliciting students' prior knowledge and helping them to articulate this mostly tacit knowledge more

9

clearly). Early lessons use familiar examples to help students develop understanding of how and why the contemporary social system functions as it does with respect to the cultural universal being studied.

2. The units consider how the technology associated with the cultural universal has evolved over time. Lessons on this historical dimension illustrate how human responses to the cultural universal have been influenced by inventions and other cultural advances.

3. The units address variation in today's world in the ways that the cultural universal is experienced in different places and societies. Along with the historical dimension, this geographical/cultural dimension of the unit extends students' concepts to include examples different from the ones they view as prototypical. This helps them to place themselves and their familiar social environments into perspective as parts of the larger human condition (as it has evolved through time and as it varies across cultures). In the language of anthropologists, these unit components "make the strange familiar" and "make the familiar strange" as a way to broaden students' perspectives.

4. The units include physical examples, classroom visitors, field trips, and especially, children's literature selections (both fiction and non-fiction) as input sources.

5. The units include home assignments that call for students to interact with parents and other family members in ways that not only build curriculum-related insights but engage the participants in enjoyable and affectively bonding activities.

6. The units engage students in thinking about the implications of all of this for personal, social, and civic decision making in the present and future, in ways that support their self-efficacy perceptions with respect to their handling of the cultural universal throughout their lives. Many lessons raise students' consciousness of the fact that they will be making choices (both as individuals and as citizens) relating to the cultural universal under study. Many of the home assignments engage students in decision-making discussions with other family members. These discussions (and later ones that they often spawn) enable the students to see that they can affect others' thinking and have input into family decisions.

Our units address many of the same topics traditionally taught as part of the expanding communities curriculum. However, they are designed to be far more powerful than the ostensibly similar units found in contemporary textbooks. They focus on the elementary and familiar in that they address fundamental aspects of the human condition and connect with experience-based tacit knowledge that students already possess. However, they do not merely reaffirm what students already know. Instead, they help students to construct articulated knowledge about aspects of the cultural universal that they have only vague and tacit knowledge about now. They also introduce students to a great deal of new information, develop connections to help them transform scattered items of information into a network of integrated knowledge, and stimulate them to apply this knowledge to their lives outside of school. For more information about the rationale underlying the units, see Brophy and Alleman (1996).

Developing the Unit Plans

In developing unit plans, we began by generating a list of big ideas about the cultural universal that might become the major understandings around which to structure the unit. The initial list was developed from three major sources: (1) social studies education textbooks written for teachers, standards statements from NCSS and other social studies–related professional organizations, and the writings of opinion leaders and organizations concerned with education in history, geography, and the social sciences; (2) ideas conveyed about the cultural universal in elementary social studies texts and in fictional and nonfictional literature sources written for children; and (3) our own ideas about which aspects of the cultural universal are basic understandings that students could use to make sense of their social lives. As we developed and discussed this basic list of key ideas, we revised it several times. In the process, we added some new ideas, rephrased existing ones, combined those that appear to go together, and sequenced them in a way that made sense as a list of lesson topics for the unit.

Once we were satisfied with the listing and sequencing of big ideas, we began drafting lesson plans. We elaborated the big ideas in considerable detail and considered ways in which they might be applied during in-class activities and follow-up home assignments. We also shared tentative plans with Barbara Knighton and other collaborating teachers. Barbara critiqued what was included and contributed specific teaching suggestions, such as identifying places where she might bring in some personal possession to use as a prop, read a children's literature selection that we had not considered, or add a learning activity.

Sequencing the Lessons

Typically, a unit begins with consideration of the cultural universal as it is experienced in the contemporary United States, and especially in the homes and neighborhoods of the students to be taught. Subsequent lessons bring in the historical dimension by considering how human response to the cultural universal has evolved through time. Later lessons bring in the geographical, cultural, and economic dimensions by considering how human response to the cultural universal has varied in the past and still varies today according to local resources and other aspects of location and culture. Still later lessons bring in the personal and civic efficacy dimensions by involving students in activities calling for them to consider their current and future decision making with respect to the cultural universal and to address some of the social and civic issues associated with it. Finally, a review lesson is developed as a conclusion to the unit.

Looking across the unit as a whole, the sequence of instruction:

1. Begins by building on students' existing knowledge, deepening it, and making it better articulated and connected (to solidify a common base of valid prior knowledge as a starting point).
2. Broadens their knowledge about how the cultural universal is addressed in the context most familiar to them (contemporary American society).
3. Extends their knowledge to the past and to other cultures.
4. Provides opportunities to apply what they are learning to present and future decision making as individuals and as citizens.
5. Concludes with a review.

Our Approach Compared to Alternatives

We have noted that our response to the widely recognized content problem in primary-grade social studies is to retain cultural universals as the unit topics but develop these topics much more thoroughly than they are developed in the textbook series, and with better focus on big ideas. Others have suggested different responses. We briefly mention the major alternative suggestions here, both to explain why we do not endorse them and to further explain our own position.

Cultural Literacy/Core Knowledge

E. D. Hirsch, Jr. (1988) proposed cultural literacy as the basis for curriculum development. He produced a list of more than five thousand items of knowledge that he believed should be acquired in elementary school as a way to equip students with a common base of cultural knowledge to inform their social and civic decision making. We agree with Hirsch that a shared common culture is needed, but we question the value of much of what he included on his list of ostensibly important knowledge. Furthermore, because it is a long list of specifics, it leads to teaching that emphasizes breadth of coverage of disconnected details over depth of development of connected knowledge structured around powerful ideas.

Subsequently, educators inspired by Hirsch's book have used it as a basis for developing the CORE Curriculum, which encompasses science, social studies, and the arts. The social studies strands are built around chronologically organized historical studies, with accompanying geographical and cultural studies. First graders study ancient Egypt and the early American civilizations (Mayas, Incas, Aztecs). Second graders study ancient India, China, and Greece, along with American history up to the Civil War. Third graders study ancient Rome and Byzantium, various Native American tribal groups, and the thirteen English colonies prior to the American Revolution. Because it is divided by grade levels and organized into World Civilization, American Civilization, and Geography strands, the CORE Curriculum is a considerable improvement over Hirsch's list of assorted knowledge items as a basis for social studies curriculum in the primary grades. However, it focuses on the distant past. We think that cultural universals have more to offer than historical chronicity as a basis for introducing students to the social world. Also, we believe that an approach that begins with what is familiar to the students in their immediate environments and then moves to the past, to other cultures, and to consideration of the future constitutes a better-rounded and more powerful social education than an exclusive focus on the past that is inherently limited in its applicability to students' lives outside of school.

History/Literature Focus

Kieran Egan (1988), Diane Ravitch (1987), and others have advocated replacing topical teaching about cultural universals with a heavy focus on history and related children's literature (not only historical fiction but myths and folktales). We agree with them that primary-grade students can and should learn certain aspects of history, but we also believe that these students need a balanced and integrated social studies curriculum that includes sufficient attention to powerful ideas drawn from geography and the social sciences. Furthermore, we see little social education value in replacing reality-based social studies with myths and folklore likely to create misconceptions, especially during the primary years when children are struggling to determine what is real and enduring (vs. false/fictional or transitory/accidental) in their physical and social worlds. Thus, although fanciful children's literature may be studied profitably as fiction within the language arts curriculum, it is no substitute for a reality-based social studies curriculum.

Issues Analysis

Many social educators believe that debating social and civic issues is the most direct way to develop dispositions toward critical thinking and reflective decision making in our citizens (Evans & Saxe, 1996). Some of them have suggested that primary-grade social studies should deemphasize providing students with information and instead engage them in inquiry and debate about social policy issues. We agree that reflective discussion of social issues and related decision-making opportunities should be emphasized in teaching social studies at all grade levels. However, we also believe that a heavy concentration on inquiry and debate about social policy issues is premature for primary-grade students whose prior knowledge and experience relating to the issues are quite limited.

In this first chapter we have presented the rationale for our approach to primary-grade social studies, identified six key components that are common to all of our units, and described how we develop the units and assess their effectiveness through classroom tryouts. In Chapter 2 we will share experienced-based suggestions about how to prepare to teach the units and bring them to life in your classroom.

2

Implementation
Preparing for and Teaching the Units

Preparing to Teach the Units

Based on our experiences with Barbara Knighton and other teachers, we suggest the following as steps that you might take in planning to incorporate our units into your curriculum. (Barbara also has some tips to pass along, which she does in the introductions to each unit and each subsequent lesson.)

Initial Planning and Scheduling

We suggest that you begin by reading through the unit several times to familiarize yourself with its goals, resources, content, and activities. Then begin making plans for how to fit the unit into your schedule; how to gather the needed instructional resources and arrange for potential classroom visitors or field trips; and how to adapt the unit to your grade level, your students' home cultures, and your local community.

We have organized each unit as a series of "lessons," but you should expect considerable variation in the time needed to complete these lessons. The content and activities that we have included within a given lesson are grouped together because they develop a common set of connected big ideas, not because they are expected to take a particular amount of time to complete. Some lessons may require two or three class sessions (or more, if your sessions are very short).

To maximize the coherence of the units, we recommend that they be taught forty to sixty minutes each day, five days per week, for three to four weeks. This probably exceeds the amount of time that you ordinarily allocate to social studies as a daily average, although you probably allocate at least that much time to science and social studies combined. If you are not doing so already, we recommend that you adopt a practice followed by Barbara and many other primary-grade teachers: Instead of teaching both science and social studies each day for twenty to thirty minutes, alternate these subjects so that you teach only social studies for three to four weeks for forty to sixty minutes per day, then shift to science for the next three to four weeks for forty to sixty minutes per day. This will simplify your instructional planning and classroom management, as well as make it possible for you to provide your students with more sustained and coherent instruction in both subjects.

Adapt Plans to Your Students

You should also consider whether the plans might need to be adapted to suit your grade level. If you teach in kindergarten or first grade, you may want to omit or plan substitutes for certain activities, especially those that call for writing. (Alternatively, you could provide extra support for your students' writing, such as by posting words that they are likely to want to use but not know how to spell.) If you teach second or third grade, you may want to plan some application activities that go beyond those currently included in the unit. You are in the best position to judge what to teach your students about the topic and how they might best apply what they are learning in and out of school. However, in making any changes or additions to the unit plans, keep the major goals and big ideas in mind.

Think about ways to adapt or enhance the unit to connect it to your students' home cultures and to resources in your local area. Do some of your students' parents work in occupations related to the cultural universal? If so, this might provide opportunities for fruitful classroom visits (by the parents) or field trips (to their work places). Do some of your students come from cultures that feature traditional artifacts related to the cultural universal (materials written in a variety of languages, items used in family celebrations, and so on)? If so, these students or their parents might be invited to bring the items to class and explain them. Are there stores, factories, museums, government offices, historical landmarks, and so forth located in your area that relate to the cultural universal? If so, you might exploit these potential instructional resources by obtaining information or materials from them, by arranging for people who work there to visit your class, or by arranging for your class to visit the sites. When your class is receiving a presentation from a parent or other visitor, or is visiting a site, you can use your own comments and questions to help guide the presentation and connect it to the unit's big ideas. (If possible, provide presenters with a list of these big ideas ahead of time.)

Gather Resources

You will need to gather the resources needed to teach the unit. Most of these are materials already available in the classroom or common household items that you can bring from home, but some are children's literature books that you will need to purchase or borrow from a library. If you are unable to obtain a recommended book, you may wish to search for a substitute, enlisting the help of local librarians if possible. Before including a book in your plans, however, read through it to make sure that it is suitable for use with your students and worthwhile as a resource for developing one or more of the unit's big ideas. Also, consider how you will use the book:

Will you read it all or only certain parts?

Will one copy be enough or should you try to get a copy for each table of students?

If you read from a single copy, will you leave the students in their seats and circulate to show illustrations, or will you gather them in a closely compacted group on a rug and show the illustrations to the whole group as you read?

Will the book be left in some designated place following the reading so that individual students can inspect it?

If you are considering supplementing or substituting for the children's literature selections identified as resources for the unit, we have a few guidelines to suggest based on our experiences to date. First, children's literature (as well as videos, CD-ROMs, and other multimedia resources) can be useful both as content vehicles and as ways to connect with students' interests and emotions. Nonfictional children's literature is most useful in teaching about how and why things work as they do and how and why they vary across cultures. Fictional sources are more useful for reaching children's emotions, as in reading and discussing stories about homeless people or about a child who volunteers at a soup kitchen.

However, not all children's literature selections that are related to a unit's topic are appropriate as instructional resources for the unit. For example, we originally intended to use Diane Siebert's (1987) rhymed text *Truck Song* to introduce one of our transportation lessons. At first glance, the text appeared to present an ideal opportunity to integrate a content source drawn from language arts: It is cleverly written and deals directly with trucking, which is a prominent component of the lesson in question. *Truck Song* is a light-hearted, romanticized, and fanciful version of a trucker's journey—so much so, however, that we became concerned that it might implant misconceptions about how truckers carry out their jobs. For example, the author omitted punctuation from the text to give readers an impression of what it is like to drive without stopping (implying that this is what truckers normally do). We doubt that this feature of the text will have its intended effect on readers, but even if it did, it would create an impression of truckers as carefree ramblers (when in reality, truckers must not only obey the same traffic laws that apply to everyone else but also comply with many additional laws regulating the trucking industry). In this and several other respects, the text's portrayal of the trucker's journey is inaccurate as a portrait of the life of a long-distance truck driver. Consequently, we decided that although the text might be worth studying in language arts, its content was not sufficiently supportive of social studies goals to justify its inclusion in our transportation unit.

Problems such as these frequently lead us to drop children's literature selections from our unit plans. In some cases, their deficiencies are obvious (e.g., content or illustrations that are so dated as to be misleading, or that focus on the exotic and convey ethnic stereotypes instead of helping students to appreciate cultural variations as intelligent adaptations to time and place). However, some deficiencies are more subtle and recognized only when problems occur as they are used during class (e.g., the language is too difficult or fanciful, or the content or illustrations tend to derail the class from key ideas into side issues). When such problems appear in nonfictional selections, some of the books still can be used by presenting their most useful parts and omitting the rest. However, fictional selections usually have to be either read all the way through or omitted entirely.

Add Learning Activities

You also may wish to supplement or substitute for some of the learning activities or home assignments included in the unit plans. We believe that any activity considered for inclusion in a unit should meet all four of the following basic criteria: (1) goal relevance; (2) appropriate level of difficulty; (3) feasibility; and (4) cost-effectiveness. Activities have goal relevance when they are useful as means of accomplishing worthwhile curricular goals (i.e., intended student outcomes). Each activity should have a primary goal that is important, worth stressing, and merits spending time on. Its content base should have enduring value and life-application potential. This criterion is typically met when the activity is useful for developing one of the big ideas that anchor the unit's content base.

An activity is at the appropriate level of difficulty when it is difficult enough to provide some challenge and extend learning, but not so difficult as to leave many students confused or frustrated. You can adjust the difficulty levels of activities either by adjusting the complexity of the activities themselves or by adjusting the amount of initial modeling and explanation and subsequent help that you provide as you engage the students in the activities.

An activity is feasible if it can be implemented within whatever constraints apply in your classroom (space and equipment, time, student readiness, etc.). An activity is cost-effective if the learning or other benefits expected to flow from it justify its costs in time and trouble for you and your students and in foregone opportunities to schedule other activities.

In selecting from activities that meet these primary criteria, you might consider several secondary criteria that identify features of activities that are desirable but not strictly necessary:

1. Along with its primary goal, the activity allows for simultaneous accomplishment of one or more additional goals (e.g., application of communication skills being learned in language arts).
2. Students are likely to find the activity interesting or enjoyable.
3. The activity provides an opportunity to complete a whole task rather than just to practice part-skills in isolation.
4. The activity provides opportunities for students to engage in higher-order thinking.
5. The activity can be adapted to accommodate individual differences in students' interests or abilities.

Along with these criteria, which apply to individual activities, we suggest additional criteria for the set of activities for the unit taken as a whole:

1. The set should contain a variety of activity formats and student response modes (as another way to accommodate individual differences).
2. Activities should progressively increase in levels of challenge as student expertise develops.
3. Students should apply what they are learning to current events or other aspects of their lives outside of school.
4. As a set, the activities should reflect the full range of goals identified for the unit.
5. Where students lack sufficient experiential knowledge to support understanding, learning activities should include opportunities for them to view demonstrations, inspect artifacts or photos, visit sites, or in other ways to experience concrete examples of the content.
6. Students should learn relevant processes and procedural knowledge, not just declarative or factual knowledge, to the extent that doing so is important as part of developing basic understanding of the topics.

The key to the effectiveness of an activity is its cognitive engagement potential—the degree to which it gets students thinking actively about and applying content, preferably with conscious awareness of their goals and control of their learning strategies. If the desired learning experiences are to occur, student involvement must include cognitive engagement with important ideas, not just physical activity or time on task. In short, the students' engagement should be minds-on, not just hands-on.

If an activity calls for skills or response processes that are new to your students (e.g., collaboration within a pair or small group, writing in a journal) you will need to provide them with modeling and instruction in how to carry out these processes and with opportunities to practice doing so. In this regard, we recommend that you introduce new processes or skills in the context of applying already-familiar content. Young learners often become confused if they are asked to cope with both new content and new skills at the same time (or they become so focused on trying to carry out the activity's processes successfully that they pay little attention to the big ideas that the activity was designed to develop).

The success of an activity in producing thoughtful student engagement with important ideas depends not only on the activity itself but on the teacher structuring and teacher-student interactions that occur before, during, and after it. Thus, an important part of making an activity successful as a learning experience is your own:

1. Introduction of the activity (communicating its goals clearly and cueing relevant prior knowledge and response strategies).
2. Scaffolding of student engagement in the activity (explaining and demonstrating procedures if necessary, asking questions to make sure that students understand key ideas and know what to do before releasing them to work on their own, and then circulating to monitor and intervene if necessary as they work).
3. Handling of debriefing/reflection/assessment segments that bring the activity to closure (during which you and the students revisit the activity's primary goals and assess the degree to which they have been accomplished).

For more information about designing or selecting learning activities, see Brophy and Alleman (1991).

Plan Your Assessment Component

We view assessment as a basic component of curriculum and instruction that should be an ongoing concern as a unit progresses, not just as something to be done when the unit is completed. Also, the goals of assessment should include generating information about how the class as a whole is progressing in acquiring the intended learnings and about ways in which curriculum and instruction may need to be adjusted in the present or future, not just generating scores that will provide a basis for assigning grades to individual students.

You might begin by assessing your students' prior knowledge before you start teaching the unit. You can use some or all of our interview questions for this purpose (these are provided in the introduction to each unit), or else formulate your own questions. Such preassessment will provide you with useful information, both about valid prior knowledge that you can connect with and about gaps, naive ideas, and misconceptions that you can address specifically as you work through the unit. It may suggest the need for additional physical artifacts, photos, or other props or visuals, or for more extensive explanations of certain points than you had anticipated providing.

To promote accomplishment of this broad assessment agenda, we have embedded informal assessment components within most lessons, and we have included a review lesson at the end of each unit. However, you may want to add more formal assessment components, especially if your students will be participating in state- or district-wide social studies testing. Also, you may want to include relatively formal assessment (i.e., tests that carry implications for grading) as a way to communicate high expectations for student engagement and effort in social studies activities and as a way to convey to students and their parents that you consider social studies to be just as basic a curricular component as language arts, mathematics, and science.

In any case, we recommend that you focus on the major goals and big ideas when planning a unit's assessment components. This includes affective and dispositional goals, not just knowledge and skill goals. It may require you to use alternative forms of assessment instead of—or in addition to—conventional tests. In this regard, bear in mind that a great deal of useful assessment information can be gleaned from your students' responses to ongoing in-class activities and home assignments. These responses frequently will indicate that certain points need reteaching or elaboration because several students are confused about them. For more information about assessment in elementary social studies, see Alleman and Brophy (1997, 1999).

Prepare the Parents

Most of the lessons include home assignments calling for students to interact with parents or other family members by discussing some aspect of how the cultural universal is experienced or handled within their family (and then recording some key information on a brief response sheet to be returned to class and used as data in follow-up discussion). It will be important to alert the parents to this feature of the social studies units and elicit their cooperation in completing the home assignments and seeing that their children return the data sheets the next day. If your school

Dear Parents,

This year we are taking part in a new exciting way to learn social studies. Our units of study will be based on cultural universals. A cultural universal is something that is common to children around the world, such as communication, transportation, or family living. By using the cultural universals, we are able to help children first connect the learning to their own lives and then learn more.

Within each unit, we will look at the many parts of the cultural universal and how it ties to important social studies topics like history, careers, geography, economics, and more. Our hope is to have students who are more excited and motivated to learn about the world within their reach and far away.

Our first cultural universal unit will be communication. During this unit, we will be starting with a discussion of the basic forms of communication and their functions to build students' beginning knowledge. Then we will have several lessons about mass media and propaganda, as well as nonverbal forms of communication. We will also learn about inventions, careers, economics, and more.

As parents, you will be asked to contribute your knowledge in this area as well. Some home assignments might involve locating symbols in your neighborhood, logging your family's TV viewing, or even interviewing people who work in the communications field. Another way to help with our learning is to ask your child often about our communication lessons and share your own thoughts about the topics we discuss.

If you have any questions about this unit or the cultural universals, please feel free to drop me a note or call. Thank you for your help in making this unit successful.

Mrs. Knighton

FIGURE 3   Model Letter to Parents

schedules parent orientation meetings early in the school year, this would be a good time and place to explain the social studies program to them in person. In any case, before beginning your initial unit, send the parents an informational letter (see Figure 3). Subsequently, in sending home the data retrieval sheets for individual home assignments, be sure to include sufficient information to enable parents to know what to do as they interact with their child to accomplish the assignment successfully.

Some teachers become concerned when they hear about our home assignments. However, we have found that most parents not only cooperate by taking the time needed to complete the requested activities with their children, but enjoy doing so, see the activities as valuable, and express considerable enthusiasm for them. There are several reasons for this. First, the assignments do not require any special preparation or demanding work from the parents. Mostly, they involve family members in activities that are nondemanding for the parents, interesting and informative for the children, and enjoyable for both (e.g., talking about how much time the family spends using various forms of mass media, discussing how the family can use environmentally responsible transportation, talking about who their ancestors were, or talking about what relatives, friends, or neighbors do in jobs relating to the cultural universal under study).

In addition to personalizing the unit's content and providing additional opportunities for students to construct understandings of it and communicate about it, these home assignments engage the parents and children in conversations that support family ties and enhance their appreciation for one another. The children learn many things about their parents' past lives and decision making that help them to know the parents more fully as individuals, and the parents learn a lot about their children's ideas, interests, and capabilities. Parents commonly report that these interactions have helped them (and other family members, such as older siblings) to develop enhanced respect for their child's insights and reasoning abilities, and that interests that the child expressed during these interactions subsequently led to other shared activities. When you communicate with parents about the home assignments, do so in ways that encourage the parents to look forward to experiencing these interesting and emotionally satisfying interactions with their children, not just to "helping them with their homework."

Theory and research on learning suggest that exposure to new information is of most value to learners when it leads them to construct understandings of big ideas that are retained in forms that make them easily accessible for application in the future. This is most likely to occur when learners have opportunities not just to read or hear about these big ideas but to talk about them during interactions with others. The home assignments embedded in our units create important extensions to the discourse that occurs in the classroom by providing opportunities for your students to engage in additional knowledge construction at home during content-based interactions with parents and other family members.

The home assignments allow students to connect what they learn in social studies class to their lives outside of school. We want students to be able to use the social knowledge and skills that they are learning whenever these are applicable. Doing this consistently requires, along with accessible knowledge and skills, self-efficacy perceptions and related beliefs and attitudes that orient students toward drawing on their social learning and using it to inform their thinking and decision making about personal, social, and civic issues. Our home assignments (and the subsequent topic-related interactions that they tend to engender) will help both your students and their family members to appreciate the students' developing capabilities for engaging in informed discussions about the social world, reasoning about the trade-offs embedded in potential alternative courses of action, and developing plans or making decisions accordingly. Typically, self-efficacy perceptions become enhanced as students begin to discover and appreciate their own growing expertise and as family members begin to display increased respect for their knowledge and informed opinions.

For more information about out-of-school learning opportunities in social studies, see Alleman and Brophy (1994).

Arrange for Pairing with Older Students

A few of the suggested in-class activities call for pairing your primary-grade students with older, intermediate-grade students who come to your class for the occasion and act as mentors, helping your students to meet the activity's requirements. Pairing with older mentors is especially helpful for kindergarten or first-grade students whose writing skills are limited. During these activities, the mentors help the younger students to generate and clarify responses to questions, then record the responses. Ideally, each pair of students will engage in sustained conversation about the questions, and the older students will develop and explain their own answers to the questions along with helping the younger students to do so.

Both students typically benefit from these pair activities. The older students tend to enjoy and take satisfaction in helping the younger students to develop their thinking, and the younger students benefit from the presence of a partner who provides both needed assistance in carrying out the activity and an authentic and responsive audience for their ideas. An added bonus is that the warm, affective tone of these interactions tends to carry over and contribute to a positive interpersonal climate in the school as a whole.

If you want to include these mentor/pair activities, you will need to make arrangements with one or more intermediate-grade teachers. (Ordinarily it is best to work with a single intermediate-grade class, both to simplify the planning involved and to make it possible for the same pairs of students to work together throughout the year.) Initially, this will require explaining the general purpose and nature of these activities and negotiating agreement on a general plan. Subsequently, prior to the implementation of each pair activity, the teachers will need to prepare their respective classes for participation by explaining (and, perhaps, modeling or role-playing) what will be accomplished during the activity and how each of the participants is expected to fulfill his or her role.

Establish a Social Studies Corner or Learning Center

If you have room in your classroom, we recommend that you develop a social studies corner or interest center. At minimum, this should include a wall display of key words, photographs, student products, and so forth connected to the unit topic, along with a collection of related books and other materials that students can inspect during free times in class or take home at night. Ideally, the social studies area would be a more complete learning center, equipped with a table, some chairs or a rug, maps and a globe, and physical artifacts for students to inspect; activities for them to complete; or opportunities for exploration or enrichment using print materials, CD-ROMs, or other learning resources. The area should also include materials previously used during lessons that your students might wish to inspect at their leisure, such as children's literature selections or photos or artifacts that connect people, events, places, or institutions in your community to the cultural universal under study.

Because each of our units includes a historical dimension, we recommend that you display a time line along one of the walls of your classroom. The units typically address human responses to the cultural universal "long, long ago" (cave dweller days), "long ago" (seventeenth or eighteenth centuries, or Native American/Pilgrim/pioneer days), and "today" (especially in the contemporary United States). Your time line might be composed of connected sheets of construction paper that stretch for five to fifteen feet horizontally, with key words and photos or symbols depicting developments in human responses to each cultural universal that characterized each of these three time periods (and perhaps others in between, such as the early twentieth century).

Additional items can be added to the time line (on a new row) each time a new social studies unit is taught. These can be occasions for looking across units to revisit some of the big ideas, especially common threads such as development over time and variation across locations and cultures in human response to cultural universals. Ideas about what to display on the time line can be found in the historical text and charts included in each unit.

Teaching the Units

Our units are built around featured big ideas that are elaborated in some detail, sometimes in language that you might use to present information to your students. This format makes these sections easier to follow by eliminating phrases such as "Explain to your students that . . ." However, their script-like appearance is not meant to imply that you should use them as scripts by reading or reciting them to your students. They are meant only as background information to inform your lesson planning. Ordinarily you would explain or elicit this information as you develop the content with your students, but not read or recite it directly from our lesson plans. You will also need to adapt the material to your students and your local situation by placing it into a context that includes your own and your students' experiences, photos and artifacts from your local community, and references to current events and local connections.

In the process, bring the unit to life by showing or telling your students about your own past or present involvements with the cultural universal (e.g., "My favorite mode of transportation is ____"; "Here's a photo of my family celebrating my sister's first birthday."). Barbara Knighton uses this personalized approach to great advantage in her classroom. Her students are fascinated to learn details about her personal life and background, and the modeling she provides as she shares this information encourages her students to share productively about topic-relevant aspects of their own lives. This kind of sharing also enhances the authenticity and life-application potential of the material, especially when the teacher explains the reasons for personal decisions (e.g., about what to watch on TV, how to get to a vacation destination, etc.).

Another way for you to personalize and communicate enthusiasm for the content is to share your own responses to the in-class activities and home assignments. This will provide you with additional opportunities for modeling engagement with the big ideas and contributing responses that will stimulate your students' thinking. In this regard, it is important to make sure that your students carry out the home assignments in collaboration with their parents or other family members and bring back the completed data sheets the next day, and that you follow up by displaying the data and leading the students through a discussion of its meanings and implications (typically at the beginning of the next day's social studies period). Students should understand that you view the home assignments as an integral part of social studies, that you expect them to complete the assignments faithfully and return the data sheets the next day, and that the information on these data sheets will be reviewed and discussed as part of the next lesson.

In developing unit content with your students, you will need to find an appropriate balance between showing/telling key ideas, trying to elicit these ideas through questioning, and providing opportunities for your students to discover them through their engagement in activities and assignments. Traditional ideas about teaching emphasized transmission approaches in which teachers (or texts) do a lot of explaining and students are expected to remember or copy this input and retrieve it later when answering recitation questions or filling out worksheets. More recent ideas about teaching emphasize social constructivist methods, in which teachers focus more on asking questions and leading discussions than on showing/telling, and students are expected to collaborate in constructing knowledge as they discuss issues or debate alternative solutions to problems.

Exclusive reliance on transmission approaches is unwise because it bores students and unwittingly encourages them to emphasize low-level rote memorizing strategies instead of processing what they are learning more actively. However, exclusive reliance on social constructivist approaches also is unwise. It can be inefficient and confusing, especially if the students do not have much accurate prior knowledge and therefore end up spending a great deal of their class time carrying on discussions that are based on false premises and laced with naive ideas and misconceptions. Counterproductive discussions of this kind often occur when primary-grade students (who are still undergoing cognitive development) are prematurely asked to discuss topics about which their prior knowledge is limited, poorly articulated, and distorted by naive ideas or misconceptions. Consequently, we recommend that you begin most units and lessons with instruction designed to establish a common base of accurate knowledge (relying more heavily on showing and telling at this stage) and then gradually shift into more emphasis on questioning and discussion as students' expertise develops.

Even when doing a lot of showing and telling to establish a common base of knowledge, however, try to avoid extended "lecturing." Use more of a narrative (storytelling) style to develop explanations, and spice your presentations with frequent references to examples from your own life, your students' lives, or current events. Also, break up extended "teacher talk" segments and keep your students actively involved by asking questions, pausing to allow students to discuss a point briefly with partners or table-mates, or asking them to indicate understanding (or readiness to provide an example) by raising their hands, touching their noses or ears, and so on. Bear in mind that although your students usually will lack articulated knowledge about the topic, they will have personal experience with many of its aspects. You can keep making connections to this experience base as you develop big ideas, both to enhance the meaningfulness of the content for your students and to keep them actively involved as the lesson progresses.

On days when you will be making a home assignment, be sure to leave enough time at the end of class to go over the assignment with your students. Explain and model how they should present it to their families and show how they might respond to one or two of the questions on the data sheet. Your students should go home feeling confident that they know what the assignment requires and how they (working with family members) will respond to it.

Also, do the home assignment yourself. This allows you to "bring something to the table" the next day when you summarize and lead discussion of the data. In addition, it communicates through modeling the importance of the home assignments and some of the thinking involved in applying social studies learning to our lives outside of school; it alleviates potential concerns about invasion of privacy (because you are sharing your life, too); and it helps your students and their families to get to know you as a person in ways that promote positive personal relationships.

Unit 1: Communication

Introduction

· ·

To help you think about communication as a cultural universal and begin to plan your teaching, we have provided a list of questions that address some of the big ideas developed in our unit plans (see Figure 1). The questions focus on what we believe to be the most important ideas for children to learn about communication. These include communication as a universal human need and the functions that it fulfills for us; methods of and limitations on communication in prehistoric times and among preliterate people who lived more recently; the impact of major inventions (writing, the printing press, radio, television, telephones, computers) on communication; communication by infants and among people who are blind or deaf; how people communicate when they do not share a language; how the environment and culture shape vocabulary; the invention of new words; reasons for using symbols instead of words on certain traffic signs and other public notices; how the postal system works; why people read newspapers; and the workings of the television industry.

To find out what primary-grade students know (or think they know) about these questions, we interviewed almost one hundred students in Grades K–3. You may want to use some or all of these questions during preunit or prelesson assessments of your students' prior knowledge. For now, though, we recommend that you jot down your own answers before going on to read about the answers that we elicited in our interviews. This will sharpen your awareness of ways in which adults' knowledge about communication differs from children's knowledge, as well as reduce the likelihood that you will assume that your students already know certain things that seem obvious to you but may need to be spelled out for them.

1. Today we're going to talk about communication. That's a big word—do you know what it means? [If not, tell the child that communication means talking to people or sending them messages.]

2. All over the world, people communicate by sending messages or talking. Do they do that just because they like to, or do they need to? . . . When would be a time that people needed to talk? . . . How would our lives be different if we couldn't talk to one another? [If necessary ask, "Would our lives be better or worse? . . . Why?"]

3. Some animals communicate by making noises; for example, dogs bark at each other. But we don't have to bark—we can talk. What does talking allow us to do that dogs can't do? . . . Is talking better than barking? . . . Why?

4. Back in time, the earliest people lived in caves. How did those people communicate? . . . Did they have any other ways to communicate? [If talking is not mentioned, ask, "Could cave people talk to each other?"]

4a. [To be asked if the student's response to Question 4 implied that cave dwellers used spoken language] Was there ever a time when people didn't have language—when they didn't know how to talk to each other? . . . How did those people communicate?

5. Before Columbus first came to America, the only people who lived here were members of different Native American tribes. How did the Native Americans communicate? . . . If the chief of one village wanted to get a message to the chief of a village five miles away, how would he do it? [The intention of these questions is to see if students understand that Native Americans had oral but not written language. If the student mentions smoke signals, ask what the chief would have to do if it were a rainy day. If the student mentions shouting or beating drums, say that the second chief was too far away to hear this. If the student says that the chief would have to walk or ride to the other village, ask if he could get a message there without leaving his own village. In general, probe to see if the student understands that the chief would have to send someone to deliver the message personally at the other village.]

6. Did the Native Americans have libraries? . . . Why not? [If yes, say, "Tell me about the books that were in the Native Americans' libraries."]

6a. [To be asked if the student's response to Question 6 emphasized the lack of bricks or some reason other than that Native Americans lacked written language.] Did the Native Americans have books? . . . Why not?

7. [With children who answered Question 6 by saying that Native Americans did have libraries or books, prepare them for Question 7 by explaining that Native Americans did not have libraries because they couldn't write their language,

so they had no books.] if the Native Americans couldn't write, how could they pass on what they had learned about hunting or farming? [If necessary, ask: Suppose that a Native American man was out hunting and found a new hunting ground. How could he communicate that to the rest of his tribe?]

8. For a long time, people could speak, but they couldn't write. Then, alphabets and writing were invented. How did the invention of writing change the world? . . . What did writing bring people that they didn't have before?

9. Let's think about communication in the time of George Washington. If George Washington was in New York and he wanted to send a message to Benjamin Franklin in Philadelphia, how could he do it? [If the student correctly says that Washington would write a letter, ask how he would get it to Franklin. If the student says that he would mail it, ask: Did they have mail back then like we do now? . . . So what would he have to do to get the message to Philadelphia?]

10. Think about the very first books that were ever made. What do you think those first books looked like? . . . When the people made those first books, how did they make them?

11. For a long time, anything that was put down on paper had to be written by hand—even books. Then, the printing press was invented, and people could print newspapers and books like we have today. How did the invention of the printing press change the world? . . . What did printing bring people that they didn't have before?

12. Another important invention was the telephone. How did the telephone change the world? . . . What did the telephone allow people to do that they couldn't do before?

13. How do babies and young children learn to speak their language? . . . [If the student just says something like "from their parents," ask what the parents do.] Sometimes a young child knows what he wants to say, but doesn't know the words. What can he do? . . . For example, if the child wants to go outside but doesn't know the word *outside*, what could he do?

14. Here, we only have a few words that we can use to describe different kinds of snow, like *snow,* or *sleet,* or *slush.* But up in Alaska, the Eskimos' language has a lot of different words that they can use to talk about a lot of different kinds of snow. Why is that? . . . Why do the Eskimos have more words for snow than we do?

15. Can people communicate with each other if they don't speak the same language? . . . How? [If student says no or cannot explain, ask, "When Columbus and the Native Americans first met, were they able to communicate somehow?. . . How?] [If student does not know, ask,

Continues

FIGURE 1 (Continued)   33

"What if you visited France—would you be able to communicate with French people who didn't know English?"]

16. Some people are deaf—they can't hear. Can deaf people communicate? . . . How? [If the student only mentions sign language or other nonverbal means, ask, "Can deaf people talk?"] [Also, if the student fails to mention lip-reading, ask, "If a deaf person were sitting here watching you talk, could she understand what you were saying?"]

17. Some people are blind—they can't see. Can blind people communicate? . . . How? [If necessary ask, "Can blind people read? . . . How?"]

18. Are there some words that we use today that didn't exist fifty years ago? . . . What are some examples? [If the child says no, probe by asking, "Does anyone ever invent new words . . . What are some words that might be pretty new?"]

19. Sometimes communication is done with symbols instead of words. [Show examples, ask for meanings, and if necessary, tell the student that the symbols mean "Railroad crossing ahead" and "No bicycling."] Why are these symbols used instead of words? [If the student only explains why the sign is there but doesn't explain why the sign has symbols instead of words, probe for the latter explanation.]

20. My brother lives in Chicago and I want to send him a birthday card. What do I have to do to send him the card? . . . OK, I put the card in the mailbox. Then what happens to it? . . . Then what? [Probe to see if the child understands the following steps: I put the card in my mailbox; the card is taken to my local post office; it is sorted and grouped with other mail headed for the Chicago; this mail is trucked to the airport and put on a flight to Chicago; there, it is trucked to my brother's post office; there, it is sorted by mail routes; then the mail carrier assigned to my brother's route delivers the card to his home.]

21. Let's talk about newspapers. Why do people read newspapers—what's in them? . . . What else is in the newspaper? [If no response, ask, "Does someone in your family read the newspaper? Why does _____ read the paper?"]

22. How is a newspaper made? What do they do first? . . . Then what? [Take whatever the student tells you and probe forward or backward from there, but in particular, see if the student knows (1) who decides what words to use and how they compose their stories (e.g., get the news and then type a report into a computer); and (2) how this is made into a newspaper (e.g., printed on a printing press).]

23. An important invention at the time was radio. How did radio change the world? . . . What did radio bring to people that they didn't have before?

24. Another important invention was television. How did television change the world? . . . What did television bring to people that they didn't have before? [If it seems worth doing so, probe to see if the child has any understanding of how these inventions made instantaneous mass communication possible and eventually shrunk and homogenized the world.]

25. Let's talk about how television works. Suppose one of the astronauts came here to your school to talk to the kids. Now if Channel 6 found out about it, they would say, "Wow—that's big news! One of the astronauts is coming to talk to the kids at the school—let's show that on our six o'clock news!" What would they have to do? [If necessary, ask, "What would a TV station have to do to show that on its news program?"] [Probe to see if the student understands that the station would have to come to the school and videotape the talk, then take the tape to the station to edit. Also, see if the student has any explanation for how the tape then is "put on TV."]

26. Besides the news, television brings us a variety of entertainment shows. What's your favorite show? . . . OK, let's take _____. Where do they make _____, and how does it get to us, on our TV? [Probe for details, especially to see if the child understands that the shows are taped in Hollywood or elsewhere, then later broadcast through a network to local stations. If the student says that they make videos and then send them to local stations, ask about live shows, like sports events, that we can watch as they unfold.]

27. We have to pay for some TV channels, like HBO, but other channels are free. Why is that? Why are some pay and some free? [If necessary, ask, "You know, another thing about television is that they keep interrupting their programs to show commercials. Why do they have all those commercials on television?"] [If the student says that commercials provide a break so the performers can get ready for the next scene, point out that TV channels show commercials during movies that are already made, so they must have some other reason for showing commercials. If the student says that the sponsors want to show commercials because they want people to buy their products, accept this but probe further to ask why the television channels let these companies show their commercials.]

28. Television programs sometimes get cancelled—the networks take them off the air and put on something else instead. Why do they do that? [Probe to see if the student is aware of the importance of program popularity and connects this to ratings and then to income from sponsors. If the student initially talks

Continues

FIGURE 1 (Continued)   35

about reasons a show would go off the air only temporarily (tornado, etc.), clarify that you refer to permanently getting rid of a show. If necessary, use the student's favorite show as an example: "Well, you like to watch _____. Someday the people who run the channel that shows _____ might say, 'we don't want to show _____ anymore—let's get rid of it.' Why would they do that?"]

29. Have you heard of electronic mail, or email? [If yes, ask, "What is it? . . . How does email work? . . . Why might someone want to use email instead of regular mail?"] [probe for two possible reasons: it's faster and it's less trouble because you don't need stamps, envelopes, etc.]

If you want to use some of these questions to assess your students' prior knowledge before beginning the unit, you can do this either by interviewing selected students individually or by asking the class as a whole to respond to the questions and recording their answers for future reference. If you take the latter approach, an option would be to embed it within the KWL technique by initially questioning students to determine what they know and what they want to find out, then later revisiting their answers and recording what they learned. An alternative to preassessing your students' knowledge about topics developed in the unit as a whole would be to conduct separate preassessments prior to each lesson, using only the questions that apply to that lesson (and perhaps adding others of your own choosing).

Children's Responses to Our Interviews

Only about a fourth of the students could define communication adequately, but most of them could speak knowledgeably about it once told that communication involves talking or sending messages to other people. The students were generally aware that communication is a basic need, although this was not as clear and obvious to them as it was for food, clothing, and shelter. Even so, a heavy majority said that humans need to communicate, and most of these were able to give examples of when and why communication needs arise. Students recognized the need for communication most clearly with respect to emergencies or situations in which one is trying to learn or carry out a job. However, some students also noted the need for communication to express feelings, and they tended to suggest that life would be worse without communication because we would be lonely and isolated from others.

Most students were able to identify one or more ways in which our lives would be worse if we couldn't talk: it would be more difficult for us to get and share information; we would have to use sign language, read lips, or communicate in writing; or we would be isolated from others and unable to share our feelings. Some students expressed the misconceptions that lip-reading and writing would have developed in humans even if they did not possess the ability to speak.

About four-fifths of the students understood the basic idea that talking is better than barking because speech allows for more subtle and differentiated communication than barking does. However, some of them overestimated what occurs in the minds of dogs, assuming that their thoughts and attempts to communicate are verbally mediated. Students appeared to progress from believing that dogs think and communicate just like humans except that they use a different "language," to not crediting dogs with verbally mediated thought but recognizing that they can communicate different "messages" through different forms of barking, to recognizing that although barking has some communication value, it is much more limited than language. Only two students specifically noted that human speech mechanisms allow us to produce a much greater variety of sound combinations in our speech than dogs can produce in their barking.

The next set of questions asked about communication among preliterate people. Almost two-thirds of the students said that cave people communicated through speech, although almost as many said that there was a time when people did not have language. Among those who depicted cave people communicating through spoken language, only thirteen clearly indicated that this language would have been much different from the one we use today. More than a third of the students suggested that cave people communicated through sign language or pantomime, a fifth mentioned writing or drawing (typically envisioning artwork on cave walls or primitive maps or directions scratched on the ground), and a sixth said that cave people grunted, growled, or made other vocal noises but did not communicate through speech. In our previous interviews, the students' responses to questions about cave people often drew from what they had seen on *Alley Oop* or *Flintstones* cartoons. Perhaps their exposure to these cartoons led many of the students to say that cave people spoke to one another pretty much as we do today.

Most of the students understood that Native Americans communicated through speech, although a majority of them assumed that the people spoke English instead of their own languages. Also, only a minority of them understood that Native American languages were spoken but not written, so the people who spoke them did not possess books or communicate across distances by sending written notes. Many students thought that Native Americans did or could have engaged in reading or writing. Some thought that they did not because their interests lay elsewhere. Others understood that they could not, but thought that this was because they lacked writing materials or the knowledge and wherewithal to make books or build libraries (i.e., rather than because they lacked the alphabetic principle). A few students thought that whatever writing Native Americans did on walls or the ground (or on bark, etc.) involved language, and a few of those who said that they communicated in sign language seemed to think that they used the same sign language used today (i.e., American sign language).

The next questions addressed students' appreciation of writing as a fundamental, world-changing invention. About half of them were able to explain why this invention was so basic, such as by noting that writing made it possible for people to communicate across distances, facilitated their learning, and made it easier for those who could not speak or hear to communicate with others. The students were less successful in applying this understanding to contrasting the distance communication options available to George Washington with those available to a preliterate Native American tribal chief, primarily because they often were unclear about when Washington lived and which inventions were available at the time. Consequently, some students thought that Washington and Franklin could communicate only through face-to-face interactions, but others thought that they could use communication or transportation devices that were not invented until much later. Fewer than half understood that Washington could send Franklin a written message, and only about a third understood that Washington's message delivery options would not include anything like today's American postal service.

The students typically depicted the earliest books as written in longhand on primitive forms of paper, perhaps using feather pens or ink made from berry juices. With the exceptions of a few who thought that the typewriter had been invented before the printing press, the students who were able to answer Question 10 understood that until the printing press was invented, making books was a laborious process that required printing or writing the text in longhand (and perhaps illustrating it by hand as well). Most of them spoke of the printing press as bringing benefits to those who manufactured books (less work required, less tiring on the hands) or improving the appearance of the text (easier to read because it was printed in typeface instead of written in cursive, less likely to get smudged, and more likely to have color or illustrations). Thus, most students emphasized a micro-level purview focused on the individuals involved in manufacturing or reading particular books, rather than a macro-level purview that included recognition of the printing press as a fundamental invention that triggered significant changes in the human condition around the world. Only one-sixth of the students noted that the printing press made it possible for people to make multiple copies of text with greater speed or ease and/or for more people to read more books.

The students were more successful in answering the question about how the invention of the telephone changed the world. A majority said that the telephone made it possible for people to converse without being face-to-face or to communicate across distances without having to write letters. Apparently, it was much easier for the students to envision the nature and implications of communication in a world without the telephone than in a world without the printing press.

The next question assessed students' ideas about how babies learn to talk and how they communicate their ideas when they lack specific vocabulary. The students generally understood that language is acquired both through specific instruction and through general exposure to communication from and among significant others in one's environment. They also understood that a young child who lacked relevant vocabulary would probably try to communicate needs by getting adult attention and point-ing, gesturing, or attempting to say the word.

The students were less knowledgeable about indirect influences on vocabulary development. About half of them were unable to give a satis-factory response to the question about why the Eskimos' language has more words for snow than ours does. The other half were able to say that this was because the Eskimos live in a snowy environment, although for many of them, this was a brief guess that they could not elaborate on. Few students noted that the Eskimos needed to pay careful attention to snow and perhaps differentiate various subtypes for survival reasons, and none made a general statement to the effect that people need to pay close atten-tion to their environment in order to thrive in it.

The next questions asked about communication among people who do not share a common language or who are handicapped by sensory defi-cits. The students found it difficult to visualize and talk about communi-cation among people who do not share a common language, and some of them resisted the premise of the question by suggesting that the people might have some words in common, that they could communicate through writing, or that they could verbally explain to the other people that they did not understand their language. Fewer than half of them un-derstood that communication under these circumstances initially would depend primarily, if not solely, on gesture or sign language (although with time, the people might teach each other their languages). Rephrasing the question to focus on examples (Columbus and the Native Americans or the student on vacation in France or China) made it easier for the students to respond, but most of their responses still involved attempts to under-mine the premise of the question (they could use an interpreter), unrealis-tic suggestions (they could exchange written messages), or solutions that would take a great deal of time and thus not accomplish immediate com-munication goals (teach each other their languages).

The students varied considerably in their knowledge about the com-munication abilities of deaf and blind people. The younger ones tended to exaggerate the scope of these handicaps, such as by thinking that deaf or blind people cannot communicate at all or that blind people also are un-able to speak or to hear. Older students usually understood that deaf people may be able to read lips and that they can express themselves through speech, sign language, or writing, as well as that blind people can carry on conversations and read Braille materials. A few students displayed somewhat detailed knowledge, usually based on personal experiences with deaf or blind people (e.g., that although deaf people can talk, their speech is usually not as clearly articulated as other people's speech, or that people who become deaf after childhood are more likely to learn to speak well than people who were born deaf).

At least among students who understood that deaf and blind people can communicate, the responses concerning these people tended to be accompanied by expressions of empathy and recognition that these are otherwise normal people who have sensory deficits. There was no disparagement of these people or suggestion that they are generally weird, scary, or mentally defective.

Most of the students understood that languages expand as new words are coined, although fewer than half of them could suggest examples of words that entered our language within the last fifty years, and only one-fifth generated examples that were all accurate (applying a generous definition of accuracy). Most of the suggestions were technical or popular culture examples that in fact were introduced relatively recently or else incorrect examples that nevertheless were associated with good reasoning processes (e.g., scientific terms suggested on the grounds that most things scientific were discovered recently, *robe* because it is used following a shower and showers are relatively recent).

When shown drawings of "Railroad crossing ahead" and "No bicycling" signs, almost all of the students understood their meanings. However, more than a third of them were unable to suggest a reason these signs would employ symbols rather than words to convey their meanings, and many of the others gave responses that focused on the whims of the sign maker (e.g., not wanting to take time to write out the words). Only thirty-five of the ninety-six students clearly understood that symbols are used on these signs because they are quicker and easier to read than verbal messages (and universally interpretable regardless of the person's literacy level or native language).

When asked about the steps carried out by post office personnel in delivering a birthday card sent from Lansing, Michigan, to Chicago, most students were able to provide at least some details but only 40 percent generated responses that we considered to be both complete and accurate. Most students began by talking about obtaining the card, signing it, placing it into an envelope, addressing the envelope, and putting it in the mailbox, then went on to say that the card would be taken to their local post office, transported to Chicago, and then processed at a Chicago post office where it would be assigned to a delivery route. Minorities of students added other details. Some of these were accurate, such as that the sender would place a stamp on the envelope, the local post office would cancel the stamp and sort the outgoing mail, and the card would be placed with other mail headed for Chicago. However, one-fifth of the students thought that the same mail carrier who picked up the card at the sender's house would travel to Chicago and deliver it personally, and another fifth suggested that upon arrival at Chicago, the card would be taken directly to the addressee's house without being first taken to a post office for processing.

Responses to this question once again illustrated the micro-level purview of most of the students. Their answers tended to be guided by images of postal services being rendered by just one or a very small number of individuals who handle all aspects of the work personally, not images of the post office as a huge organization that employs hundreds of thousands of people who each work on just a subset of the steps involved in picking up, processing, and delivering mail.

The students' responses to questions about newspapers were interesting because they reflected the shifts that have taken place in recent years in the roles and relative prominence of newspapers vis-à-vis other communication media. The students' ideas about newspapers were generally valid as far as they went, but most were vague about how stories are composed, edited, collated, and transformed into printed newspapers. Few students understood that newspapers fulfill unique functions by covering a much greater range of information than is covered on the television news and going into greater depth on the material covered in common. In fact, some thought that newspapers get all or at least most of their content from television and that they function as primary news sources only for people who do not watch the news on television (as well as backup sources for people who miss their usual news programs on particular days).

Most students were unaware of the news-gathering functions of newspapers. Only a few clearly understood that reporters proactively develop stories rather than just receive what people convey to them.

Despite being fuzzy or confused about the processes and technology involved in creating newspapers, the students had generally accurate ideas about what is found in them and why people read them. They viewed newspapers primarily as sources of entertainment and information about local sports, weather, and shopping or leisure time options, along with coverage of events not significant enough to be covered on television. None mentioned editorials, and only a few suggested that newspapers provide deeper coverage than that found on television. Those who mentioned reading the newspaper themselves tended to provide more sophisticated responses to the interview as a whole, even though many of these students said that their newspaper reading was confined to the comics.

Questions about broadcast media indicated that the students were very familiar with radio and television in their current forms, so they could talk about how radio brings us music, news, and weather and television brings us entertainment as well as news and weather reports and allows us to see the events being broadcast. However, their responses showed little awareness of the fact that the broadcasting and instantaneous communication features of these media have "shrunk" and homogenized the world in many respects.

The students did not show much knowledge of how radio changed society when it was first introduced and popularized. In particular, only a few of them were aware that prior to television, radio served the same kinds of nightly entertainment functions for people that prime-time television serves today. Most of the students expressed awareness that television was an improvement over radio because it allowed people to see in addition to hear what was being broadcast. Otherwise, however, their explanations about what television brought to people focused on its delivery of cartoons and other entertainment rather than its delivery of news and information.

Questions about the creation and broadcasting of television programs showed that the students possessed good knowledge about the people but not the electronics involved in bringing television shows into our homes. They understood that a local station would send out personnel to videotape an event that it wanted to cover for its news program, and many of them displayed at least some knowledge of how entertainment shows or cartoon shows are made. However, few of them understood much about what is involved in broadcasting a taped news event, and even fewer understood that broadcasting is accomplished by transmitting wave signals through the air to antennas or other receivers. Some made reference to receiving television programs via cable but did not consider how the programming gets to the local cable company. Others understood that the cameras recording an event would have to be connected somehow to the television sets in viewers' homes, but were vague about what this connection might be. Only nine students made reference to transmission of signals through the air, and only a minority of these had clear ideas about the nature of these signals.

The students did not know much about the economics of television. The minority who were able to respond when asked why we have to pay for some television channels but not others mostly suggested that the pay channels provide programming that is especially new (particularly movies), expensive to produce, in high demand, or of high quality. A few also noted that people who live in areas that get poor reception must pay for cable services if they want good reception. A few thought that we pay for adult entertainment, for programs that come from farther away, or for programs that require more electricity than others.

Few students had awareness of commercial television as a business (i.e., a mechanism for delivering viewers to watch commercials). About a fourth had no idea why television stations show commercials, and most of the rest thought that they do so as a form of public service, as a favor to companies, or as a way to provide the people who make the show or the viewers who watch it with breaks in between segments. Only nine students understood that companies pay television stations to run their advertisements, and few if any clearly understood that commercial television stations are profit-making enterprises that generate income from sponsors because they deliver viewers for their advertisements.

The students also did not understand the importance of ratings and the bottom line as influences on networks' and local stations' decisions about programming. Only nine students indicated that a network or station would not make money if enough people didn't watch a show, and all of these students were thinking of people who pay for cable services rather than people watching programs on free channels. No student said that if a program failed to attract enough viewers, the network/station showing it would lose money because it could not sell enough advertising time or charge enough for broadcasting the ads. Nor did any student show understanding that stations must pay for the programs they show, that they recoup these costs (and make profits) from the fees they charge for broadcasting advertisements along with the shows, or that how much they get for these ads depends on how many people watch the show.

Consequently, instead of linking decisions about changes in programming to ratings and income, the students linked them to other causes. These included the ideas that the people involved in making the show were tired of doing it, had run out of ideas, or were no longer able to work well together; the network executives or local station managers want to serve their viewers by taking off programs that they do not watch anymore or scheduling new ones that they think the viewers will like; or programs are eliminated because their content is too raunchy or frightening to children. In general, the students depicted network and local station executives as service-oriented people managing a public trust, not as people running businesses strongly influenced by bottom-line numbers.

The last question dealt with electronic mail. Fewer than half of the students had heard of email and could say something specific about it, but most of what these students were able to say was accurate. A majority said that email works by computer and is delivered much more quickly than conventional mail, and a minority said that email is typed rather than handwritten or that it is easier to use because it doesn't require stamps, envelopes, or trips to the mailbox.

Overall, the data showed consistent tendencies for increases in knowledge across the K–3 grade-level range. Also, higher achievers tended to provide more sophisticated responses than lower achievers, although these differences were much smaller than the grade-level differences. Gender differences indicated that girls tended to know more about communication in the cave days, about how young children learn to talk and what they are likely to do to try to indicate their needs when they lack relevant vocabulary, about the communication abilities of deaf and blind people, and about how newspapers are made, but boys tended to know more about what is to be found in newspapers, about how television shows are made and broadcast, and about electronic mail.

Overview of Communication Unit —Barbara Knighton

Communication was one of the more difficult cultural universals for my students, because their prior knowledge was limited and what they did know was not organized and was difficult to access. This can be a challenging unit, but it conveys information that is very interesting to students.

To help make this unit more successful, spend extra time with the first two lessons. This will allow students to develop stronger building blocks and create a common vocabulary. Be sure to take plenty of time to brainstorm several different types of communication, so that they have a broad view of what communication is. Use the main ideas to drive your instruction and assessment, especially in these early lessons.

Post the lists and charts that you create as you brainstorm information together. These can be used later to spark class discussions. We often referred to the lists when we needed new ideas or examples. Also, they were helpful to use as reminders when reviewing before each new lesson.

Parent involvement in this unit includes a variety of tasks, ranging from brainstorming lists and writing paragraphs to interviewing people and filling out charts. The information supplied by families often helps to provide instruction during the next lesson. Be sure to put a clear deadline on each assignment so that families know when to return it.

This is a terrific unit in which to involve an older class of students. These buddy students help your students to write journal entries and assist with rereading and listening to students. This also provides great practice in reading and writing for the older students. Start with just a couple of buddies at a time and work out a plan that fits your schedule and class the best.

Finally, review each of the lessons carefully before you teach. I found that although I already knew much of the information, the important part is connecting it to the previous lessons. Make sure that you know the main ideas and structure your instruction and assessment to support those ideas.

Lesson 1

Communication: What Is It?
Why Is It So Important?

Resources

- Pictures, books, and electronic sources and computer in an interest center focusing on communication
- Strips of paper with questions related to communication posted throughout the classroom
- Pictures that illustrate means of communication and their functions
- Three-by-five-inch cards for student questions
- Means of Communication Chart (see Table 1)

Children's Literature

Brandenberg, A. (1993). *Communication*. New York: Greenwillow Books.

General Comments

To launch this unit, collect the instructional resources and display visual prompts as a means of generating interest in the topic. Post questions (written on wide strips of paper) around the room or on the bulletin board. For example:

What is communication?

Why is communication important?

What means of communication can you name?

How has communication changed?

How does communication vary across cultures?

What is your favorite means of communication?

What careers exist in the area of communication?

What would you like to learn about communication?

General Purposes or Goals

To help students: (1) become aware of the possible questions to be answered about communication; and (2) understand what communication is and why it is important.

Main Ideas to Develop

- Communication is the exchange of information, ideas, feelings, and attitudes through speaking/listening, writing/reading, electronic media, and other signs and symbols.

- Communication allows us to exchange ideas more quickly and directly than we would be able to otherwise, thus making it easier for us to collaborate on common tasks.
- By enabling us to exchange our thoughts and feelings, communication allows us to construct common understandings and build friendships.

Teaching Tips from Barbara

This lesson is especially important to help students create a definition of communication. Be sure to help them move past the idea that communication always involves talking or words. After the class discussion and reading the book *Communication*, I allowed the students time to talk with each other before we brainstormed a list of various means of communication.

Starting the Lesson

Pose questions regarding communication. Sample questions might include What is communication? Why is it so important? After a preliminary discussion of these questions, refer students to the questions posted around the room and show the class the bulletin board that has been started that depicts what communication is and illustrates why it is so important to us, as well as other aspects of this cultural universal that will be addressed during the unit. Use this visual as a springboard for generating interest in the unit as well as introducing the importance of communication in our lives. On 3X5 cards, write and post some of the students' comments as well as theories or speculations that surface regarding communication.

Suggested Lesson Discussion

[Share all or part of the book *Communication* by Brandenberg. It provides some of the big ideas that will be addressed during the unit, including the key ideas for Lesson 1.]

Communication is a big word. It is sharing knowledge, telling news, expressing feelings, and being heard. It takes two to communicate—one to say something and one to listen and respond. We communicate through language by speaking words, listening to words, writing words, and reading words.

We all need to express ourselves. Before babies learn to speak words, they communicate in other ways. Before people learned to write, they communicated through sounds, signals, pictures, and so on. Even today, we use signs and symbols to communicate. We often communicate without words. If we can't speak someone's language, we use body language, gestures, and so on.

Communication is the exchange of information, ideas, feelings, and attitudes through speaking and listening, writing and reading, electronic media, and other signs and symbols. [Post these major understandings on the bulletin board or at some other appropriate site and ask students (as a class) to list all of the means of communication that they have used or see in their classroom at this moment. Ask for "thumbs up" when students are ready to provide an example. Place the list on the white board.]

Examples might include talking (asking teacher for a direction), crying (when a student skinned his knee on the way to school), using symbols (in math or in writing journal entries), clock (for telling time), telephone book (for reading), map (for locating), and so on. [If time permits, ask for means of communicating that they have used at home and/or on the way to school. List. Retain the list for use with the history of communication lessons.]

[After the list has been compiled, ask the students to assist in completing a chart focusing on means of communication and why each is so important. See Table 1 for an example.]

TABLE 1   Means of Communication Chart

1. **Radio**	It gives us information about sporting events and scores. It gives us a weather report. It keeps us informed. It helps us figure out what to wear to school (rain gear). It gives us information about what is happening in the world.
2. **Telephone**	Allows us to interact directly with people all over the world. Allows us to share information immediately.

Activity

After completing the chart as a class, ask each table (group of four) to decide which means of communication the group thinks is the most important and why. Have students signal with "thumbs up" when the table is ready to respond.

Summarize

• Communication is the exchange of information, ideas, feelings, and attitudes through speaking, listening, reading, writing, electronic media, and other signs and symbols.

• There are many means of communication.

• Communication helps us in many ways.

Assessment

Have each student draw a picture representing the most important thing she or he learned about communication in this lesson. Use upper-grade mentors or posted word cards reflecting the big ideas, if necessary, to assist the students in writing the captions that express the major understandings.

Home Assignment

Encourage the students to share with family members their pictures and captions representing what was learned in this introductory lesson. Then as a family project, have them compile a list of means of communication found at home (e.g., video, TV, talking, book, newspaper, written directions for fixing a TV dinner, etc.).

Dear Parents,

We are beginning a unit on communication. We would like to have you, as a family, discuss the means of communication that you have in your home and compile a list of at least five such means to be shared at school (e.g., video, telephone, newspaper, directions for making a hot casserole dish for dinner, etc.). Thank you!

Sincerely,

FIGURE 2   Model Letter to Parents

Lesson 2

. . . .

Means and Functions of Communication

Resources
- Figure 4: Means and Functions of Communication Chart
- Pictures illustrating the various functions of communication
- Pictures illustrating means of communication
- Props (e.g., newspapers, maps, medicine bottle with directions, food pyramid, nutrition label from cereal box or bread wrapper, birthday or other greeting cards, articles of clothing from various cultures)
- Copies of Figure 4: Means and Functions of Communication Chart (for Activity)
- Word cards: functions of communication (packets for Activity)

Children's Literature
Brandenberg, A. (1993). *Communication*. New York: Greenwillow Books.

Brandenberg, A. (1984). *Feelings*. New York: William Morrow & Co.

Rich, S. J., Crocker, E. M., Langford, H. G., & Rosborough, K. (1996). *Sending Messages*. Bothell, WA: The Wright Group.

General Comments
The focus for this lesson is functions of communication that are universal and shared across cultures. Communication is everywhere and very important in our lives, yet we often take it for granted. This lesson is intended to help students appreciate its importance and realize how our lives are different from those of our ancestors because of major advances in communication.

General Purposes or Goals
To help students understand and appreciate: (1) the functions of communication; (2) how the functions are revealed; and (3) how we depend on these functions in our lives.

Main Ideas to Develop
- Communication is a basic need.
- Communication is used to give us information and ideas, help us express feelings and attitudes, entertain us, keep us safe (protect us), provide directions, help us stay healthy, and help us make choices.
- Culture is an important factor to be considered in our communication activities.

- Our ability to satisfy our needs and wants depends in part on our ability to communicate.

Teaching Tips from Barbara

This lesson makes connections between the outside-of-school world and the definition that you created in the first lesson. I found the Means and Functions of Communication Chart to be very beneficial. We filled it out together and then students had a chance to work with the chart as a home assignment. It's worth the extra time it takes to spend two days on this lesson and make sure that your students have the building blocks they need.

Starting the Lesson

Follow up the home assignment from Lesson 1 by asking students to share means of communication that they found at home. List them in the first column (Means) of Figure 4, p. 54: Means and Functions of Communication Chart.

Then ask what each means of communication does for us. How does it help us? List the responses in the second column (Functions).

Suggested Lesson Discussion

We have several means of communication that fulfill each function. For example, radio, television, the Internet, newspapers, and magazines all keep us informed.

[After filling in the chart with ideas acquired through the home assignment as well as through students' observation of their classroom surroundings, show the class objects, drawings, symbols, etc. and continue with the discussion and recording of information in the appropriate categories (Means and Functions)]. Following are examples that might be included:

- Newspaper—Keeps us informed. It is news printed on paper. It tells people what is going on around the world. There are many different kinds of newspapers: daily (metro/regional), weekly (local/neighborhood), special interest (business, school, church, club, newsletters).
- Map—A medium for locating places and determining their distance and direction from other places (especially this place). Maps are used by people employed in many different careers (e.g., truck drivers, pilots, businesspeople, engineers, etc.).
- Medicine bottle label [show a medicine bottle]—Helps keep us safe by telling us when to take the medication and explaining precautions.
- Videotape—Entertains or informs us.

[Show the food pyramid and the label from cereal or bread wrapper.]

The food pyramid is a symbol that reminds us what foods are good for us. The kinds of foods that are most nutritious include dairy products, eggs, meat, beans, poultry, nuts, fruits, vegetables, and grains. The lower you go on the food pyramid, the more servings you should have. Labels on food packages tell us about the ingredients and about nutrients, vitamins, fats, etc.

Communication can also be used to tell people how we feel. [Share a birthday card and a sympathy card. Read the narrative and explain that putting our feelings into words can be difficult. Refer to *Communication* and *Feelings*, both books by Brandenberg.] Some things are hard to say, but it's a relief when you say them.

Sometimes we communicate how we feel by the colors we wear. [Show articles of clothing.] The same color may mean different things in different cultures. For example, white is often worn by American brides, and black often means mourning or death; however, in Japan, black is worn by brides, and in India, white means mourning or sadness.

Activity

Have each table group discuss which means of communication it thinks is most important and why. Use the Means and Functions of Communication Chart as a reference. Have groups give "thumbs up" when ready to share the response with the class.

Optional   Provide a blank copy of Figure 4 to each group. Provide each table with several word cards naming functions of communication. As you verbalize and post on the class chart a means of communication, have each table select the appropriate function word cards and hold them up. Place a checkmark in the appropriate Functions columns on the chart. For example, when you post "television," tables with word cards for the following functions should hold them up: "keeps us informed," "gives us direction," "helps keep us safe," "entertains us," "helps keep us healthy," and "helps us make choices." Students can then fill in their own chart. Allow time for discussion.

Summarize

- Communication is a basic need.
- It provides us with information and ideas, helps protect us, helps keep us healthy, provides directions, and helps us express our feelings.
- People all over the world communicate.
- Culture is an important factor to be considered in our communication activities.

Assessment

As a class, write a collective journal entry that focuses on the most important ideas acquired about the means and functions of communication. Duplicate the entry for students to bring home.

Home Assignment

Have each student read the class journal entry to an older sibling or adult, then review the list (see the Means and Function Chart) of means of communication that are available in his or her home. Have them circle the means that seems to be the most important and discuss why. Then have them discuss which one costs the most and why. Send home copies of Figure 5 for recording responses. Encourage the students to share family responses with their peers.

Dear Parents,

Your child has a journal entry that she or he would like to read to you. It is a class summary of what was learned today about communication. We also would like you or an older sibling to review with your child the list compiled by the class naming the means of communication that are available in our homes. Then decide which seems most important and why. Discuss which one costs the most and why. Encourage your child to share family responses with his or her peers during our next class session. A form for recording the information has been enclosed. Thank you!

Sincerely,

FIGURE 3 Model Letter to Parents

MEANS	KEEPS US INFORMED	GIVES US DIRECTIONS	HELPS KEEP US SAFE	ENTERTAINS US	HELPS KEEP US HEALTHY	HELPS US INTERACT WITH OTHERS	HELPS US MAKE CHOICES	OTHER
1.								
2.								
3.								
4.								
5.								
6.								
7.								
8.								
9.								
10.								

Figure 4 Means and Functions of Communication

© 2002 by Janet Alleman and Jere Brophy from Social Studies Excursions, K–3: Book Two. Portsmouth, NH: Heinemann.

Means of Communication We Have In Our Home

1.   6.

2.   7.

3.   8.

4.   9.

5.   10.

(a) The means of communication our family thinks is most important is

_____

_____

(b) We think it is most important because

_____

_____

(c) The means of communication that we have in our home that costs the most is

_____

_____

(d) It is most expensive because

_____

_____

FIGURE 5   Means of Communication Form

Lesson 3

Changes in Communication over Time

Resources
- Pictures depicting what means of communication existed long, long ago (cave dwellers); long ago (pioneers); and today (when possible, have duplicates so some can be used for preassessment and others for the lesson)
- Time line for bulletin board—see *World Book Encyclopedia* for a great time line depicting the highlights of the history of communication
- Table 2: Means of Communication: Long, Long Ago; Long Ago; and Today

Children's Literature
Brookfield, K. (1993). *Book*. New York: Alfred A. Knopf.

Corke, D. (1994). *Messages Without Words*. Bothell, WA: The Wright Group.

Ellwood, H. (1996). *The Story of Books*. Bothell, WA: The Wright Group.

"Highlights in the History of Communication." (1996). *World Book Encyclopedia*. (Vol. 4, pp. 880–887). Chicago: World Book, Inc., Scott Fetzer Co.

Koehler, L. (1995). *Internet*. Chicago: Children's Press.

Merbreier, W. C. (1996). *Television*. New York: Farrar, Straus, & Giroux.

General Comments
The intent of this lesson is to develop a sense of wonder and interest in how people have communicated over time. Students will step back in time and look at pictures and listen to narratives that express the evolution of communication. They will come to realize how much easier it is to communicate today and how most Americans enjoy a range of communication choices.

General Purposes or Goals
To develop an understanding and appreciation of: (1) how communication has changed over time; and (2) how modern technology has enhanced the variety of communication methods available to us.

Main Ideas to Develop
- People very long ago had very limited means of communicating (e.g., grunting, gestures, drawings on walls), and, because of the lack of records, our knowledge about their culture is limited.

- People long ago used limited verbal communication (i.e., they didn't have many words) and nonverbal means such as smoke signals and markings on trails.
- Communication methods have evolved over time because of expansions of spoken language and inventions of written language, printing/books, telegraph, telephone, television, computer networks, and so on. This has made for a more complete and accurate preservation of certain communications (original dependence on oral tradition, then writing and printing, now videos and other electronic preservation).
- Electronic media have now made it possible for communication to be instantaneous (no more dependence on face-to-face oral exchange or hand-to-hand exchange of written materials) as well as worldwide (no more need for physical travel across space).
- Cultural diffusion via communication has become faster and more complete, shrinking and homogenizing our world.

Teaching Tips from Barbara

I especially needed to review the content before I taught these lessons. You will be sharing a great deal of information as you create the time line. I suggest that you move quickly through the information the first time and plan to review the completed time line before you begin the next section. Also, you will bring out more about many types of communication included in the time line as you lead discussions in later lessons. For example, you mention signs and symbols in the time line and later there is a whole lesson devoted to the topic.

Starting the Lesson

Begin the lesson by discussing the home assignment. Then show a series of pictures illustrating communication. Ask for student volunteers to put them in the order in which they were invented. Post on a board near the official time line. This will be a way of assessing prior knowledge and misconceptions. Explain that during the lesson they will be able to figure out if the pictures were ordered correctly or if changes need to be made.

Suggested Lesson Discussion

Long, long ago, people lived in caves or simple huts. They depended on their environment for satisfying their basic needs. Because we have no written records, we can only speculate about how they communicated. They undoubtedly made grunts and other noises or used signals because they had no real language. They did leave a few messages (e.g., lines, drawings on walls), and scientists have made guesses regarding their meaning. [As you share the story of changes in communication over time, use a time line and add pictures or drawings illustrating key points or make a time line on the board and add words and sketches as you share the story.]

The earliest people probably communicated much like animals—using grunts or shouts but not words or sentences. Several thousand years ago, people somehow learned to use sounds, each of which meant something special to other people. These were the first words. They slowly learned to put the words together to form language. People still had two big problems: They could not communicate over distances and as soon as a person spoke, the words vanished. People began to use runners to solve the first problem. Over time, people have kept trying to find faster ways to carry messages [see time line]. To solve the second problem, people first invented ways to preserve their ideas by making pictures. Later, written languages developed out of such artwork (pictures of Sumarians → hiero-glyphics → alphabet).

In America, Native Americans began using sign language. Sign language progressed from representational pictures to abstract symbols. However, it remained primarily representational in that the pictures/symbols were attempts to depict (represent visually) the things they stood for, rather than using more abstract symbols (signs) to stand for them.

The symbol usually had a clear connection to the thing it stood for—the form of an object, the movement of an action, or the placement of something. Sign language is a rich means of communication. It was used during powwows to hold the attention of the listeners, by war parties whose success depended on silence, and during bison hunts. Pioneers used sign language when trapping, when acting as guides and scouts, and when trying to communicate with Native Americans, who did not speak their language.

Commonly used signs included *me, you, up, down,* and *come.* These are intuitive and natural (another universal sign is the act of placing a finger vertically against the lips, meaning *silence*). The Plains tribes had signs for actions, emotions, and daily life. Among these signs were the following:

action: to break—Close both hands, hold them fairly close together and raise them. Then spread them, with the right hand tipping to the right, the left hand to the left, suggesting breaking.

emotion: to forgive—Raise both hands, closed except for extended thumbs and index fingers, to shoulder level, with palms facing the person addressed. Then move the hands forward, each describing a semicircle.

daily life: house/home—With the hands open and placed against the chest horizontally, interlock both sets at right angles to one another.

The Native Americans also used smoke signals to send messages in clear weather, although they could not use this method at night or when it was raining or snowing. Early means of sending messages had many limitations.

Pioneers learned a lot from the Native Americans, including their methods of sending messages. When the pioneers came to America, they brought with them both a spoken language and a written language that had been developed many, many years before in the Old World.

Before the development of writing, people kept all the things they knew in their heads. It became difficult to remember all that information. Writing is a way of storing information and passing it on to other people who might be far away in distance and time.

It was not invented by one person, but it evolved naturally in different places at different times from the need to keep accounts or record events. It takes many forms from simple picture writing to scripts that represent the sounds of a language. Writing is found today on a range of materials—from paper to pottery [see pp. 6–7 in *Book*].

Optional [The following is quite detailed and you might wish to delegate to an upper-grade level.]

The earliest forms of writing were sets of pictures of animals and everyday objects. These are called pictograms, and they date back to about 3000 B.C. Later, ideograms (symbols that represent ideas) were developed [see pp. 8–9 in *Book*]. Still later, more sophisticated signs were developed. In some cultures such as the Chinese, these are still used today [see pp. 10–11 in *Book*].

The Egyptians developed hieroglyphs, which is a system of writing. Pictorial symbols are used to represent meaning and sounds or a combination of them. It was a slow way to communicate, but later an entire alphabet was developed. [Show pp. 12–13 of *Book*.] Today, people around the world use alphabets more than any other form of writing. Alphabets are collections of letters that stand for the sounds used in spoken language. The alphabet is the quickest and most efficient way to write. You need only twenty-six letters to write all the words in the English language. One letter represents a sound in the language, and the letters are combined to make words. [Show pictures on pp. 14–15 in *Book* and demonstrate how much quicker and easier it is to write *dog* or *cat* than it is to draw one.]

Once people started to keep written records of trade, agriculture, and major events, they needed a constant supply of material to write on. At first, they used natural materials such as wood, bamboo, or bone, but these were difficult to write on and were not practical. The ancient Egyptians found they could make an excellent material for their written documents from the papyrus plant. When the supply of papyrus began to run out, people looked for a substitute. The result was parchment, which was made from animal skins. Until paper reached the West (from China) in the Middle Ages, parchment was the most important writing material.

The best paper is made from plants that have a lot of cellulose in their fibers, or from rags made from natural materials such as cotton or linen.

For centuries, books were written by hand on papyrus, parchment, or paper. Even with many scribes working together, only a small number of books could ever be made. Pictures have always been used in books, either to add information or to make the text more attractive. The first illustrated books were probably from Egypt. [See *Book*, pp. 48–49.] The artwork, like the inscription, was done by hand. [End of optional section.]

At first, writing was done only by a few highly skilled scribes; however, people soon realized that to survive in the modern world, everyone needed to be able to write. The invention of printing did much to encourage the skill of writing. Printing made books available to many people (i.e., not just rich people who could afford handwritten manuscripts), and readily available books encouraged people to learn to read and write.

Also, the introduction of the postal services in the late eighteenth century (1775) brought an increase in letter writing, and written communication grew rapidly. In countries where schooling was compulsory, there was no longer a barrier to literacy. It became expected that every student would learn to read and write.

Today, students have a huge choice of books to read for pleasure, but this has not always been the case. For hundreds of years, there were no books written especially for children, who, if they could read at all, had to make do with books written for adults. Later, there were grammar books and spelling books. About 250 years ago, publishers began to produce alphabet books, rhyme and fairy tale books, animal books, and so on.

Optional The first writing was all done by hand, so it was slow and time-consuming. Then in 1867, Christopher Scholes invented the typewriter. [Show picture on p. 58 in *Book*.] The first typewriters were large, heavy, and had hundreds of moving parts. Later these manual typewriters were replaced by electric ones, and today electric typewriters have been replaced by computerized word processors [show pictures]. Note: Some people still prefer typewriters and some still do a lot of their writing by hand.

Libraries in ancient Egypt and Babylonia were our very first storehouses of knowledge. The records were on clay tablets and papyrus rolls. Books as we know them today were rare. It was not until the twentieth century that large public libraries existed. [End of optional section.]

Pioneers could write letters. However, because there were no trains or airplanes, the information was received very slowly. Letters and newspapers had to be hand carried from one village to another. Communicating with families back in Europe could take weeks or even months because the letters had to travel on horseback over land, then cross the ocean by ship, and then be carried on land again.

One of the most important inventions that improved communication was the telephone. It was invented in 1876 by Alexander Graham Bell [place on time line] after many, many months of trying and failing. In the last 125 years, lots of improvements have been made in the telephone. [Show pictures of the first telephone and the modern telephone.] For a long time, someone who made a call had to give an operator the number of the person that was being called. The operator then connected the proper phone lines. Today we can dial directly anywhere in the world, without the help of an operator.

Another important invention was the radio, invented by Guglielmo Marconi in 1895. [Place on time line.] He figured out a way to send radio signals through the air. For the first time ever, people were able to hear about events as they took place. As time passed, radios provided entertainment as well as information (quiz shows, situation comedies, and dramas, just like on prime-time television today). There were no pictures, so people just had to imagine what things looked like. Many families continue to rely on the radio for the news and entertainment today (mostly music or "talk radio" shows).

In 1936 [place on time line], the first regular television broadcast took place in the United States. Like a radio, a television set uses an antenna to receive the wave signals sent out by the television station. The television set changes the signals into the pictures that we see and the sounds that we hear. In the 1930s and 1940s, only a few people could afford television sets, there were only a few programs, and the pictures were in black and white. In 1953 [place on time line], color television became available. Today, television is available across the globe, except in the most isolated places. Even families with very simple lifestyles have access to television. It is not uncommon to see a television antenna on top of a houseboat or a grass hut.

Televisions keep us in touch with news and events as they are occurring around the world. We can see and hear the leader of another country make a speech, watch a special show about life in Mexico or China, or see athletes competing in the Olympics.

In 1969, 723 million people worldwide watched a man walk on the moon [place on time line]. In 1972 [place on time line], the first national cable channel was available; in 1975, video cassettes were available; in

1982 [place on time line], there was a boom in cable television; in 1994 [place on time line], TV services from direct broadcast satellites were inaugurated. [Mention that many students' parents didn't have videos and cable TV when they were children.] In the future, it is possible that our contacts with any life on other planets will be on television. That is because television signals that shoot out from the earth travel on forever. If there are living creatures on some planet at the end of the galaxy, and if they have developed a TV technology similar to ours, they might be watching our television shows, just as we might someday be watching theirs.

Another major change in communication has occurred in the last thirty years—the spread of computers and the Internet. The Internet began in 1969 [place on time line] with only four computers owned by the Department of Defense. Connecting with the Internet through a computer today, you can get information from books and magazines housed in libraries that are made available electronically from around the world. [Show *Internet* and read excerpts. Illustrate using a computer and discuss with the students based on their level of computer literacy.]

Activity

Revisit the display of pictures that student volunteers put in order prior to the lesson. Have each table decide if any changes need to be made and if so, why. Then turn to the more comprehensive time line with pictures and words that was developed during the lesson. Ask each table to decide which event/invention on the time line seems most important and why. Conduct a class discussion.

Activity

As a large-group activity, have the class complete a blank chart titled Means of Communication: Long, Long Ago; Long Ago; and Today (see Table 2) and then as a group, draw tentative conclusions.

TABLE 2   Means of Communication: Long, Long Ago; Long Ago; and Today

LONG, LONG AGO	LONG AGO	TODAY
Grunts	Smoke signals	Computer
Noises	Trail markings	Fax
Drawings on walls	Oral language	Television
	Written language	
	Books	
	Telegraph	

Summarize

- People long, long ago had very limited means of communicating.
- People long ago used limited verbal communication and nonverbal means such as smoke signals and markings on trails.
- Communication methods have greatly expanded because of much increased spoken language and inventions such as the printing press, telegraph, telephone, radio, television, computers, and so on.
- Electronic media have now made it possible for communication to be instantaneous.

Assessment

With you as the key player/facilitator, pantomime and/or role-play with the class selected scenarios regarding means of communication across time—the changes that have occurred, the range of choices we enjoy today, etc. Allow time for discussion after each enactment.

Scenario #1 Cave dweller communicating to another person that she is tired.

Scenario #2 Native American communicating directions for growing corn to a pioneer.

Scenario #3 Native American communicating the need to build a house as a source of protection from the weather and from animals.

Scenario #4 Pioneer children communicating to family what they are learning in school.

Scenario #5 Pioneer family wanting to get a message to someone in a nearby village.

Scenario #6 A first grader wanting to find out from his grandmother living in Florida what the weather is like there today.

Scenario #7 A first grader's parents ordering a new jacket from a catalog. (The company's customer department is located in another state.)

Scenario #8 A first grader wanting to find out whether or not there is school today (it has been snowing and blowing all night).

Home Assignment

Encourage each student to have a conversation with his or her family about the changes that have occurred in communication during the family's lifetime. For example, they could discuss means of communication that were very popular in the past (radio, telegraph) that are used less today. Have the family write a paragraph describing these changes that could be shared during the next class session. If elderly individuals are available, have students use their experiences as additional resources.

Dear Parents,

We have been discussing changes in communication over time. Please share and discuss with your child changes that have occurred during your family's lifetime. For example, when you were a child, you might have had only a black-and-white television and your family might have sent long-distance messages by telegraph. Please write a paragraph describing these changes that your child can share during our next class session.

If elderly relatives or neighbors are available, please ask them to share their experiences. Responses from them regarding changes in communication over the years would be welcomed. Thank you!

Sincerely,

FIGURE 6   Model Letter to Parents

Lesson 4

. . . .

Types of Communication: Personal Interactive and Personal Delayed Interactive

Resources

- Telephone
- Pictures depicting types of communication: interactive and delayed interactive
- Table 3: Types and Means of Communication Chart
- Pictures of face-to-face communication, gestures, sign language, early telephones
- Picture illustrating how the telephone works
- Sample artifacts (e.g., letter, email message, greeting card)
- Time line focusing on changes in communication over time
- Computer/screen with email capabilities
- Chart: Steps in Postal Delivery
- Packets of cards with words and/or pictures illustrating the various means of communication

Children's Literature

Ardley, N. (1995). *How Things Work*. London: Dorling Kindersley.

Greene, L., & Dicker, E. (1982). *Sign Language*. New York: Franklin Watts.

Hockman, H. (Ed.). (1993). *Great Inventions*. New York: Dorling Kindersley.

Houghton Mifflin. (1991). *I Know a Place*. (First Grade Text). Boston: Author.

Koehler, L. (1995). *Internet*. Chicago: Children's Press.

McPherson, J. (1996). *Hello, Hello, Hello*. Bothell, WA: The Wright Group.

Mooney, M. (1991). *Taking Jason to Grandma's*. Bothell, WA: The Wright Group.

Parsons, J. (1994). *My Letter*. Bothell, WA: The Wright Group.

Sandler, M. (1996). *Inventors*. New York: HarperCollins.

Williams, R. (1990). *Call 911*. Bothell, WA: The Wright Group.

General Comments

The focus for this lesson will be on two of the major types of communication: interactive (face-to-face and telephone conversations), and delayed interactive (exchange of letters, email, greeting cards, postcards, etc.). The lesson will address the trade-offs that these communication types offer.

General Purposes or Goals

To help students understand and appreciate: (1) the two types of communication addressed (interactive and delayed interactive); and (2) the trade-offs involved in using each of the types.

Main Ideas to Develop

- Communication is a basic need.
- There are three majors types (groupings) of communication: (1) personal interactive types (face-to-face and telephone conversations); (2) personal delayed interactive types (exchange of letters, fax, email, greeting cards); and (3) mass communication (radio, television, the Internet).
- Personal interactive, personal delayed interactive, and mass communication are enjoyed by people all over the world.
- In isolated or underdeveloped areas, there are places where some types of personal interactive communication such as telephone conversations are not available. There are also places where personal delayed interactive communication does not exist or is extremely limited because of geographic and/or socioeconomic circumstances.

Teaching Tips from Barbara

This lesson let me know which students were beginning to understand and internalize the idea of communication. I started the lesson by defining interactive, or personal, communication, then sorted interactive communication into delayed and immediate. The scenarios were a powerful way to review the information in the lesson. I also used the scenarios as sponges to help fill transition time.

Starting the Lesson

Share the results of the home assignment. Show a series of pictures illustrating interactive and delayed interactive communication. Ask questions such as "What can you tell me about these pictures?" Assess prior knowledge, conceptions, and misconceptions.

Suggested Lesson Discussion

There are three major types (groupings) of communication: interactive, delayed interactive, and mass communication.

This lesson will focus on interactive and delayed interactive communication. In interactive communication, you can hear the other person at the time the message is being sent. In delayed interactive communication, you can send or receive messages, but you must wait for a response.

[Introduce the Types and Means of Communication Chart (Table 3). Indicate that the class will complete the chart during the next two or three days as the lesson unfolds.]

TABLE 3 Types and Means of Communication

INTERACTIVE	DELAYED INTERACTIVE
Face-to-face	Letter
Telephone	Postcard
Gestures	Greeting card
Sign languages	Email
	Fax

[Model and demonstrate each means as you introduce and explain it.]

Face-to-face communication is as old as the human race. For a long time, it was one of the few means people had available for communication. You often hear people say, "I like to see who I'm talking to. I like to look into their eyes and see their reactions." Advantages to face-to-face communication include a close look at the feelings/reactions associated with the words, an immediate response, and a sense of closeness. These are important, for example, in developing social relationships. [Elicit other advantages of face-to-face communication.] Face-to-face communication is often referred to as *interactive communication*.

The telephone is another means of interactive communication. It does not have the face-to-face option, although scientists promise this feature will be available soon through videophones. However, many people do not think that such a feature would be a good thing because "it would take away our privacy."

In 1876 [point date out on time line], Alexander Graham Bell made the first telephone call from one room in his house to another. Bell's mother and wife were both deaf and Bell had been interested in sound for many years. [Show pictures of early telephones, illustrating how they worked.]

A microphone in the mouthpiece of the sending telephone changes the sound of your voice into an electric signal. This electric signal travels through the telephone lines to the receiving telephone. In the receiving telephone, a vibrating membrane in a small loudspeaker in the earpiece converts the signal back into the sound of your voice. [See p. 67 of *Great Inventions* for illustrations and p. 158 of *How Things Work* for a more detailed explanation.]

The telephone is a very useful means of communication. It enables people to share personal, interactive communication across both short and long distances. If you had lived before the telephone was invented, you could have written letters to your grandmother in Florida, but the only way you could have spoken to her directly would have been for one of you to travel to visit the other.

Optional   [Discuss with the students telephone etiquette and the proper use of the telephone in emergency situations (the information they should provide when calling for help). Have students role-play situations involving using telephone etiquette and calling 911. You should take an active role in facilitating the enactments and role-plays.] [End of optional section.]

Gestures are nonverbal personal interactive means of communicating. People learn to use gestures to communicate at times when speech might be impossible or inconvenient. [Model using the following gestures: *be quiet, come here, stay away, good-bye.* Discuss the reasons for using gestures. Responses might include communicating during a noisy event (crowd could not hear the call, so referee uses signals), keeping the message secret from others, wanting to communicate with one person without disrupting an ongoing activity.]

Sign language is considered a personal and interactive but nonverbal means of communicating. It is a language that has been created for people who cannot hear sound. They learn to associate meaning with signs created by the hands. Sometimes the mouth and facial expressions are used as well. Sign language can be learned just like Italian, French, Russian, and other languages. [Demonstrate the use of sign language. See *Sign Language* by Greene and Dicker. See also Lesson 9.]

A letter or greeting card is an example of a personal delayed interactive means of communication. You can send or receive a letter or card from near or far; however, you do not personally talk with the other party. Imagine that you are sending a letter to a pen pal in Mexico. [Use the Steps in Postal Delivery chart.]

STEPS IN POSTAL DELIVERY
1. Write a letter and enclose it in a stamped, addressed envelope.
2. Drop it into the mailbox.
3. Postal worker picks up letter and takes it to the post office.
4. Sort mail at U.S. post office.
5. Transport mail to the airport by U.S. mail truck.
6. Put mail for Mexico on a jet.
7. Jet flies to Mexico, crossing a border between the two countries.
8. Mail is unloaded at airport in Mexico.
9. Postal truck transports mail to Mexican post office.
10. Mail is sorted.
11. Mail is delivered.
12. Letter is received.

This process takes several days; therefore, when people are considering how to send a message they have to think about the time factor. Also, not all people in the world have the range of choices that we have. Instead of sending a birthday greeting by letter or card that you make, you could decide to call. Calling far away might require you to pay a lot more money, although a nice card and the postage needed to mail it could cost more than a brief phone call.

Email is another way to send and receive messages. Just as the post office delivers the mail to your house address, a computer network delivers messages to your email address.

One difference between a message sent through the postal service and a message sent by email is the time that it takes. [Review the steps of the postal system; use *My Letter* by J. Parsons; then demonstrate the use of email.] With email, you type your message with an address at the top and press a few keys to send it. [Watch the message being sent. Time it.] The message will probably reach its destination (a computer) in a matter of seconds, although the receiver may not pick up your message right away.

The "roads" that connect the computers are cables and wires—sometimes the same wires that give you telephone service. Because electronic mail travels so quickly, people who like to use it sometimes refer to the postal system as "snail mail." Electronic mail has other advantages too: It's often cheaper than regular mail and it doesn't require envelopes, stamps, or trips to the mailbox.

Activity

Provide each table with a series of cards with words and/or pictures that illustrate the various means of communication. Have each group sort them into two types: personal interactive and delayed interactive. Allow time for discussion.

Summarize

- There are many means of personal interactive and personal delayed interactive communication.
- Long, long ago, face-to-face communication was the only personal method. Today we have many more choices.
- We decide what means of communication to use based on our purpose, location, and cost/convenience factors.

Assessment

Revisit the Types and Means of Communication Chart that the class has partially completed. Using brief scenarios, ask for "thumbs up" when the students are ready to identify which *means* of communication and what *type* will most likely be used.

Scenario #1 I have an emergency. The stove is on fire and I need to get a message to the fire department.

Scenario #2 My friend has just been hit with a baseball. He fell over and I think he has fainted. We need to call a doctor.

Scenario #3 My friend has a birthday next week. I want to wish him happy birthday.

Scenario #4 My friend is deaf. I want to tell her what we are having for lunch.

Scenario #5 We are playing basketball; it's an exciting game and the crowd is noisy. The coach wants us to take a time-out.

Scenario #6 I want to get some information about food groups from my aunt. I know she isn't home until late tonight; however, I need to get a message to her today.

After the group assessment, have each student write two sentences explaining the most important idea he or she acquired from the lesson. Encourage the students to share their responses with the class and with at least one family member.

Home Assignment

Encourage each student to share what she or he learned about interactive and delayed interactive communication. Then with an older sibling or adult, have the student talk about one means of personal interactive or personal delayed interactive communication that's very important to the family and why. The students should be prepared to share the response with the class during the next lesson. Send home a copy of the Types and Means of Communication chart.

Dear Parents,

I have sent home a copy of a chart labeled Types and Means of Communication that we discussed in class today. Encourage your child to share what he or she learned. Then talk about one means of personal interactive or personal delayed interactive communication that is very important to your family and why. Make sure your child is ready to share your family's ideas with our class during our next lesson. Thank you!

Sincerely,

FIGURE 7   Model Letter to Parents

Lesson 5

Mass Communication

Resources

- Word card—Mass Communication
- Pictures and examples of mass communication (e.g., local daily, regional, or national newspapers, school newspapers, radio, television, etc.) and chart for displaying them
- Time line
- Example of a ballad
- Picture of first printing press
- Chart: Types and Means of Communication (from Lesson 4)
- Pretaped commercial (e.g., Nike)
- Television newscast (optional)
- Radio (If possible, show an early model and a more contemporary model.)
- Ads (for example, newspaper, magazine, article of clothing with corporate logo)
- Figure 9, Data Retrieval Sheet

Children's Literature

Ardley, N. (Ed.). (1995). *How Things Work*. London: Dorling Kindersley.

Harris, R., & Harris, C. (1993). *Making Your Own Newspapers*. Holbrook, MA: Bob Adams.

Hockman, H. (Ed.). (1993). *Great Inventions*. New York: Dorling Kindersley.

Jaen, P. (1996). *Watching TV*. Bothell, WA: The Wright Group.

Merbreier, W. C. (1996). *What's Behind What You See?* New York: Farrar, Straus, and Giroux.

Petersen, D. (1983). *A True Book: Newspapers*. Chicago: Children's Press.

Quantock, R. (1993). *The School Newspaper*. Bothell, WA: The Wright Group.

Sandler, M. (1996). *Inventors*. New York: HarperCollins.

General Comments

The focus of this lesson will be on mass communication. Included in this category are news and information, entertainment (movies, videos, television), and persuasion and advertising that are available in both print and visual forms. Students will have the opportunity to discuss and examine examples of mass media and begin to understand how they impact our lives. Students also will begin to appreciate the global nature of modern society due to the developments in mass media.

General Purposes or Goals

To: (1) help students understand and appreciate means of mass media, their characteristics, and the trade-offs involved in using each type; and (2) provide students with opportunities to examine the means of mass media and begin to understand and appreciate how they influence people's lives.

Main Ideas to Develop

- Mass communication is one of the three major types.
- Within that category are many means (e.g., newspapers, magazines, radio, video, movies, television, etc.).
- Mass communication has many purposes: (1) to provide news and inform; (2) to entertain; (3) to persuade; and (4) to facilitate global connections.
- Mass media are accessible in almost every part of the world; however, socioeconomic factors affect an individual's level of access.
- The mass media we select should be based on our needs/goals.

Teaching Tips from Barbara

After this lesson was completed, I had my students help me create a bulletin board showing the three major types of communication. This enabled us to tie the information from Lessons 4 and 5 together. My students actually found it easier to sort communication into two groups, interactive and mass communication. To complete the assessment, I gave each student three index cards with the letters *N, R,* and *T,* standing for newspapers, radio, and television. It was quicker and easier to complete this way.

Starting the Lesson

Share and discuss the home assignment. After briefly reviewing the terms *personal interactive* and *personal delayed interactive,* display a word card that says "Mass Communication." Ask the students to explain what that means and how they think it would differ from personal communication. Ask the class to give examples of mass communication. List their responses. Ask them to provide ideas regarding the possible advantages of mass communication. Disadvantages? List their responses. Revisit the lists at the conclusion of the lesson.

Show pictures and examples of mass communication. Mass communication allows people all around the world to receive the same programs and messages. Refer to the types of mass media listed on the data retrieval chart for the home assignment. Indicate that this lesson will focus on newspapers, radio, and television, but note that there are many other examples, and as a part of their home assignments, students will be able to talk about these as well.

Suggested Lesson Discussion

The mass media that we select should be based on our communication needs/goals. What do we need/want? How much time do we have? How much can we spend? Are there other considerations?

Newspapers [Show several local, regional, or national newspapers, the school newspaper, and so on. Allow the students to examine the examples.] A newspaper is news printed on paper. It tells people what is going on in your local area, in the world, or with a special group (school newspaper). [Use a newspaper to show and describe the sections. Pick out appropriate articles and read/paraphrase the copy.]

People who gather news and write stories for newspapers are called *reporters*. The very first reporters (town criers) traveled around shouting out announcements or telling the news in songs or poems because printing and newspapers hadn't been invented yet. Their songs or poems were called *ballads*. [Show a ballad.] Later, handwritten notices were posted in town squares. Then the first printing press was invented [show picture]. This machine printed many copies of written stories set in type. The first real newspaper was printed in London, England, in 1665. [Point out this date on the time line.]

The first successful newspaper in the United States was printed in 1704. [Point out on time line.] It was called the *Boston News Letter*. [Show picture from *A True Book: Newspapers*.] It was very small—the size of a notebook page printed on both sides. In the early days (1700s), one person did all the jobs: reporter, editor, printer, seller, and so on. Benjamin Franklin ran a one-man newspaper [show picture of Benjamin Franklin from *A True Book: Newspapers*]. Most of the news in the first American newspapers was taken from the larger English newspapers that were brought to America on ships that traveled very slowly. By the time these newspapers reached America and the news was reprinted, it was several months old. For example, the death of a king or other famous person was old news by the time it reached our country.

In 1833 [show year on time line], the *New York Sun* was the first newspaper to print the day's news (i.e., put out a new edition each day). It was also the first one to use advertisements. Gradually, street sales, newsstands, and home delivery became available.

Putting a newspaper together takes many people who do a variety of jobs.

Optional [Invite a resource person from a local newspaper to share its "story" accompanied with video footage or a photo-essay that illustrates the jobs accomplished in each department.]

Editorial Department   People gather news and prepare stories.

- Reporters write stories about news they have gathered.
- Photographers take pictures to go with the stories.
- Some editors read the stories to make sure they are "correct."
- Other editors decide what stories should be printed, and where.

Mechanical Department   This is the department that prints the news.*

- Edited stories are put in type (typesetting).
- Photographs are developed.
- The type and pictures are put in place, following the layout determined by the editorial department.
- When everything is in place, the newspaper is printed and the copies are trucked out to be sold or circulated.

Business Department   This department takes care of the business of the newspaper.

- It sells advertising space to stores, companies, or individuals [show and read selected ads of various kinds].
- One of this department's main jobs is to sell the newspaper in stores, machines, newsstands, or through home deliveries (by carriers). Some newspapers are delivered through the mail (because people like to read the newspaper from another state or country).
- This department also takes care of paying the bills and keeping records.

Modern newspapers can print news from anywhere in the world almost as soon as it happens. When a news event takes place somewhere, the story is typed into a computer and sent to newspapers around the world. Organizations that distribute these stories to newspapers are called news services, such as the Associated Press or United Press International.

Several careers are associated with newspapers. [Show pictures to illustrate these careers.] These include reporters, photographers, editors, advertising sales, and printers.

Optional   [This is an excellent opportunity for a combined social studies and literacy project involving making a class newspaper. See *Making Your Own Newspapers* packet.]

Radio   Another means of mass communication is the radio. [Ask students how many listened to the radio before they came to school. If they did, what do they view as advantages? Disadvantages? If not, why not? What advantages might it have over newspapers? Disadvantages?]

---

*Much of the mechanical work is now handled electronically. Computers, printers, and digital cameras are rapidly replacing typesetting and manual layouts.

[Show a radio. Turn it on. Listen to the news for a brief period. Discuss its use as a source for news for a student who is just beginning to read. Then show pictures found on pp. 10–11 of *Great Inventions* and briefly explain how a radio works. Point to the time line, indicating that radio was invented more than one hundred years ago.]

In 1887, Henrich Hertz discovered that a big electric spark sends out invisible waves of electricity called radio waves. They travel so fast that they could go around the earth seven times in one second. In 1894, Guglielmo Marconi had the idea of using radio waves to send messages, and it worked [see pp. 10–11 in *Great Inventions*; p. 82 in *Inventors*; p. 147 in *How Things Work*].

The sound comes out of the speaker which is behind a fabric grille. The speaker has a membrane—sort of a drumhead—that is shaken by the electrical signals. The shaking of the membrane makes the sounds we hear. Valves are tubes that make the electrical signals stronger. The antenna wire plugs in here [see diagram in *Great Inventions*]. When the radio waves reach the antenna wire, they are turned into little electrical signals. Before TV, people used to gather as a family and listen to radio news and entertainment shows at night.

Television   The most popular form of mass media today is television. The first TV went on sale to the public in 1939 [point to time line]. [Ask students how many watched TV before they came to school today. Why? Why not? Have a brief discussion focusing on what they view as advantages and disadvantages of television compared to other forms of mass media. Record the responses on a chart.] Television is affordable; it provides the same opportunities that newspapers and radio provide plus lots of pictures; it's entertaining (e.g., adventure, comedy, cartoons, drama, movies, etc.). Television news is usually more current than that found in a newspaper. However, the typical newscast does not provide the depth found in some newspapers. Sometimes you don't hear the "story" because you are so busy looking at the pictures.

[Using pictures and drawings from *What's Behind What You See?* and *How Things Work*, briefly explain how a television works.] Television sends signals through the air. It changes what a camera views into an electrical signal that can be sent through the air to a TV set, which converts the signal back into visual images. This brings into our homes the sights and sounds of distant countries and the best and worst of people's ideas and adventures.

[If time permits, have the class watch a portion of a newscast. Compare it to the coverage in a newspaper. Point out the use of commercials—their role and the reasons for their inclusion. (Use a pretaped commercial to illustrate.)] Companies whose ads are shown on TV pay the TV stations to show the ads. That's why free TV is free—the costs of making and showing the programs are paid for by the advertisers. We get the programs free, but we have to get the ads, too.

Advertising is making a product or service known and appealing to the public in hopes that people will want to purchase it. Advertising appeals to one or more of our needs (e.g., safety, love, esteem, self-actualization, aesthetic, and the need to know). The cost of advertising is passed on to us—the consumers—by adding its cost to the price of the product.

Commercials are intended to influence the viewer. This is called *persuasion*. The companies who advertise their products pay a lot of money to do so—much more for television ads than for newspaper or radio ads. When you watch an ad on television, ask yourself: Does it present information about the product or good reasons that you should buy it? Just show the product? Suggest that using the product will make you more popular? [Elicit examples.]

[Show the students a Nike (or other name brand) shoe or clothing article and explain that in addition to TV commercials, many companies communicate who they are on their clothing. They also advertise in newspapers, magazines, etc.]

Activity

Pair/Share—Have students think about one important thing they learned about mass communication and share it with a partner. Then discuss as a large group. List responses on the white board.

Summarize

- There are many forms of mass communication.
- The most popular is television, which provides us with the widest range of entertainment choices and opportunities to learn about the weather, news, and sports.
- We make choices regarding mass communication based on our needs and wants.
- While television is a relatively inexpensive means of entertainment for most of us, we can be influenced by it (through commercials) to spend more money on certain products than we might have otherwise.
- Mass communication provides broadcasters with the ability to send the same programs or messages to people all over the world.

Assessment

Briefly describe a use of mass communication and ask the students to give "thumbs up" when they are ready to name the means that they would use. [Option: Provide each student with an answer sheet and ask the students to record their responses (N = newspaper, R = radio, T = television).]

1. Individuals most concerned with having people of all ages protect the environment by conserving our forests would probably get their message out by _____. (R, T)

2. Companies most interested in getting their audiences to visualize their products, identify with people who use or support the products, and ultimately buy the products would probably use the _____. (T)

3. Individuals most interested in an in-depth story about their favorite basketball team would probably use the _____. (N)

4. People most interested in being entertained for the evening would probably pick _____. (T)

5. People most interested in receiving an update of the national news while driving would probably select the _____. (R)

6. People most interested in listening to music on the way to work would probably select the _____. (R)

7. People interested in the weather report would choose _____. (N, R, T)

8. People wanting to find out about the entertainment in their city this week would probably choose _____. (N, although R and T might also have coverage)

9. Advertising a car or house for sale (or trying to find one) _____. (N)

10. Finding out about supermarket sales this week _____. (N)

11. Finding out what movies are in town this week _____. (N)

12. Finding out if their school is closed due to a storm _____. (R)

13. Hearing the latest music releases _____. (R)

Home Assignment

With the help of an older sibling or family member, ask each student to keep an accounting of what type and how much mass media she or he uses during the next week—and (optional) the type of content/programming included. Tell them to be prepared to share the results with the class. Along with the note to parents, send home copies of the Data Retrieval Sheet (Figure 9) for recording the information.

Dear Parents,

We have been learning about mass communication. During the next week, please assist your child in keeping track of the types of mass communication he or she uses and how much time is spent using each. The enclosed data retrieval sheet will help you keep good records. Be sure your child is ready to share the results with the class on _____. Thank you!

Sincerely,

FIGURE 8   Model Letter to Parents

Mass Media: Types and Amounts of Time Spent

	Sun.	Mon.	Tues.	Wed.	Thurs.	Fri.	Sat.
Type of Mass Media			Time Spent				
Newspaper	___	___	___	___	___	___	___
Purposes (optional)	___	___	___	___	___	___	___
Radio	___	___	___	___	___	___	___
Purposes (optional)	___	___	___	___	___	___	___
Television	___	___	___	___	___	___	___
Purposes (optional)	___	___	___	___	___	___	___
Other (Internet)	___	___	___	___	___	___	___
Purposes (optional)	___	___	___	___	___	___	___

FIGURE 9 Data Retrieval Sheet

Lesson 6

A Trip to a Television Station

Resources
- Permission slips for field trip to local television station
- Map layout of the television station
- Photos of television station—exterior and interior
- Television Tour Activity Sheets (Figure 11)
- Pencils and clipboards

Children's Literature
Civardi, A. (1985). *Things People Do*. London: Usborne.

Merbreier, W. C. (1996). *Television—What's Behind What You See*. New York: Farrar, Straus, & Giroux.

Gano, L. (1990). *Television—Electronic Pictures*. San Diego, CA: Lucent.

General Comments
The intent of this lesson is to take the class on a field trip to a local television station and make some planned observations regarding station layout, the types of activities carried out at the station and their complexity, and the types of workers needed to deliver television programming to our homes, as well as to begin thinking about some of the indirect and direct costs associated with television. You, and perhaps parent volunteers as well, should previsit the television station to work out the logistics of the trip, consult with the manager, and "walk through" the student activity sheet.

General Purposes or Goals
To develop understanding and appreciation of: (1) the layout of the television station; (2) the range of activities associated with television programming; (3) the nature of the tasks involved and the types of workers needed to bring us a variety of television programs; and (4) the costs involved in the television industry—and what we pay for indirectly or directly.

Main Ideas to Develop
- Most broadcast TV stations are a part of a national chain of stations called a network. The network provides programs for its member stations to share. Local stations produce some of their own programs, but most of the day is filled with network programming.

- In the control room, the director communicates with the people in the studio via microphone. The engineers work with the studio lights and microphone. They make sure the picture being shown is clear and sharp and that the sound is good.
- The layout of the television station is planned to enable the workers to ensure that the programming is handled professionally.
- There is a range of jobs that need to be done at the television station.

Teaching Tips from Barbara

Because of time constraints, we were unable to do this field trip, but it would be very valuable. Instead, we were able to have a local TV weatherman visit our class. He shared information about the weathercasts and showed some of the equipment. He even allowed students from the class to videotape us for the newscast.

Starting the Lesson

Discuss the home assignment. Introduce the lesson with an outline map showing the route to the local television station, a photo of its exterior, and several photos of the various rooms (e.g., reception, newsroom, control room, sound stage, etc.).

Talk about the roles, norms, and expectations of the workers and the students on tour. Role-play guidelines to follow when on field trips. Provide each small group of students and volunteers with a pencil and a simple activity sheet attached to a clipboard (see Figure 11).

If possible, organize each table as a group and assign each group a parent volunteer to conduct an overall "broad brush" tour of the television station to observe the layout and types of work being done. Depending on the local station's tour plan, small groups might rotate through various operational centers or the large group might move through as a whole. Make sure students have a clear understanding of station rules. Show students copies of the activity sheet that will be completed at the end of the tour. Establish the expectations.

Suggested Lesson Discussion

[Information that will be shared during the tour will include, but may not be limited to, the following.]

Most broadcast TV stations are part of a national chain of stations called a *network*. The network provides programs for its member stations to share. Local stations produce some of their own programs (especially local newscasts), but most of the day is filled with network programming delivered to affiliates by satellite (i.e., the station receives microwave signals that travel through the air).

Local TV stations have to pay their employees who produce local programs. They also have to pay the network for the programs that it sends to them. The stations get the money to pay these and other costs by charging companies who want to televise commercials advertising what they offer. The stations can charge more for advertising on programs that draw large audiences than on programs that draw smaller audiences, so TV programmers specialize in trying to figure out what style of program will attract the largest number of viewers at a particular time during the broadcast day. The programmers study reports on such things as age, gender, and interests, and they try to learn as much as they can about all programs in production. For example, early morning programming is split between cartoons and wake-up news shows. This is a time when families are getting ready for school or often preparing to go to work, so the different television stations offer choices—for parents to catch up on the news or for kids to be entertained by cartoons as adults shower, for example.

Prime time follows about an hour after the evening news. It's the time when more members of the family are available to watch television. The goal for every station is to get the biggest audience possible and keep that audience until bedtime. A thirty-second commercial on a network program during prime time costs a company more than one hundred thousand dollars—more than most families earn in a whole year. If your family buys the product being advertised, your family is paying indirectly, because companies pass along their advertising costs when they set the prices for their products.

Control Room   A look into the master control room reminds us how complicated the television operation really is. Every button means something different! Engineers in the master control room control all video and sound received, produced, and broadcast by a station. In many ways, the master control tower is something like the airport's control tower—except at the local TV station, there are many runways "in," but only one runway "out," which is the broadcast channel.

Row upon row of small television screens show the master control engineer programs and commercials coming in from the studios, the news vans, the helicopters, and the network.

The sound, picture, and color quality of every program are checked and adjusted here. The control room is cool because sensitive electronic equipment can slow down or give out if it overheats.

Hundreds of commercials are loaded into these giant videotape decks. The tapes are pulled up, played, and returned to their appropriate slots, all by computer.

An engineer programs the entire day's schedule into the computer. The schedule is revised if a commercial is added or dropped, or if a program runs long or short. If a big news story comes in, the engineer can cut into a program and insert a news bulletin. The master control engineer also records all programs produced locally. All incoming programs from the satellite dishes on the station lawn or roof are also taped.

Newsroom   Another section of the television station is the newsroom. The newsroom team goes out on assignments, puts stories together, and plans the show. Here you see the reporter, video editor, camera operator, and producer. There is a studio team that consists of on-air anchors and the studio crew, which includes the director and engineers who get the show on the air. [Observe the crew in action.] Reporters get the story by going to the site and interviewing people; videocam operators go with them and record video; editors decide what is most important or of most interest to viewers, how much time to give each story, and what to show and say; sales representatives sell advertising space. These key jobs all have parallels at newspapers. It takes about forty people eight hours (more than the amount of time you spend in school in a day) to put together a half-hour news show.

[If time permits, show the students the mini television station on wheels in the parking lot.] It can send local news stories back to the station as they are happening. The pictures are recorded by the video camera at a remote site, sent back to the station as microwave signals, and broadcast directly to TV viewers.

Sound Stage   [A tour of the sound stage is optional.] Sets are designs created to look like a dining room, an office, or a certain place (e.g., garden, desert, etc.). Outdoor sets are equipped with overhead machines to produce rain and snow effects. A camera crew, producer, and director work with actors and actresses (who have learned their scripts) to provide the television audience with a show.

Activity

At the conclusion of the field trip, have students work in groups to complete the Television Tour Activity Sheet (see Figure 11). Discuss the responses.

Summarize

- Television is our most popular form of mass communication.
- Local television stations produce some of their own programs, but most of the days and evenings are filled with network programming.
- There is a range of jobs that need to be done at a television station.

- The layout of the television station is planned to enable the workers to do their jobs in professional ways.
- We pay for television directly as well as indirectly.

Assessment

Provide each table with a different open-ended starter for a paragraph related to the field trip. You may wish to invite upper-grade mentors or adult volunteers to serve as recorders. Examples of open-ended starters:

1. Going to the local television station was interesting because _____

   _____

2. The jobs at the television station that seemed most interesting were

   _____ and _____ [select two] because

   _____

3. To be a local newscaster you need to _____

   _____

4. The control room at the local television station can be described as

   _____

5. The newsroom at the local television station can be described as

   _____

6. It would be fun working in a news van because _____

   _____

7. We pay for television directly as well as indirectly by _____

   _____

Home Assignment

Compile and copy the group paragraphs (assessment) and encourage the students to read them to one or more family members. Then, as a family, have them discuss and decide what the most interesting job at a television station might be and why.

Dear Parents,

As you know, our class visited a local television station. Please spend a few minutes with your child as she or he reads the group paragraphs that summarize interesting aspects of the trip. Then together discuss what your family thinks would perhaps be the most interesting job at the television station and why. Children will be asked to share the responses during our next lesson. Thank you!

Sincerely,

FIGURE 10 Model Letter to Parents

1. Describe the local television station.

_____

_____

_____

2. What types of work do you see being done at this television station?

_____

_____

_____

3. Name three activities that go on in the control room.

   1. _____

   2. _____

   3. _____

4. Name three activities that go on in the newsroom.

   1. _____

   2. _____

   3. _____

5. What is the purpose of the news van?

_____

_____

6. What indirect costs are "tacked on" to what we buy as the result of watching television?

_____

_____

Explain. _____

7. What did you learn by visiting the station?

_____

_____

_____

FIGURE 11 Television Tour Activity Sheet

© 2002 by Janet Alleman and Jere Brophy from *Social Studies Excursions, K–3: Book Two*. Portsmouth, NH: Heinemann.

Lesson 7

Careers in Communication

Resources

- Photos and drawings of a range of careers associated with communication
- Interview schedule for eliciting responses regarding careers related to communication (Figure 13)
- Upper-grade mentors
- Role-play cards: secretary, special reading teacher, speech therapist, librarian, school psychologist, etc.

Children's Literature

Brandenberg, A. (1984). *Feelings*. New York: William Morrow & Co.

Christelow, E. (1995). *What Do Authors Do?* New York: Clarion Books.

Civandi, A. (1985). *Things People Do*. London: Usborne.

Guthrie, D., Bentley, N., & Arnsteen, K. (1994). *The Young Author's Do-It-Yourself Book*. Brookfield, CT: The Millbrook Press.

Johnson, N. (1989). *All in a Day's Work*. Boston: Little, Brown & Co.

Maynard, C. (1997). *Jobs People Do*. New York: Dorling Kindersley.

Quantock, R. (1993). *The School Newspaper*. Bothell, WA: The Wright Group.

General Comments

For this lesson, students will visit one of four sites in the school to learn about the careers of four workers they often see but don't know very much about: for example, school secretary, school librarian, special reading teacher, school psychologist, speech therapist, and so on. Students might visit these sites as a total class or in small groups. Students will pose as reporters like those they met during their field trip to the television station. They could audio- or videotape the interview and take photos. The class might also engage in additional dialogue about other careers related to communication. If some parents' careers are related to communication, this would be a good time to invite them to the class to describe their work. This lesson provides a wealth of opportunities for natural integration with literacy (e.g., an author could be invited to the school and either make a formal presentation or serve as a resource for one of the groups to interview).

General Purposes or Goals

To develop: (1) understanding and appreciation for the diversity of career opportunities involved in communication; (2) understanding of the roles of people who work in communication and the costs associated with their work; and (3) a sense of efficacy regarding the possibilities for pursuing existing careers in communication or even creating new ones.

Main Ideas to Develop

- We depend on many people for giving and receiving communication.
- Communication workers provide us with a range of services that impact our daily lives.
- We pay for the services that these people provide to us.

Teaching Tips from Barbara

An easy way to record the information from the interviews is with a tape recorder or video camera. That way your students don't have to focus on reading or writing skills. If possible, break your class into small groups and have each group interview separately. Then take a day to "screen" the videos and look for similarities between the interview answers.

Starting the Lesson

Discuss the home assignment. Then review the field trip experience to the local television station. Review the types of workers at the television station and the work they do.

Large-Group Discussion and Activity

[Show a picture of a reporter.] Television stations, radio stations, and newspapers all have men and women who serve as reporters. Their responsibility is to get information and write it up for inclusion in newspaper articles or radio or TV news reports. One technique that a reporter uses is the interview. Sometimes a reporter prepares questions in advance and other times he asks the questions as they come to mind. The reporter takes notes, uses a video camera or tape recorder (if the story will be used in a news program on radio or television), and/or takes photographs to use if it will be presented in the newspaper or a magazine. Today you will serve as reporters. [Give each student or each upper-grade mentor an interview schedule, or have the class generate questions to gather information from people in their school who have careers related to communication.] Sample questions that might be used:

1. What is your name?
2. What is your job?
3. Describe your major responsibilities.
4. What do you like most about your work?
5. What is the most frustrating part of what you do?
6. What educational background prepared you for your profession?
7. Can you show us examples of what you do?
8. What else do you want to tell us about your work?

[One plan would be for each student or small group to have an upper-grade mentor to serve as the scribe. The mentors could also record the conversations (audio- or videotape) as well as serve as the photographer. For literacy, the early elementary students with their mentors could write up and present their stories.]

Suggested Lesson Discussion

[This format can be used for gathering data from the secretary, special reading teacher, speech therapist, librarian, and psychologist.]

Secretary   The secretary communicates face-to-face, by telephone, by email, by fax, by letter, and so on. It is very important that the secretary listen carefully to others so that she can accurately record the message. She needs to know which means of communication she will use, given the urgency of the message, its length, the location of the person expected to receive it, and other factors. The secretary performs many duties every day that require communication.

Special Reading Teacher   The special reading teacher helps students who have difficulties with letters and sounds, maybe because they are from a different culture, have difficulty seeing or hearing, or have a unique learning problem.

Speech Therapist   The speech therapist helps students with their oral communication problems by teaching them to hear and pronounce the sounds of a language. Sometimes students need special assistance because they come from another culture, or perhaps they have difficulty hearing sounds and words.

Librarian   The librarian spends most of her day with written forms of communication. However, many of the libraries today have expanded into media centers emphasizing sound and sight—auditory and visual. The librarian decides what to purchase for the school's collection, then stamps each purchase with the school's logo and assigns it a unique number so as to know where it is kept and where to return it after it has been borrowed.

Psychologist   The psychologist usually works with individuals or small groups. One major responsibility is to encourage children to express themselves verbally and to examine how they feel and explain why. Psychologists spend a lot of time listening. [The book *Feelings* would be a useful resource for the psychologist portion of this lesson.]

[If an author were to serve as one of the resource people for this lesson, either as an interviewee or a presenter, an appropriate sequence of literary lessons might focus on how to write, illustrate, and produce your own book. The literacy tie-in might be especially appealing given the reading and writing emphasis in the early grades.]

Optional   [*The Young Author's Do-It-Yourself Book* emphasizes how to write, illustrate, and produce your own book. This can serve as a valuable resource. The authors emphasize and illustrate writing fiction and nonfiction, editing, illustrating, binding, and promotion. They all have impressive backgrounds that are closely associated with the lives of young children. The book is an excellent resource to use in promoting writing as a career as well as in guiding students in authoring their own stories, drawing their own pictures, and producing their own books.]

[Another children's book, *What Do Authors Do?*, could be read to students. The illustrations are humorous; however, the ideas are basic. Christelow shows how authors develop their ideas into books and then find publishers for them. The dedication and patience that writing requires and the help supplied by friends, family, editors, designers, and printers are expressed in this source.]

Activity

Allow time for each individual or group and the upper-grade mentor to work on the "stories" gleaned from the interviews. This activity will take more than one class period.

Summarize

- We depend on many people for personal and mass communication.
- All of these people need special skills and are paid by the institution or company associated with them.
- Communication workers, many of whom are found in our school, provide us with a range of services that impact our daily lives.

Assessment

Using role-play cards and yourself as the key role-player/facilitator, have a student select a card, describe the communication career opportunity observed in the school, explain what the work involves, and tell whether it would be a job that he or she might like to try someday. Why or why not? [Note: Several students could play the same role, each building on previous responses. Example: Role—librarian. This person assists students in finding written, oral, and visual communication to explain an idea, describe a place, meet a person, etc. This person needs to go to college to learn how to make good decisions regarding instructional materials for students, etc.]

Home Assignment

Encourage students to share with their families stories gleaned from the interviews with the people in their school who have careers related to the communication field. Then encourage families to talk with friends, neighbors, and relatives engaged in work related to personal and/or mass communication. Send home copies of Figure 13 for recording highlights of these discussions. Communication workers include the following:

Television station personnel

Radio station personnel

Designers of communication devices (telephone, fax), stage sets, etc.

Programmers

Salespeople for ads, commercials

Newspaper and magazine personnel

Authors, publishers

Equipment repair personnel

Researchers

Stage managers, actors, actresses, lighting engineers

Secretaries, receptionists, librarians

Dear Parents,

We have been talking about careers in communication. Your child, with the help of an upper-grade mentor, interviewed an individual in our school who is in the communication field. Please encourage your child to share his or her news story. Then, assist your child in talking with someone else who is in the communication field. A partial list of possibilities along with a worksheet for recording the information have been enclosed. Your child will be asked to share his or her information during an upcoming class session. Thank you!

Sincerely,

FIGURE 12   Model Letter to Parents

NAME _____

I talked with _____ about his/her work in communication.

His/her jobs include _____

_____

_____

_____

_____

_____

Special skills needed to do a good job include _____

_____

_____

_____

_____

This work is important because _____

_____

_____

_____

_____

_____

I would/would not like to do this job someday because _____

_____

_____

_____

_____

FIGURE 13   Careers in Communication Worksheet

© 2002 by Janet Alleman and Jere Brophy from *Social Studies Excursions, K–3: Book Two*. Portsmouth, NH: Heinemann.

Lesson 8

Signs and Symbols: Nonverbal Communication

Resources
- Set of flash cards illustrating popular signs and symbols
- Figure 15: The Language of Signs and Symbols
- A range of examples illustrating signs and symbols (music score, card games, stop sign, aircraft logo, military uniform, and sports logos)
- Picture of a control panel on a vehicle
- Maps (road, weather)
- Blueprints
- Firefighter's hat

Children's Literature
Adkins, J. (1978). *Symbols: A Silent Language*. New York: Walker & Co.

Corke, D. (1994). *Messages Without Words*. Bothell, WA: The Wright Group.

Fronval, G., & Dubois, D. (1978). *Indian Signs and Symbols*. New York: Sterling.

Gibbons, G. (1993). *Puff . . . Flash . . . Bang: A Book About Signals*. New York: Morrow.

General Comments
The focus of this lesson is signs and symbols, often referred to as a *silent language* or *nonverbal communication*. Students will be intrigued by the mystery of unspoken language that can show warnings, give instructions, direct traffic, and result in enjoyment or entertainment (e.g., game of hearts; music notations that are exact and express specific moods, feelings, etc.).

General Purposes and Goals
To help students understand and appreciate: (1) the functions that symbols play in communication; (2) the universal meaning of many signs and symbols (e.g., stop sign, nonsmoking sign); and (3) the power of symbols (by observing and using them).

Main Ideas to Develop
- The language of signs and symbols has no words, but it can shout warnings, give instructions, direct traffic, or serve as the focus for games (e.g., hearts and other card games).
- Some symbols are pictures, some are shapes that began as pictures, and some are pure designs not meant to look like anything.

- Signs and symbols are important means of communication. To visitors from other parts of the world, they can be more understandable than written words.
- Some signs and devices can become so familiar that we forget they are from the silent language of symbols (e.g., math symbols). Games have many signs (e.g., hearts). Striped shirts of referees and black suits for umpires are symbols of their functions.
- Signs and symbols are powerful means of providing society with information nonverbally.

Teaching Tips from Barbara

Once again, this is a good lesson for students to practice their sorting skills. Along with sorting, however, they should be asked to support their answers using logic. I found actual examples of signs and symbols to use with the lesson. Afterward, they were added to the bulletin board display. Students continued to be "on the lookout" for other examples to add to the display as the unit progressed.

Starting the Lesson

Begin the lesson by sharing the results from the home assignment, then ask students to review the difference between verbal and nonverbal communication. Indicate that during this lesson, you are going to talk about examples of nonverbal communication. It is often referred to as a silent language because although it does not involve words, it can warn us, give us directions, direct traffic, or guide us in our decision making.

To further stimulate interest and engagement regarding signs and symbols in our lives, take a walking trip through the school building or around the block. Have students spot signs and symbols that give warnings, provide instructions, direct traffic, and so on. Return to the classroom and begin filling in the chart (see Figure 15).

After the field trip observations have been recorded, continue the lesson by describing other signs and symbols that we use in our lives. Use pictures and objects to represent the signs and symbols being described. Whenever possible, contextualize the example (e.g., skull and crossbones on a bottle of poison).

Suggested Lesson Discussion

[Show examples of signs and symbols.]

The language of symbols has no words, but it can show warnings, give instructions, direct traffic, and guide us as we play cards.

Some signs and symbols are pictures; some are shapes that began as pictures; and some are pure designs not meant to look like anything. Some are new; some have existed a long time; some change. Even our letters are symbols—signs that represent sounds. They came from stylized pictures of objects that carried their respective sounds in ancient Egypt— or wherever men and women began to write.

Symbols are an important part of communication. To visitors from other parts of the world, they can be more understandable than written words (e.g., universal traffic and traveler information signs). Some signs and devices can become so familiar that we forget that they are from the silent language of symbols [show math symbols and hearts (card game)].

Music is a great achievement of sign language. If you decide to play a musical instrument, you will probably learn to read music as well. Written music uses a special system of symbols instead of words to show how a piece of music is played. The notes that you play appear as oval shapes, often with stems and tails on a group of lines called a staff. These lines cover the normal sound range of human voices, with the highest notes at the top of the staff and the lowest notes at the bottom [see p. 28 in *Messages Without Words*].

Signs can be insistent or urgent [show a picture of a control panel on a vehicle].

Maps are sheets full of guiding symbols [show a map]. Maps show features that help travelers find their way. Some maps tell us what the weather is or is going to be like. Architectural drawings [show a blueprint] are kinds of maps. A blueprint is more than a picture; it's a guide to construction, a detailed reference for material and measurement.

Road signs are symbols [show a road sign]. The meaning must be clear in an instant, from a distance, and through rain, snow, or fog. Often people are driving quite fast, so road signs need to be read quickly. Drivers also need to be told about situations and possible dangers that they might encounter as they travel [see pictures on pp. 8–9 in *Messages Without Words*].

If you visit a national or state park to go camping, hiking, or skiing, you are likely to come across signs that tell you about the area. Some signs give warnings of danger and others point out special facilities for visitors. Many of these signs use pictures or symbols instead of words. The same pictures or symbols also appear on maps of the area to show where you can camp or picnic, what activities you can enjoy in the area, and ways that you can take care of the environment [see pp. 14–15 in *Messages Without Words*].

Hats [show firefighter's hat] flags, ringing of bells, horns, and so on also are examples of symbols. Symbols can represent careers, places, events, and more.

In an international airport, people from all over the world can be found as travelers. Special signs help people find their way around. These signs often use pictures or symbols instead of words to give directions. Symbols can speak to all travelers [see *Symbols*, pp. 20–21. Show pictures of these symbols. Also see p. 13 in *Messages Without Words*.].

For example, each airline paints a design or logo on its aircraft to help identify the airline. This logo is also on the passengers' tickets and the luggage check-in point for the airline [show examples].

Inside the airport terminal, signs using pictures or symbols point in the direction of airport facilities such as restaurants, public telephones, and ground transportation. Many of these signs appear at airports all around the world and can be recognized by people of many different nationalities [see p. 12 in *Messages Without Words*].

Military groups have insignia—symbols to help them recognize other members of their group—as well as other groups [show military uniform or picture].

Stamps or marks are other symbols (e.g., seal on document, family coat of arms, animal brand, tattoo) [show logos of local sports teams, towns, companies, universities, etc].

Trademarks are modern symbols. They lure us to buy certain products or products made by certain companies [show Nike shoe].

Symbols have several advantages: they are compact; they are legible at a distance or through difficult circumstances; they allow images to stand for much behind them (e.g., flag, corporate logo); and in many situations, they help people who cannot read a language different from their own to get the things they need (e.g., find a telephone, a restaurant, the restrooms at an airport, the nearest hospital, etc.).

Optional   Signals are another way of communicating. People use them to say things to each other without using spoken or written words. We see or hear most signals. For example, we see a light flashing from the lighthouse or we hear the car horn sound. We see the traffic light turn red or the police car's red light flashing. We hear the church bell ring and the ambulance's siren scream. We see the football referee throw both hands above his head. All of these are signals.

Thousands of years ago, ancient Romans set fires on mountaintops to send messages over long distances. These signals were often called beacon fires.

Later in time and in other parts of the world, people used drums to send messages. A tribesman might beat out a signal on his drum to send a message to a nearby village that there was about to be a great feast. In some parts of the world, drums are still used for sending messages.

During pioneer times, Native Americans were known for developing some creative ways of sending messages. For example, at the end of the growing season, they would send a message that the harvest was about to begin. They had no telephones, radios, or televisions, so they would communicate the message by starting a fire, covering it with a wet blanket, and then quickly pulling it from the smoking fire. A puff of smoke would quickly rise toward the sky. Other Native Americans used columns of smoke for signals. One column of smoke meant "pay attention." Two columns meant "all is well." Three columns of smoke meant "danger."

During the American Revolution, cannons were used as signals. They were intended to send the message that troops must move forward. Lanterns were also used as signals. One lantern meant enemies were coming by land, two if by sea.

Today we have many other sight signals. Lights are signals we see every day. A traffic light tells drivers what they should do. Some cars stop at intersections and others go through. Cars and trucks have light signals such as turn signals, brake signals, and so on.

At a railroad crossing, a sign blinks on and off to warn drivers not to cross the track because a train is coming.

Light signals guide boats and ships. Flares are used to signal for help. For example, if a car breaks down, the driver parks it at the side of a highway, places a flare next to it, and waits for help.

Flags can be used for signaling. Some flags show meaning through color and design. For example, at a racetrack a checkered flag is used to signal to a driver that he has completed the race. In America, the United States flag is often lowered from the flagpole to half-mast to indicate that an important person has died.

Hand signals are often used. For example, a finger over the mouth means "be quiet." At some sporting events, referees communicate "time-out" by making a T with their hands.

Many kinds of sound signals are a part of our everyday lives. For example, a person might whistle for the dog to return home, a teacher might blow a whistle to communicate that recess is over, and a train whistle communicates "stay off the track." Sirens usually mean that there's an emergency and we should get out of the way.

Bells are also sound signals. An alarm clock signals that it's time to get up; a school bell rings to communicate that it's the beginning of school; the doorbell rings to communicate that someone is at the door; and the telephone rings to tell you that someone wants to talk. In a theatre lobby, a chime might tell the audience that the concert is about to begin.

Sometimes bells are warning signals, telling there's a fire nearby or a burglar is trying to get into a house or car. Bells are sometimes used as safety signals, for example, to guide captains of boats into harbors on foggy nights.

Horns are still another kind of signal. They can be used to announce the arrival of guests, to indicate that it's time to get up, or to signal to other drivers or to pedestrians that they need to get out of the way.

Many signals are important in our daily lives. Often we don't think much about them, yet they help us understand our world (from Gibbons, 1993, *Puff . . . Flash . . . Bang: A Book About Signals*).

DEFINITIONS

Sign—A thing that tells you what to do (e.g., stop sign). It is an object with words. It displays information.

Symbol—A representation. It is something that stands for something else (e.g., skeleton head with crossbones means poison).

Signal—A sound or movement (gesture) that instructs you.

Activity

Table Talk—Using the collection of examples (used during the lesson) illustrating signs and symbols, ask each table to select one and as a group identify it as a sign or symbol. Have students explain when and how it is used and why it is important. Allow time for sharing and whole-group discussion.

Summarize

- The language of signs and symbols (often referred to as nonverbal communication) is a very important way to communicate.
- Many signs and symbols cut across all cultures.
- Signs and symbols provide warnings and give information and directions.

Assessment

Using a series of flash cards that depict signs and symbols, ask students to give "thumbs up" when they can identify the sign or symbol and explain why it is important.

As a class, write a group paragraph as a flip-chart journal entry focusing on the important things the children learned about signs and symbols. Duplicate the paragraph and encourage students to share it with family members.

Home Assignment

Give students blank copies of Figure 15 and ask that an older sibling or parent help them record signs and symbols that they find in their neighborhood, at home, while shopping, and so on. Each student will share his or her responses with the class.

Dear Parents,

We have been learning about signs and symbols, often referred to as silent language or nonverbal communication. Please take a few minutes with your child while she or he reads a paragraph focusing on the important things that she or he has learned about this topic. Then review the Language of Signs and Symbols chart enclosed. Perhaps you or another member of your family can assist your child in recording signs and symbols found in your neighborhood. Your child will be asked to share the results with his or her classmates. Thank you!

Sincerely,

FIGURE 14   Model Letter to Parents

List and/or draw signs and symbols that you find that help us in the following ways. Some may fit under more than one category.

GIVE WARNINGS	GIVE INSTRUCTIONS	SHOW FEATURES	DIRECT TRAFFIC	HELPS US PLAY GAMES	IDENTIFY PROFESSIONS OR WAYS OF LIFE	OTHER
Flashing red lights on police car	Fasten seatbelt	Restaurant exit	Green, yellow, red traffic light	Draw three cards (directions)	Barber pole	

FIGURE 15   The Language of Signs and Symbols (Nonverbal Communication)

© 2002 by Janet Alleman and Jere Brophy from *Social Studies Excursions, K–3: Book Two*. Portsmouth, NH: Heinemann.

Lesson 9

Communication: Languages

Resources

- Chart of greetings in several languages (for example, see Greetings from Around the World, Chart FS 2417, 1991, Frank Schaffer Publications)
- Table 4: Comparing languages (sound, sign language, and Braille)
- Signing alphabet
- Braille samples
- Upper-grade mentors
- Pictures illustrating signing and reading Braille
- Cassette tape recorder and tape to demonstrate speaking Spanish

Children's Literature

Feder, J. (1995). *Table. Chair. Bear. A Book in Many Languages*. New York: Ticknor & Fields Books for Young Readers.

Greene, L., & Dicker, E. B. (1982). *Sign Language*. New York: Franklin Watts.

Parker, S. (1989). *Living with Blindness*. New York: Franklin Watts. (Teacher Reference).

Spier, P. (1980). *People*. New York: Delacorte Press.

Taylor, B. (1989). *Living with Deafness*. New York: Franklin Watts. (Teacher Reference).

General Comments

This lesson is intended to be very interactive, with discourses centered around other languages that depend on speaking and on feeling/touching.

General Purposes or Goals

To develop an understanding and appreciation for languages that are based on speaking, observing, or touching.

Main Ideas to Develop

- Language is the symbol system that people use to show what they think and how they feel.
- Most, but not all, languages are based on sound. Language also can be based on signs that are observed or patterns of dots that are felt.
- Language is an expression of culture.

Teaching Tips from Barbara

High school language students are another great resource for this lesson. The foreign language instructors will often offer extra credit to students who will work with the elementary students to learn a few phrases and words. Songs are another fun way to introduce foreign languages and even sign language.

Starting the Lesson

Begin the lesson by reviewing the home assignment, then demonstrate speaking in Spanish (or another language), signing for the hearing impaired, and reading Braille. Ask, "What do these activities have in common?" Explain that they are all forms of communication. As the lesson unfolds, prepare a chart illustrating the similar and dissimilar characteristics of spoken languages, signing for the hearing impaired, and Braille for the visually impaired (see Table 4).

Suggested Lesson Discussion

If you are reading the journal entry on the flip chart that we wrote for the last lesson, and understanding the words, you have language. Your language is English. A language is a symbol system that people use to show what they think and how they feel. Most languages are based on sound. English-speaking people have a special sound system; Spanish- and Japanese-speaking people have other sound systems. When the sound system of language is understood, there is communication. Almost everybody can speak, but there are more than two hundred different main languages spoken around the world, plus countless variants and dialects spoken in smaller groups.

[Have students learn greetings from around the world. Use the Frank Schaffer Publications chart titled Greetings from Around the World. Introduce the students to how the greetings are written. Optional: Share *Table. Chair. Bear. A Book in Many Languages* by Jane Feder. In this playful introduction to languages, familiar objects from a child's bedroom are presented in thirteen languages and illustrated with folk art.] Language is an expression of culture.

Language is one way that people communicate with each other. It is usually transmitted through speech. Most people learn a language by first hearing it spoken and then imitating it.

However, some people cannot hear sound, or they hear so little that what they do hear makes no sense to them. These people are called *deaf* or *hearing impaired.* Without special help in communication and language use, hearing impaired people have difficulty expressing themselves and understanding what people are saying.

Sign language is a visual way to communicate, based on symbols that are seen rather than heard. Finger spelling (manual alphabet) has a special sign representing each letter in the alphabet. Formal signs are another part of the sign language system. Pantomime, or the telling of a story with body movements, is also part of the sign language system.

Signs may represent spoken words, but not every spoken word has a specific sign. A sign may be the symbol for one word or several words. For example, the sign for *dog* always means *dog;* however, the sign for *beautiful* also means *lovely, pretty, nice-looking, handsome,* and so on. Sometimes there is no way to indicate exactly what the signer has in mind unless the word is finger spelled or spoken as it is signed.

Some signs are very easy to understand because they look like the object they represent. For example, the sign for *house* [demonstrate] is made with two hands formed into the shape of a room. The sign for *ball* is made with the hands slightly cupped and the fingers touching in the shape of an imaginary ball.

Some signs for objects show an action connected with the object. For example, the sign for *milk* is made by squeezing the two hands alternatively [demonstrate] as if milking a cow. The sign for *butter* is made by using two fingers on the right hand to spread imaginary butter onto the palm of the left hand, which represents a slice of bread.

Action signs often symbolize action words. For example, the sign for *drive* is made by pantomiming the action of turning a steering wheel [demonstrate]. The sign for *jump* uses two fingers on the right hand to symbolize the legs of the jumper. The "legs" then "bounce" as if jumping up and down on the left palm. Each sign is formed on the basis of three characteristics: shape of the hands, position of the hands, and movement of the hands.

In recent years, sign language has been recognized as another language, and it is growing rapidly across the United States. Many hearing adults are going to school to learn to sign because they want to work with hearing impaired people or because they have family members or a friend who is hearing impaired. Others learn it because they have a desire to communicate with a group they could not communicate with before.

You will have the opportunity to learn to use sign language to communicate your name. [To do this, have upper-grade mentors or adult volunteers learn the signs in advance model and tutor the early elementary students. Students will have an opportunity to practice until they can use sign language to communicate their names to the class and to their family as part of the home activity.]

Just as hearing impaired people have a language, so do the visually impaired. Visually impaired or blind people can hear language, but they cannot see it, so they need another way to read it. Louis Braille (1890–1952) invented such a language. By feeling raised patterns of dots with their fingertips, people who are visually impaired can read texts written on a special Braille typewriter. [Show students a sample of Braille. If possible, have them read their names—or at least an English greeting—in Braille.]

Activity

Table Talk—Have students talk about the things they learned about languages. As a class, complete Table 4. Discuss their distinct characteristics. Address these questions: Which would be most difficult to learn? Why?

Summarize

- Language is a symbol system that people use to show what they think and how they feel.
- Most languages are based on sound. A certain combination of sounds has a certain meaning.
- English-speaking people have a special sound system.
- Spanish- and Japanese-speaking people have other sound systems.
- Language is the main way people communicate with each other.
- Language is usually transmitted through speech, although sign language is transmitted by sight and Braille is transmitted by touch.

Assessment

Have each student prepare a journal entry that reflects his or her choice regarding what type of new language he or she would want to learn and why. Begin by surveying the class and preparing a bar graph depicting student preferences. Then have students provide written reasons for their choices. Discuss ways of learning the new languages. Encourage students to share their journal entries with their families as a part of the home assignment.

Home Assignment

Encourage each student to read the journal entry to family members. The student should then be prepared to communicate a greeting in another language, use sign language to communicate his or her name, and explain the sample words written in Braille.

Some good questions for family discussion would be "What would be the value of learning at least a few words in another language? Which language would we choose? Why? Where could we get information?" Have families put together a simple plan for learning a few words in the language.

TABLE 4   Comparing Languages

SOUND	SIGN LANGUAGE	BRAILLE
Spoken	Based on shapes by hands, position of hands, and movement of hands.	Based on raised patterns of dots that are interpreted as words/sentences.
Transmitted by sound through speech	Transmitted by sight. Shapes and movements of hands are observed by receiver.	Transmitted by touch. It is based on symbols that are felt rather than heard.
Culturally oriented	Finger spelling, formal signs, and pantomime are all part of a sign language system.	By feeling raised patterns of dots with their fingertips, people who are visually impaired can read.

Dear Parents,

We have been learning about languages, which are symbol systems people use to show what they think and how they feel. Encourage your child to read his or her journal entry, explaining what new language he or she would like to learn and why. Then as a family, discuss what would be the value of learning at least a few words in another language. Where would you get information that would help you learn the new language? Your child will be asked to share the highlights of your discussion during our next class session. Thank you!

Sincerely,

FIGURE 16   Model Letter to Parents

Lesson 10

Communication: Being a Responsible Citizen

Resources
- Photos or pictures of children and adults with special needs (e.g., elderly person with cane, teenager in a wheelchair)

Children's Literature
Quantock, R. (1993). *The School Newspaper*. Bothell, WA: The Wright Group.
Senisi, E. (1998). *Just Kids*. New York: Dutton Children's Books.

General Comments
This lesson is intended to raise students' consciousness regarding responsible citizenship by helping them to become aware of their own personal power in acknowledging and responding to diversity and what they can do to contribute. They may not yet be capable of working independently to improve the human condition, but under adult guidance, they can get a sense of what it means to "help."

This lesson is built around a beautiful contemporary children's book titled *Just Kids*. The story is based on a true incident at an upstate New York school. The author tells of the experiences of a girl who visits a special-needs classroom and gets to know and understand the kids there.

(Note: *Just Kids* probably cannot be read and discussed in a single session, so you can select sections for the lesson focus or spread the text and discussion over two class periods.)

Main Ideas to Develop
- Communication and understanding go hand in hand.
- We do not have to leave our classroom or school to find people who have special needs—needs that we can help satisfy by learning to communicate with them.
- By coming to understand how people respond to their special situations, we can become more supportive and helpful to our peers who have special needs.
- Sometimes people need special assistance to help them overcome disabilities. This special assistance might come in the form of professional people, volunteers, peer help, or donations of money or goods for special equipment. Communication serves as an underlying theme.
- Sometimes when we are unfamiliar with what we see, we misinterpret it. These misinterpretations can be eliminated through better communication.

Teaching Tips from Barbara

The information in this lesson is more important than ever. Our school district has adopted a character education curriculum that ties to this lesson well. I chose to expand the lesson beyond its suggested parameters of special-needs kids. We also included new students, people who like different things, and people of different races. We wrote about ways to make everyone feel welcome in our class.

Starting the Lesson

Begin the lesson by discussing the home assignment. Lead into this lesson by saying, "Sometimes when we are unfamiliar with what we see, we misinterpret it." Explain a reaction you had the first time you saw a very, very short adult or an individual who had lost an arm, for example.

Suggested Class Discussion

Under these circumstances, we might laugh. We might try to avoid the person or situation. We might say negative things to others. This can be really unfair! We need to find ways to learn about these situations—read about and get to know people who are in some ways different from ourselves, and take positive actions to help others and also give us practice in being respectful, kind, caring, and more forgiving.

[Introduce the class to *Just Kids*.] In almost every school, there are children with disabilities, some more observable than others. The book is based on a true incident in an upstate New York school. Cindy, who is the main character in the story, misunderstood some of her peers, made fun of them, and made them feel bad. It is an example of misinterpreted communication. Cindy has been asked to visit these children in their class, so that she may learn more about them, better understand and appreciate them, and learn how to communicate with them.

In the story, Cindy meets children with autism, ADHD, epilepsy, and learning disabilities. She learns that they work just as hard as she does, but sometimes their bodies and brains just don't cooperate. She realizes that they deserve respect, friendliness, and extra support so they can achieve, too.

[Select sections of the story and lead a discussion of each of Cindy's encounters. As the conversation ensues, as a class, compile a list of what "positive citizens" in this class can do to assist others who have special needs.]

Activity

Pair/Share—Using photos or pictures to stimulate discussion, have students talk about all of the kinds of people in their community that they need to learn to communicate with (e.g., elderly person who is blind, a teenager in a wheelchair, etc.). As a class, list all of these special circumstances. Discuss what students can do in order to become better communicators with them and as a result, more responsible citizens to them.

Summarize

- Sometimes when we are unfamiliar with what we see, we misinterpret it.
- Misinterpretations can be eliminated through better communication.

Assessment

The editorial section of a newspaper is a kind of meeting ground for ideas. It can include a message from the editor, known as an editorial, as well as letters to the editor from readers. (See pp. 20–21, "Editorial," in *The School Newspaper.*) Write a group editorial for the newspaper focusing on "what we should do to make special-needs kids feel welcome" in our class, our school, on the bus, at parties, and so on. Have it published in the school newspaper or in the weekly community newspaper.

Then have each student draw a picture illustrating one thing he or she will do to assist a special-needs student in the school. Share and display the pictures.

Optional   Set up a buddy system pairing a regular and a special-needs student for a special activity or class period. Structure the time and activity according to curricular dictates.

Home Assignment

Encourage each student to take home a copy of the class editorial and read it to a family member. Then ask each family to discuss what it will commit to do in the school or community to assist someone with special needs (e.g., tutor a student who has reading difficulties, help a wheelchair-bound person when on a school field trip, arrange to take a handicapped child to the movies, participate in Special Olympics, etc.). Tell children to be prepared to share the family responses in class. Encourage families to develop action plans and enact their ideas. Seek follow-up results.

Dear Parents,

Our class has written an editorial focusing on "what we can do to make special-needs kids feel welcome" in our class, our school, on the bus, at special parties, and so on. We encourage you to have your child share and discuss the editorial with you. Then figure out what you could do as a family to assist individuals in our class or in your neighborhood who have special needs. In the process of assisting others, you will learn a lot about their specialness. Your child should be prepared to share the response with our class. Thank you!

Sincerely,

Figure 17   Model Letter to Parents

Lesson 11

Decision Making: Communicating a Cause or Publicizing a Good or Service

Resources

- Resource person from the community who is currently promoting a cause or publicizing a good or service (not for profit)
- Decision-making graphic (see Figure 18) and word cards reflecting the key points of the decision-making model
- Photos and "artifacts" of means of communication that promote causes and/or the sales of goods and services
- Family Discussion Guide (Figure 20)

General Comments

This lesson is intended to heighten students' awareness regarding the range of decisions people make when they communicate with others. This lesson will give the students a chance to promote a cause (e.g., picking up litter in the community, eating healthy every day, or publicizing an upcoming book fair, popcorn, or cookie sale, etc.). If possible, the selection should be one that naturally fits into the curriculum. This lesson can provide opportunities for natural integration with literacy.

General Purposes or Goals

To: (1) develop an understanding of and appreciation for the considerations that need to be addressed when attempting to encourage a "public" to participate in a cause or purchase a (nonprofit) good or service; and (2) engage students in a real-life experience that is meaningful and through which they can realize results.

Main Ideas to Develop

- People make decisions about whom they communicate to, what they communicate, and how they communicate.
- People with a cause to promote or a product or service to sell need to decide who the audience is, how the audience should receive the information, and what they want the audience to do with it.
- Promoting causes and publicizing sales of goods and services entails costs in terms of time, trouble, and often actual expenditures.

Teaching Tips from Barbara

I am the student council supervisor for our building. Therefore, I tied this lesson to a student council event. You might want to consider a similar idea. Our class helped to promote a T-shirt sale to raise money for two new basketball courts. This lesson also fulfilled my district's required service to community learning project. Always try to look for opportunities to make less work for you and more connections among curriculum goals and ideas.

Starting the Lesson

Begin by sharing the results of the home assignment. Underscore the importance of communication in our daily lives.

Introduce the decision-making exercise calling for promotion of a cause, product, or service. Pose this question: "What are some of the decisions we need to make in order to promote our selected cause or publicize our selected product or service?" Money you earn in a candy or popcorn sale, for example, would benefit the classroom or school. (Note: You can either complete the graphic of the decision-making model in advance and elicit examples from the students to illustrate, or construct the diagram as the class discussion ensues [see Figure 18].)

Decision Making

Decision to promote a cause or the sale of a good or service.

Whom do we want to tell?

Why do we want to tell them?

What do we want to tell them?

What do we want them to do as a result of receiving the message?

How do we want to send our message?

Television   Radio   Word of Mouth   Signs or Posters
Other

How much will it cost to send our message?

We need to consider:

Time

Trouble

Money

How will we know if we are successful with our promotion?

FIGURE 18   Sample Graphic of Decision-Making Model

Suggested Lesson Discussion

[Invite a local member of the community to share how she or he is helping promote a cause or a (nonprofit) good or service. As the visitor tells the story, ask him or her to walk through the decision-making model. Then walk the class through the decision-making model, using the following text to underscore the variables that need to be considered. Post word cards to add interest/emphasis and serve as visual sources for students' independent writing.]

As a group, we can decide if we will promote a cause or publicize a (nonprofit) good or service. Usually the decision to promote a cause is based on our strong opinion and feelings about the issue or cause at stake. If we decide to promote a good or service, usually it is because we will benefit financially. (For example, we might conduct and promote a popcorn sale and use the profits to buy library books for our classroom.) We need to think about why we want to promote or publicize something, whom we want to inform, what we want to tell them, what we want them to do with the information, how we want to communicate the information to them, and so on. [Post these considerations.] When we decide how to send our message, we need to think about actual costs of the message. For example, a spot on television might be a good medium because we would have a large audience, but it would cost a lot of money, and even if we borrowed it, we have no evidence that we could pay it back. [This conversation would help students realize that there are always trade-offs to our decisions.]

Signs and posters to promote our cause (campaign) or publicize the sale of a (nonprofit) good or service probably would be the most manageable, cost-effective (including time and trouble), and visible, given normal constraints. The class will need to decide where the signs and posters should be placed. Permission needs to be granted and certain signs such as large billboards require leasing space.

[After a strategic decision-making class conversation, have students prepare the signs and posters for their promotion. Use literacy time for preparing the communications. Ideally, class members should monitor public response. At the end of the campaign or sale, a debriefing should occur in order to evaluate the decisions and actions.]

Activity

Select a hypothetical community cause or (nonprofit) good or service to be publicized. As a class, walk through the decision-making model. Elicit student responses at each juncture. Then provide each pair of students with another hypothetical situation. Have each pair respond to each of the elements of the model and be prepared to share its responses with the whole class.

Summarize

- People make many choices about communication.
- When a group decides to promote a cause or publicize the sale of a good or service, it has many variables to consider: What is the goal? What should be communicated? Why? How much money should we spend for this promotion? What is the best way to publicize it? What do we expect to result from our communication? How will we know if it was effective?

Assessment

Have students as a class write a group story focusing on what they learned about promoting a cause or publicizing a good or service. If possible, invite a graduate student in advertising or a businessperson who uses advertising to be a guest and comment on the class story.

Home Assignment

Have each student share the group story about promoting a cause or publicizing a good or service. Then have the family engage in a discussion about the family's response to a billboard, handbill, or poster that it has located that is promoting a cause or publicizing a good or service (e.g., pancake supper, fund-raiser for a family in need, athletic or cultural event, etc.). Have each family fill out the discussion guide in Figure 20 describing its response. Have them explain how these means of communication inform and influence. Was the communication effective? Why? Why not?

Dear Parents,

Your child has been learning how to communicate a cause or publicize a good or service by using a decision-making model. Encourage your child to share the group story the class has prepared. Then engage in a discussion about your family's response to a billboard, handbill, or poster it has located that is promoting a cause or publicizing a good or service (e.g., pancake supper, fund-raiser for a family in need, or an athletic or cultural event). How did these means inform and influence? Was the communication effective? Why? Why not? Your child will be asked to share your response during our next class session. A family discussion guide has been included. Thank you!

Sincerely,

FIGURE 19   Model Letter to Parents

Use this guide and encourage students to return the completed form for a follow-up discussion.

What recent event (e.g., pancake supper, book sale, political campaign, sporting or cultural event) did you attend or hear about? _____

_____

_____

_____

_____

_____

How did you learn about it? _____

_____

_____

_____

_____

_____

Was the means of communication effective? Why? Why not? _____

_____

_____

_____

_____

_____

Optional: Look for examples of other means by which people in the community promote causes and the sales of goods and services

FIGURE 20   Family Discussion Guide

Lesson 12

. . . .

Decision Making: Mass Media (Television)

Resources
- Television set and VCR
- Taped segment of television program—your choice
- Word cards (questions to ask in deciding whether or not to view a program)
- TV program guide
- Table 5: Television Program Types Chart
- Food pyramid
- Taped commercial for a cereal
- Box of advertised cereal and at least two other cereals
- Visuals depicting propaganda techniques
- Figure 22: Accounting for Myself Form
- Figure 23: TV survey

General Comments

This lesson is intended to heighten students' awareness regarding how they spend their time. The students will have the opportunity to realize the influence that mass communication (television) has on their lives and how they can evaluate its content in order to make informed decisions.

General Purposes or Goals

To: (1) develop students' awareness of how they spend their out-of-school time and how much of it is spent with mass communication; (2) develop an understanding and appreciation of the variety of ways mass communication (television) influences its viewers; (3) develop an understanding and appreciation for the criteria they can use to evaluate television content; and (4) evaluate their own viewing habits to become wise consumers of mass media.

Main Ideas to Develop

- People make decisions about how they spend their leisure time.
- Television is the most popular means children use during their leisure time.
- Television is a great means for communicating with the masses.
- Television is used in a variety of ways to influence its viewers.
- There are numerous types of television programs.
- There are several ways to evaluate television content. Does the program inform or educate? Does it entertain? Is the entertain-

ment appropriate for the viewer's age? How will the program influence the viewer's behavior? Is the program showing reality or fantasy? What are the commercials trying to do?

Teaching Tips from Barbara

My students were most interested in the results of the survey (see Figure 23). They also enjoyed hearing about the TV rules from other families and comparing them to their own rules. After we compiled the information in a graph, we brainstormed a list of recommendations for television viewing to share with their families. Because understanding advertising techniques is challenging for children, spend plenty of time discussing this aspect with them.

Starting the Lesson

Begin the lesson by discussing the home assignment. This will raise students' awareness about the impact of mass media on their daily lives.

Suggested Lesson Discussion

Television influences its viewers in a variety of ways. It educates or informs us and it entertains us. [As the conversation unfolds, construct a chart to show a range of program types available to the viewers (see Table 5). Ask students to provide specific examples of each program type. Use the TV program guide as a reference.]

There are numerous types of programs, each of which serves one or more purposes. How might we decide what to view? Does the program educate or inform? Does the program entertain? Is the entertainment appropriate for young children? Is the program fantasy or reality? Does the program show violence? If so, how could that affect my behavior? [Show one or more live or taped television segments, and after discussing the content of the program, focus on ways to evaluate it. Post questions that you need to ask in deciding what to view.]

TABLE 5 Television Program Types Chart

Example

Commercials _____

News _____

Educational Programs _____

Comedy _____

Game Shows _____

Sporting Events _____

Drama/Mystery _____

Optional [Invite a person who in real life (by nature of the position) compares to an individual on television, for example, a lawyer. How is the profession depicted on television? Make sure the person has viewed the specified television program. As a class, discuss the distinctions.] [End of optional section.]

[After the discussion focusing on actual television programs, shift to the impact of commercials. Begin by showing an ad (taped) for cereal—a real part of students' lives and a choice that they frequently influence when family purchases are made. Discuss the contents of the ad and how it attempts to influence the viewers.] Several advertising techniques are used by companies to encourage viewers to purchase their products. [Select from the following list those most appropriate for the discussion. Use items, video-taped commercials, and magazine advertisements to illustrate.]

- Name calling—Negatively labeling a product or service to make another product or service look very positive.
- Glittering generality—Used to describe a product or service in a favorable light without citing any factual information.
- Transfer—Joining the use of a product or service with a model of glamour or popularity.
- Testimonial—A famous person or "satisfied user" endorses an idea, service, or product.
- Card stacking—Rigging the facts about a good or service by concealing contradictory information or by emphasizing favorable information.
- "Plain folks" device—Depicting the individual advertising a good or service as "one of us."
- Bandwagon procedure—Appeals to the group instinct (everyone is buying it).

[Underscore the power of suggestion. Then show the box of cereal that was advertised. Give each student a sample of the cereal to taste. Through discussion, evaluate whether or not the cereal lives up to all of the advertised claims. Also include what was not said (e.g., higher cost than some cereals, doesn't taste as good as some other brands). Compare and contrast taste with at least two other brands. Examine the nutritional value by reading the label on the box and compare to other brands. Refer to the food pyramid used in the food unit. You might bring to the students' attention that products that are very appealing to youngsters usually are advertised during programs viewed by children, and that cereals most appealing to them are placed low on the grocery shelves so they can easily locate them.]

[After comparing the cereals according to taste and nutritional value, you might compare the packaging. Show the students that cereal companies communicate lots of messages on the boxes that entice/influence a potential buyer (e.g., colorful decorations, toys/prizes inside the boxes, games, coupons, forms providing opportunities to order gifts, recipes, etc.).]

We need to use our knowledge and best thinking to make informed choices. Companies that advertise their goods and services pay a lot of money to produce the ads and broadcast them to large audiences because they want to make money by selling their goods and services.

Activity

Pair/Share—Have students brainstorm all the ideas they can think of regarding how to make better decisions about television viewing. As a class, list these ideas on the white board.

Summarize

- Television is a very popular choice during our leisure time.
- It uses a variety of ways to influence its viewers.
- We can become wise consumers of mass media (television) by thoughtfully evaluating it.

Assessment

Have each student write a letter to his or her family describing what important things he or she learned about television viewing and identifying one recommendation that he or she wants to have the family consider during future viewing (e.g., "Don't believe everything the commercials tell you. They may not be giving the whole story. For example, Nike shoes cost a lot more than other brands not advertised. Nike pays Michael Jordan to endorse its shoes"; "Some of those cartoons we watch are pretty violent"; "Let's check the television guide for some programs on nature"; "Our family should watch the news at least once a day, to learn about what's going on in the world").

Home Assignment

Encourage each student to take the letter home and share it with the family and discuss the contents. Have them discuss the importance of family members becoming more informed about television and making more intelligent choices about viewing. Encourage a family member to assist the student in keeping track of his or her television habits for a week by completing the form in Figure 22 and the survey in Figure 23.

Dear Parents,

We have been learning about the influences of television and how we can evaluate its content in order to make more informed decisions. Please take a few minutes to read and discuss your child's letter with your family.

Our class members are going to survey themselves to figure out their television viewing habits. An accounting form and a survey are enclosed. Please help your child fill out the form during the following week and then complete the survey so that his or her response can be included in the graph that our class will prepare. A copy will be sent home so you can discuss the results during a future family meeting. Thank you!

Sincerely,

FIGURE 21   Model Letter to Parents

Complete the form. List each activity you did during the specified block of time. If you watched TV, name the program.

	Sun.	Mon.	Tues.	Wed.	Thurs.	Fri.	Sat.
7–8 A.M.							
8–9 A.M.							
9–10 A.M.							
10–11 A.M.							
11–Noon							
Noon–1 P.M.							
1–2 P.M.							
2–3 P.M.							
3–4 P.M.							
4–5 P.M.							
5–6 P.M.							
6–7 P.M.							
7–8 P.M.							
8–9 P.M.							
9–10 P.M.							
10–11 P.M							

FIGURE 22   Accounting for Myself

1. What types of television programs do you watch?

• Check each of the following that you watch.

• Circle your favorite.

• Mark an X by your least favorite.

_____ news   _____ cartoons

_____ sports   _____ soaps

_____ mystery   _____ nature shows

_____ space shows   _____ music shows

_____ talk shows   _____ movies

_____ comedy   _____ other (specify) _____

_____ educational   _____

2. About how many hours of television do you watch on weekdays? _____

   _____

3. About how many hours do you watch on the weekends? _____

   _____

4. Have you seen anything on television this week that you'd like to read about?

   _____

5. Does your family watch television together?_____

   _____

6. Does your family have rules about what programs you can watch? _____

   _____

   Explain._____

7. Have you seen any programs recently that tie in with what you are studying

   in school? If so, specify. _____

   _____

FIGURE 23   TV Survey

Lesson 13

Review

Resources

- A selection of artifacts that represent the major understandings developed during the unit (bulletin boards, charts, student work, results from home assignments, etc.) (See Table 6)
- Markers and question sheets for carousel activity (optional)

General Comments

For this lesson, students will revisit the entire communication unit and review the understandings developed. The class will review the big ideas associated with the changes in communication over time, using the bulletin board time line. Posters, props, and student work used during the previous lessons will be looked at again to stimulate discussion and reemphasize key points. Invite an upper-grade class (or a delegation of parents and relatives of your students) to come to the classroom to listen to what your students have learned about communication. In other words, your students will be modeling communication through speaking, listening, viewing, and writing with another group of students. A viable option is to have the class select what it views as the most important lessons from the unit and focus on the main ideas and artifacts associated with those lessons. Another option is to engage the students in the carousel activity.

General Purposes or Goals

To: (1) draw on prior knowledge, understanding, appreciation, and applications conducted at home and at school that collectively enhance meaningfulness and continued curiosity in learning about communication; (2) revisit and reflect on the big ideas developed about communication; and (3) practice communicating with others through a range of modalities.

Main Ideas to Develop

- Communication is the exchange of information, ideas, feelings, and attitudes through speaking/listening, writing/reading, electronic media, and other signs and symbols.
- Communication allows us to exchange ideas more quickly and directly than we would be able to otherwise, thus making it easier for us to collaborate on common tasks.
- By enabling us to exchange our thoughts and feelings, communication allows us to construct common understandings and build friendships.

- Communication is a basic need.
- Communication is used to give us information and ideas, help us express feelings and attitudes, entertain us, keep us safe (protect us), provide directions, help us stay healthy, and help us make choices.
- Culture is an important factor to be considered in our communication activities.
- Our ability to satisfy our needs and wants depends in part on our ability to communicate.
- People very long ago had very limited means of communicating (e.g., grunting, gestures, drawings on walls), and, because of the lack of records, our knowledge about their culture is limited.
- People long ago used limited verbal communication (i.e., they didn't have many words) and nonverbal means such as smoke signals and markings on trails.
- Communication methods have evolved over time because of expansions of spoken language and inventions of written language, printing/books, telegraph, telephone, television, computer networks, and so on. This has made for a more complete and accurate preservation of certain communications (original dependence on oral tradition, then writing and printing, now videos and other electronic preservation).
- Electronic media have now made it possible for communication to be instantaneous (no more dependence on face-to-face oral exchange or hand-to-hand exchange of written materials), as well as worldwide (no more need for physical travel across space).
- Cultural diffusion via communication has become faster and more complete, shrinking and homogenizing our world.
- There are three majors types (groupings) of communication: (1) personal interactive types (face-to-face and telephone conversations); (2) personal delayed interactive types (exchange of letters, fax, email, greeting cards); and (3) mass communication (radio, television, the Internet).
- Personal interactive, personal delayed interactive, and mass communication are enjoyed by people all over the world.
- In isolated or underdeveloped areas, there are places where some types of personal interactive communication such as telephone conversations are not available. There are also places where personal delayed interactive communication does not exist or is extremely limited because of geographic and/or socioeconomic circumstances.
- Mass communication is one of the three major types.
- Within that category are many means (e.g., newspapers, magazines, radio, video, movies, television, etc.).

- Mass communication has many purposes: (1) to provide news and inform; (2) to entertain; (3) to persuade; and (4) to facilitate global connections.

- Mass media are accessible in almost every part of the world; however, socioeconomic factors affect an individual's level of access.

- The mass media we select should be based on our needs/goals.

- Most broadcast TV stations are a part of a national chain of stations called a network. The network provides programs for its member stations to share. Local stations produce some of their own programs, but most of the day is filled with network programming.

- In the control room, the director communicates with the people in the studio via microphone. The engineers work with the studio lights and microphones. They make sure the picture being shown is clear and sharp and that the sound is good.

- The layout of the television station is planned to enable the workers to ensure that the programming is handled professionally.

- There is a range of jobs that need to be done at the television station.

- We depend on many people for giving and receiving communication.

- Communication workers provide us with a range of services that impact our daily lives.

- We pay for the services that these people provide to us.

- The language of signs and symbols has no words, but it can shout warnings, give instructions, direct traffic, and serve as the focus for games (e.g., hearts and other card games).

- Some symbols are pictures; some are shapes that began as pictures; and some are pure designs not meant to look like anything.

- Signs and symbols are important means of communication. To visitors from other parts of the world, they can be more understandable than written words.

- Some signs and devices can become so familiar that we forget they are from the silent language of symbols (e.g., math symbols). Games have many signs (e.g., hearts). Striped shirts of referees and black suits for umpires are symbols of their functions.

- Signs and symbols are powerful means of providing society with information nonverbally.

- Language is the symbol system that people use to show what they think and how they feel.

- Most, but not all, languages are based on sound. Language can be based on signs that are observed or patterns of dots that are felt.

- Language is an expression of culture.

- A map is a medium for locating places—even places where we've never been before.
- Communication and understanding go hand in hand.
- We do not have to leave our classroom or school to find people who have special needs—needs that we can help satisfy by learning to communicate with them.
- By coming to understand how people respond to their special situations, we can become more supportive and helpful to our peers who have special needs.
- Sometimes people need special assistance to help them overcome disabilities. This special assistance might come in the form of professional people, volunteers, peer help, or donations of money or goods for special equipment. Communication serves as an underlying theme.
- Sometimes when we are unfamiliar with what we see, we misinterpret it. These misinterpretations can be eliminated through better communication.
- People make decisions about whom they communicate to, what they communicate, and how they communicate.
- People with a cause to promote or product or service to sell need to decide who the audience is, how the audience should receive the information, and what they want the audience to do with it.
- Promoting causes and publicizing sales of goods and services entails costs in terms of time, trouble, and often actual expenditures.
- People make decisions about how they spend their leisure time.
- Television is the most popular means children use during their leisure time.
- Television is a great means for communicating with the masses.
- Television is used in a variety of ways to influence its viewers.
- There are numerous types of television programs.
- There are several ways to evaluate television content. Does the program inform or educate? Does it entertain? Is the entertainment appropriate for the viewer's age? How will the program influence my behavior? Is the program showing reality or fantasy? What are the commercials trying to do?

Teaching Tips from Barbara

I chose to use the carousel activity to review the communication information because it incorporated a communication tool: posters. Be sure to take time to go back to the two big questions that started the unit: What is communication? Why is it important?

Starting the Lesson

Discuss the home assignment. Remind the class that during this lesson each student will get the opportunity to showcase what he or she has learned by explaining to guests key points from the unit.

This lesson involves going back to look at what the class has been learning and sharing your thoughts and opinions about communication before you move to the next unit. Recognize that some students still have some unfinished business—and that's fine too. For example, a student and his or her family may be extending the TV Survey (see Figure 23) or a student may be learning sign language. Some students may have elected to sign up for a foreign language class as a part of Fabulous Fridays. Periodically check on progress and ask those who are doing communication projects to share.

At this juncture, explain to the class that in pairs with their volunteer guest/guides, they will revisit the communication sites (either select ones or all) and review the key ideas acquired during the unit. This will be called a communication fair. Prior to the lesson, provide the guests/guides with a list of key ideas and conduct a walk-through in an effort to familiarize them with the goals and content (see Table 6 for suggested artifacts to include). Establish a time limit for each site visit. Have each pair of students and guest/guide work as a team. Give each team a number. Each team begins at the station with the matching number and then follows the sequence. For example, Team 4 begins at Station 4 and continues with 5, and so on. When the team completes 13, it goes to 1, then 2, and finally 3. At the conclusion, each teams returns to the station where it began.

Optional Carousel Activity

This activity is most effective in the early grades if upper-grade mentors—one per group—serve as readers/recorders. Otherwise, name one student at each table to be the scribe for the group. Give each scribe a different colored marker.

Set up the same number of stations as there are groups, each with one question about communication and chart paper for recording responses. Each group begins at the station (site) where the question (printed on a large sheet of paper) matches the color of its marker. Designate five minutes for each group to discuss and record its response. Then ask each group to move to its left, keeping its own colored marker. The tasks are to read the new question and the previous group's response (or responses, if more than one group has been at the site) and place a question mark beside any part of the response(s) that the group disagrees with or is unclear about. Then the group will discuss and record additional responses to the question. Continue this until all of the groups have responded to all of the questions and returned to the sites where they started the activity. At this point, each group should review all of the responses to the question at its station and prepare to expand on the question during a large-group discussion. During the discussion, have groups clarify responses from the carousel activity.

Questions might include following:

What is communication?

Why is communication so important to all of us?

How has communication changed over time?

What are examples of communication types?

Why is mass communication so interesting?

What can you tell us about signs, symbols, and signals—all important means of communication in our lives?

What are things we need to consider when making decisions about how we spend our time, especially television viewing time?

Large-Group Discussion and Activity

After each team has visited each of the sites, return to the large group and write a group summary regarding the highlights of the unit.

(We recommend that after each lesson the class decide what "artifacts" will be used for the review session when an upper-grade class or family and community members learn from the early elementary class. This planning/preparation should begin at the outset and be an established expectation. Extend a written invitation to the class that will visit early in the unit.)

Summarize

- Communication is a very important part of every person's life.
- There are many means, types, and functions of communication.
- Communication is needed in our work and play. It also helps keep us safe.

Assessment

As a class, write thank-you letters to the individuals who participated with you in the review lesson. Have students explain the most important thing they learned about communication and how it will help them.

TABLE 6   Communication Fair

LESSON	SUGGESTED ARTIFACTS
Lesson 1 Communication: What Is It? Why Is It Important?	• *Communication* by Brandenberg • Means of Communication Chart (Table 1)
Lesson 2 Means and Functions of Communication	• Means and Functions of Communication Chart (Figure 4) or items representing each (e.g., newspaper, map, newsletter, medicine bottle label)
Lesson 3 Changes in Communication over Time	• Time line • Means of Communication: Long, Long Ago; Long Ago; and Today (Table 2)
Lesson 4 Types of Communication: Personal Interactive and Personal Delayed Interactive	• Types and Means of Communication Chart (Table 3) • Stack of cards naming communication types with task being to categorize them
Lesson 5 Mass Communication	• Copy of assessment questions (answers provided on the back)
Lesson 6 A Trip to a Television Station	• Television Tour Activity Sheet (Figure 11)
Lesson 7 Careers in Communication	• Stories gleaned from individuals interviewed
Lesson 8 Signs and Symbols: Nonverbal Communication	• Collection of articles and pictures representing signs, symbols, and signals
Lesson 9 Communication: Languages	• Cassette tape (language representing culture) • Braille sample • Three cards illustrating signing
Lesson 10 Communication: Being a Responsible Citizen	• Class editorial "What Should We Do to Make Special-Needs Kids Feel Welcome?"
Lesson 11 Decision Making: Communicating a Cause or Publicizing a Good or Service	• Decision-Making Model—promoting a cause or publicizing a service
Lesson 12 Decision Making: Mass Media (Television)	• Questions to ask when evaluating television viewing • Class viewing habits (graph)

Unit 2: Transportation

Introduction

To help you think about transportation as a cultural universal and begin to plan your teaching, we have provided a list of questions that address some of the big ideas developed in our unit plans (see Figure 1). The questions focus on what we believe to be the most important ideas for children to learn about transportation. These include transportation as a universal human need and the functions that it fulfills for us; the evolution of transportation over time and the impact of inventions; the tendency for settlements to be built along transportation routes; the ways in which improvements in transportation have made the world "smaller"; the fundamental importance of the wheel as a basic invention; how modern life differs from earlier times as a function of improvements in transportation; the effects of building a highway through a rural community; the effects of improvements in transportation on farming and consumer access to farm products; special forms of transportation found mostly in cities (trains, buses, taxis) and what is involved in using them; how automobiles work; problems that exist in places where most people drive cars or trucks; the nature and uses of maps; the need for traffic control mechanisms; and considerations involved in traveling across national borders.

To find out what primary-grade students know (or think they know) about these questions, we interviewed ninety-six students in Grades K–3. You may want to use some or all of these questions during preunit or prelesson assessments of your students' prior knowledge. For now, though, we recommend that you jot down your own answers before going on to read about the answers that we elicited in our interviews. This will sharpen your awareness of ways in which adults' knowledge about transportation differs from children's knowledge, as well as reduce the likelihood that you will assume that your students already know certain things that seem obvious to you but may need to be spelled out for them.

If you want to use some of these questions to assess your students' prior knowledge before beginning the unit, you can do this either by interviewing selected students individually or by asking the class as a whole to respond to the questions and recording their answers for future reference. If you take the latter approach, an option would be to embed it within the KWL technique by initially questioning students to determine what they know and what they want to find out, then later revisiting their answers and recording what they learned. An alternative to preassessing your students' knowledge about topics developed in the unit as a whole would be to conduct separate preassessments prior to each lesson, using only the questions that apply to that lesson (and perhaps adding others of your own choosing).

Two-thirds of the second graders and over 90 percent of the third graders were able to define the term *transportation,* but this was true of only one kindergartener and one first grader. Compared to their responses concerning food, clothing, and shelter, the students were less likely to say that transportation is a basic need. Even so, a heavy majority of them did make this response. The students who were able to respond to these questions typically defined transportation as moving from one place to another or as a conveyance or vehicle that can be used to accomplish such movement. About two-thirds cited local travel needs (to get to school, work, a doctor's office, etc.) in explaining the need for transportation, although some students emphasized long-distance travel or said that people need transportation when they do not have a car.

The next questions assessed students' knowledge about transportation in three time periods: the cave days (prehistoric times), the pioneer days (early eighteenth century), and the present. Most of the students who responded correctly said that people walked in the cave days, although minorities said that that they rode animals, used carts or other wheeled vehicles, used *Flintstone* vehicles with stone wheels, or used modern vehicles. Only 40 percent made reference to wagons, covered wagons, buggies, or other animal-pulled vehicles in talking about the pioneer days. Other students were unable to respond, said that the pioneers used ships or that they had to walk everywhere, or said that they used modern vehicles.

Almost all of the students mentioned engine-powered vehicles in talking about transportation in modern times. In general, the students seemed to understand the progression from walking and carrying or dragging things to animal-powered wheeled vehicles to engine-powered wheeled vehicles. However, some of them were badly confused about when these progressions occurred.

1. Today we're going to talk about transportation. What does transportation mean? [If student does not know, explain that transportation refers to how people travel or get from one place to another.]

2. Is transportation just something that people enjoy, or do they need it? . . . What are some times when they need it?

3. Let's talk about transportation in the past. How did people get around way back in the days when they used to live in caves? . . . How did people get around during the pioneer days? . . . What kinds of transportation do we use now that people long ago didn't have?

4. For a long time, the Native Americans didn't have horses, but then they got horses. How did having horses change their lives?

5. For a long time, people had only horses and wagons to get around in, but then the railroad was built. What could people do after the railroad was built that they couldn't do before? [If necessary, ask, "Why would they choose to do that?"]

6. Later, highways were built. What could people do after highways were built that they couldn't do before?

7. Then, airplanes were built. What could people do after airplanes were built that they couldn't do before?

8. Some people say that all of these changes in transportation have made the world "smaller." What do they mean by that? [If necessary, ask, "How have railroads and cars and airplanes made the world smaller?"]

9. Long, long ago, people built cities near oceans or on big rivers. Why was that?

10. Later, people built cities along railroad lines. Why was that? [If necessary, ask, "why did they *want* to live by the railroad lines?"]

11. At one time, mountains made it hard for people to travel. Most people didn't even try to cross mountains, but now we cross them all the time. Why is it easier now?

12. Why was the wheel an important invention? (What could people do after the wheel was invented that they couldn't do before?) [If student starts talking about cars, ask, "What about before cars were invented—why was the invention of the wheel important?"]

13. If the first Pilgrims to come to the New World had cars, could they have used the cars to drive across the country? [If the student says yes, ask, "How would they have done it?" If no, ask, "Why not?" If the student says that trees were in the way, ask, "What if they cut the trees down?"]

Continues

FIGURE 1   Starter Questions

14. What if there were no cars today? How would our lives be different if we only had horses and wagons to help us get around?

15. What if we had trains but no cars? How would our lives be different? (How would that affect where we lived? How would we shop if we only had trains? How would it affect where we went on vacation?)

16. Suppose you lived in a small town out in the country and a big highway was built right through it. How would your town be different after the highway was built? (How would it be better? How would it be worse?)

17. Farmers produce food for people. A long time ago, farmers didn't have trucks. Then they got trucks. How did the farming business change after trucks were built? (How did trucks make things different for farmers?) [If necessary, ask, "What difference would it have made if farmers could have taken produce to market in trucks?"]

18. Apples grow here in the summer, but not in winter. But even in winter, we can buy apples. Why is that? [If necessary, ask, "So you think that the apples in supermarket were grown locally and then frozen?]

19. What kinds of transportation do you find in big cities but not in other places? (Why do a lot of people in big cities use buses or subways instead of cars?)

20. What is a taxicab? Why do people use taxicabs? Do they have to pay to use taxicabs? [If yes, ask, "How does that work? How does the driver decide how much you should pay?"]

21. How does a car work—what makes it go? [Probe for knowledge of gasoline-fueled engines.]

22. It's nice to have cars and trucks, but they create problems, too. What are some problems that exist in places where most people drive cars or trucks? [Probe for knowledge of noise, traffic, pollution, etc.] [For students who respond in terms of breakdowns of one's own car, say, "OK—that would be for your car. But I was wondering if places where there are a lot of cars have problems because there are so many cars there?"]

23. What is a map? . . . When do people need maps?

24. If people want to go to another country, can they just go, or do they have to get permission? (If they need permission, who do they have to get permission from?) [If student speaks of a child asking parental permission, ask, "Do grown-ups have to get permission to go into another country?"]

25. Why do we need stoplights on our streets? (What would happen if we didn't have them?)

The next set of questions addressed students' understanding of the ways that key innovations in transportation (the Native Americans' acquisition of horses, the building of railroads, the construction of highways, and the coming of airplanes) brought new opportunities into people's lives and "shrunk the world" by developing connections between formerly isolated places. Although inability to respond was a frequent problem, most of what was said in response to these questions was accurate or at least defensible. Most students easily grasped the big idea that each successive transportation innovation made it possible for people to travel farther, quicker, and easier than before. However, the responses focused on the ways that improvements in travel affected individuals (e.g., Native Americans would not have to expend as much energy or get as tired or footsore as they did formerly when they had to walk everywhere; when trains became available people could ride them to get places more quickly and in more comfort). Very few students answered these questions with reference to macro-level changes in society or the world at large.

When asked about how transportation innovations had made the world "smaller," the majority could not respond and most of the rest took the statement literally and said that transportation-related construction (of highways, train tracks, airports, etc.) took up a lot of space and thus reduced the space available in the world for other uses. Only two students grasped the metaphoric meaning of "made the world 'smaller'" and spoke of people now being more connected to one another, and no students mentioned, for example, that horses allowed the Plains tribes to follow the buffalo over much greater distances or that railroads, highways, and airplanes transformed the nation and the world from a collection of mostly isolated settlements into a richly connected social and economic network.

Misconceptions in responses to these questions were mostly minor and infrequent. However, several students were under the impression that trains cannot cross rivers and that all highways are literally high—that is, built significantly above the surrounding land. Other misconceptions included the ideas that Native Americans found it harder to hunt food with horses because they scared away the buffalo, that horse-drawn buggies were faster than trains, that highway travel is slow because it takes hours to get where you are going, and that it is not possible to drive from Michigan to Florida because the way is blocked by a significant body of water that one must fly over.

The next set of questions addressed students' understanding of the principle that human populations tend to concentrate along travel routes and to be bounded by significant geographical barriers, especially mountains. Here again, the students' responses tended to be accurate as far as they went but limited to a micro-level purview. Thus, they talked about early cities being built near oceans or on rivers because the people wanted to swim or play in the water, travel locally by boat, fish, or simply take aesthetic pleasure in viewing the beauty of the water or listening to the sound of the waves. Only a minority displayed awareness that water is necessary to human survival and only a few conveyed awareness that in the distant past, much exploration and long-distance travel was done on waterways.

Similarly, students generated various reasons that people might want to build cities along rail lines (because they wanted to be able to ride the train to go places, etc.), but few of them showed awareness of rail lines as vital links to other communities, sources of access to goods and markets, and so on during those times. Furthermore, some showed elements of reversed reasoning in thinking that the tracks were built first and then settlements were built along them primarily to serve the needs of the trains and their riders, not realizing that tracks ordinarily are laid to link communities to which people want to travel and the trains operate to serve the needs of the people in these communities. That is, although it is true that the opening of a new travel route tends to energize the economies of already-existing settlements along the routes and sometimes to stimulate the development of new settlements, the cause-effect chain usually begins with recognition of the need for a better travel route between two or more already-existing communities.

Finally, the students again generated various reasons that it is easier to cross mountains today than in the past (e.g., better mountain-climbing equipment, engine-powered vehicles), but few of them showed any awareness of mountains as significant barriers to transportation until the relatively recent past.

The next set of questions further probed students' understanding of historical developments in transportation, and the students' responses once again focused on micro-level events. When asked why the wheel was an important invention, a majority said that wheels are needed for vehicles and smaller numbers said that wheels allow us to move things more easily without having to drag them or to travel more quickly than we can travel in non-wheeled conveyances. These responses are accurate and most show at least some appreciation of the fundamental importance of the wheel. However, few students showed any awareness of the wheel's far-reaching impact or the ways that society at large (not just personal travel) would be very different without it.

When asked whether the Pilgrims would have been able to drive across the country if they had cars with them, a majority of the students incorrectly said that they would have been able to do so, and most of the others were unsure or only made reference to barriers such as rivers, mud, snow, or the lack of gas stations. Only fifteen students clearly understood that the Pilgrims would not have been able to drive across the country because it was a heavily forested and roadless wilderness at the time.

When asked how our lives would be different if we had only horses and wagons to get around in, most of the students who were able to respond said that travel would be slower or more difficult. However, few of them conveyed any indication that they were visualizing major changes in society as a whole. Similarly, when asked how our lives would be different if we had trains but no cars today, the students were usually able to say that travel would be less convenient, but few of them showed awareness of ways that society at large (not just personal travel) would be different.

Responses to questions about the impact of travel innovations made it clear that the students were more aware of water than of mountains as formidable barriers to long-distance travel, and they were much more heavily focused on personal travel than on the transportation of goods or raw materials. Finally, they were often vague or confused about the reciprocal relationships between the development of travel routes and the location of settlements along these routes.

Our question about the effects of building a highway through a small country town also produced micro-level responses focusing on how the highway would make it harder for individuals to get out of their driveways, create irritating noise or pollution, or allow them to get out of town more quickly. Only a few responses addressed how the highway would change the town as a whole. The students were much more aware of potential negative effects than positive ones. Except for a few references to construction of more houses or other buildings, the students seemed unaware of the effect of a highway in stimulating the local economy.

Similarly, the question about the impact of trucks on farmers elicited responses talking about how individual farmers might use their trucks but not about how the trucks transformed the nature and scope of farming as a business. Responses to the next question conveyed very little awareness of the role of transportation in bringing fresh farm products to our local stores all year round. This lack of awareness was associated with a more fundamental lack of awareness that the farm products sold in stores during the winter have been transported from other states or nations. A majority of the students harbored the misconception that apples purchased locally in the winter were grown locally, picked in the summer or fall, and then preserved for sale in the winter. Some of the students talked about chilling the apples or taking other steps to preserve them, so they at least were aware that apples eventually rot. Nevertheless, even these students were under the impression that the apples had been grown locally and preserved, not imported from elsewhere. This misconception appeared in a majority of even the third graders.

Most of the students understood that city dwellers often ride trains, buses, or subways because they do not have cars or because public transportation may be cheaper, faster, or more convenient for them than driving/parking in a congested inner city. Also, a heavy majority of the students understood that taxis are cars hired for local transportation by people who do not have a car available at the time. Older students usually knew that the fare is determined by the length of the trip as well, but younger students usually were unable to respond or could only guess how fares are determined.

When asked how a car works—what makes it go—the students typically began by mentioning the engine or gasoline or various other car parts, then went on to respond to probes by talking about the steps that the driver goes through in starting the car or causing it to begin moving. These responses were generally accurate as far as they went (you need a key to start the car, you push on the gas pedal, the engine makes the wheels turn, etc.). However, fewer than half of the students mentioned the engine, and for a majority of them, the engine was a black box. Individual students mentioned quite a number of car parts in struggling to explain what makes the car go, but these terms often were used in ways that showed that the student did not understand their meanings or functions. No student gave a clear explanation subsuming the key elements that gasoline (mixed with air) is burned within the cylinders to create explosions that move the pistons, and this piston movement in the engine is transferred to the axle to make the car's wheels move. Three students did supply partial explanations that talked about piston movement in the engine resulting in movement of the wheels and thus the car, but none of them mentioned burning of gasoline or explosions that get the pistons moving.

Several students talked about gasoline starting out in the gas tank, then traveling throughout the car, and eventually coming out the exhaust in gaseous rather than liquid form. These students understood that gasoline is necessary to the car's operation, but they had only black-box theories of the engine or other workings of the car. Again, only a few students mentioned that the gasoline is burned, and none mentioned explosions that initiate piston movement.

Not surprisingly, given their previous responses concerning the effect of building a highway through a small country town, the students (except for those unable to respond) found it easy to answer our question about problems that exist in places where most people drive cars or trucks. Most of them named at least one problem associated with a concentration of motor vehicles (accidents, traffic jams, congestion, noise, or pollution), and none communicated misconceptions.

The students also understood the nature and functions of maps. Almost all of them were able to define and/or describe maps and talk about when and why people use them. Again, no misconceptions were expressed.

When asked whether people wanting to travel to a foreign country need permission, many students initially responded in terms of children getting permission from their parents. Once this was clarified, most students said either that adults do not require permission to travel to other countries or that they need permission from airlines, hotels, or people with whom they will be staying. Only seventeen students clearly understood that travelers require permission from the governments of the countries involved. Only one student mentioned a passport and none mentioned a visa.

The last question asked why we need stoplights and what would happen if we didn't have them. This proved to be relatively easy for most students. A heavy majority said that without stoplights there would be many more accidents in our streets, and some went on to mention other factors such as that the lights make sure that people will stop for each other, that pedestrians can cross the streets safely, or that people do not travel too fast. However, few if any of the students seemed aware that stoplights also make traffic more efficient, enabling people to get to their destinations more quickly and easily than they would if traffic were not controlled.

Overview of the Transportation Unit —Barbara Knighton

Transportation was a particularly interesting cultural universal. Children have a number of unusual misconceptions, especially concerning costs and history. We were able to have many interactive conversations as the unit progressed.

This cultural universal incorporates a big idea that I used to help connect all my teaching together. All transportation serves to fill one main need: to move something from one place to another. Somewhere in every lesson, I made sure to return to that thought. In the beginning of the unit, my teaching emphasized transmission techniques, telling my students how that main idea fits in. During later lessons, I shifted emphasis to constructivist techniques, asking questions to make sure that we tied the new information to that big idea.

One of the keys to making this unit successful is using pictures with every lesson. Magazines and personal photographs help to stimulate students' interest and often spark questions and "I wonders." If you simply carry a camera with you for a few weeks before the unit starts, you will find plenty of opportunities to get good transportation photographs. Enlarging and copying pictures from the many books suggested works, too.

The pictures can also be a resource for a bulletin board or to use as writing prompts.

Another bonus with this unit is your students' ability to gather data by making observations in their daily lives. I found my students almost too aware of and excited to share the transportation information that they saw around them. By simply changing the things that you stress during a lesson, you can open a whole new can of worms and generate excitement for a new facet of transportation.

Journal writing is an important part of this unit. Students are asked to respond in writing after almost every lesson. I often model for my students before they write to give them more support. Another idea is to allow students to pair up and share their thoughts before starting to write. I had each student decorate a file folder as storage for the journal entries. By the end of the unit, you have an assessment tool and a record of the students' work.

Send a letter home briefly outlining the learning for this unit. Include the things that you'd like parents to send to school to help with the lessons. Also, suggest that parents start discussing transportation with their children to get them interested and excited about the new unit. Parent involvement in this unit focuses around family discussions. The journal entries students write as part of the lessons are great for sparking family discussions at home. I found it easiest to staple a strip of paper with the discussion question on the top of each journal page so families would know what the students had respnded to in their writing. Some families responded by adding to the journal; others simply talked about the topic (and students later shared those ideas in class). You might want to copy the journal pages before sending them home so that you have a record of your students' ideas.

Finally, be sure to keep the main ideas in mind as you teach. The more often you come back to those ideas in different discussions and in different ways, the more students will begin to internalize them.

Lesson 1

. . . .

Transportation: What Is It?
Why Is It So Important?

Resources
- Pictures and photographs that illustrate transportation
- 3X5 cards for student questions
- Data Retrieval Chart (Figure 3)

Children's Literature
Bingham, C. (Project Ed.). (1994). *The Big Book of Things That Go*. London: Dorling Kindersley.

Brown, R. II. (1987). *100 Words About Transportation*. San Diego: Harcourt Brace, Gulliver Books.

Coster, P. (1997). *Transportation and Communication*. New York: Children's Press.

General Comments
To launch this unit, collect the instructional resources and display visual prompts as a means of generating interest in the topic. Prior to the first day, post questions around the room or on the bulletin board. Good questions might include the following:

> What is transportation?
>
> Why is transportation important?
>
> What types of transportation can you name?
>
> How has transportation changed?
>
> How does transportation vary in places around the world?
>
> What careers exist in the area of transportation?
>
> What specific things would you like to know about transportation?

General Purposes or Goals
To help students understand and appreciate: (1) what transportation is, and (2) why transportation is so important.

Main Ideas to Develop
- Transportation is the movement of people and things from one place to another.
- People move from one place to another for many reasons: to work, go to school, shop, go to the post office, go to the doctor or dentist, visit relatives, worship, attend recreational events, and so on.

- Goods are moved from one place to another for many reasons: raw materials must be carried to factories to be processed; products from farms and factories must be carried to different places (i.e., markets and stores to be sold).
- Civilization has made progress as transportation has developed.

Teaching Tips from Barbara

The most important piece of this lesson is to help children develop their own definition of transportation. The students were surprised to find that there were non-motorized methods of transportation. They also were surprised to learn that goods (not just people) need to be transported. Therefore, I provided many picture examples and discussions about those types of transportation.

Starting the Lesson

Pose questions regarding transportation. Sample questions might include What is transportation? Why is it so important? How has transportation changed? How does transportation vary in places around the world? After a preliminary discussion of these questions, show the class the bulletin board that has been started that depicts what transportation is and illustrates why it is so important to us, as well as other questions that will be addressed during the unit. Use this visual as a springboard for engendering interest in the unit as well as introducing the importance of transportation in our lives. On 3-by-5-inch cards, write and post some of the students' comments as well as theories or speculations that surface regarding transportation.

Share the book titled *100 Words About Transportation* as a springboard for discussion. The illustrations focus on ways that individuals can move on their own (by foot, skateboard, bicycle); types of transportation in the city and the country; transportation vehicles used at work, on the road, in water, in the winter, in the air, in space, in distant lands, and so on. Another book, titled *The Big Book of Things That Go,* could be used to expand the discussion. Wonderful drawings illustrating the multiplicity of transportation means (on rails, at sea, in the air, etc.) are provided. Both of these books will stimulate questions, elicit interest in the topic, and create a sense of wonder about transportation and decisions associated with it.

A third book, titled *Transportation and Communication,* has an excellent section on moving people and things (pp. 6–9). The author explains how people have always traveled from place to place; however, with modernization, dramatic changes have occurred. One especially good illustration shows how a letter from the United States reaches its destination in the United Kingdom.

Suggested Lesson Discussion

Transportation is the act of moving people or goods from one place to another. Transportation takes people where they need and want to go, and it brings them the goods that they need or want. It connects people and goods all the way across the globe. Without transportation, there would be no trade, and without trade, there would be no towns or cities. Towns and cities are traditionally the centers of civilization. Therefore, transportation makes civilization possible. It brings people together and allows them to exchange goods, services, information, and more. Civilization has made progress in parallel to the development of transportation. The most modern forms of transportation on land are cars, trucks, motorcycles, trains, and buses. Passenger ships, boats, ferries, and tankers are used to transport people and goods by sea. Airplanes transport people and goods by air. They take things great distances in a short time.

Activity

Have students think about the most important things that they learned in the lesson. Have them signal by putting their hands on their foreheads when they have two or more ideas. When the class is ready, have students share ideas with partners.

Summarize

- Transportation is the movement of things and people from one place to another.
- The first humans traveled by foot; then came vehicles powered by animals and later by machines.
- The transportation of goods throughout the world is as important as the transportation of people.

Assessment

Have each student draw a picture representing the most important thing she or he learned about transportation in the lesson. Encourage each student to write two or more sentences explaining the picture and expressing the major understanding. Use the word board as a spelling prompt.

Home Assignment

Encourage each student to share with family members his or her picture and caption representing what was learned in the introductory lesson focusing on transportation. Then, as a family project, have them compile a list of transportation methods that their family has actually used. Encourage family members to use the Data Retrieval Chart in Figure 3 for compiling the information. The results will be shared during an upcoming class session.

Dear Parents,

We have just launched a new unit on transportation. Please spend a few minutes with your child discussing what he or she has learned in the introductory lesson. Begin discussing all of the methods of transportation that your family has used. Please compile a list to be shared during our next social studies lesson on the enclosed Data Retrieval Chart.

Sincerely,

FIGURE 2 Model Letter to Parents

Name _____

We are beginning a new unit on transportation. We would like to have you as a family talk about all of the methods of transportation that you have used (e.g., snowmobile, car, train, etc.). Please compile a list to be shared during our social studies class.

1.   6.

2.   7.

3.   8.

4.   9.

5.   10.

FIGURE 3   Data Retrieval Chart
© 2002 by Janet Alleman and Jere Brophy from *Social Studies Excursions, K–3: Book Two*. Portsmouth, NH: Heinemann.

Lesson 2

. . . .

Changes in Transportation over Time

Resources
- Time line for bulletin board
- Pictures depicting what types of transportation existed long, long ago (cave dwellers); long ago (pioneers); and today
- Table 1: Changes in Transportation: Long, Long Ago; Long Ago; and Today
- Globe
- Figure 5: Changes in Transportation: Long, Long Ago; Long Ago; and Today (blank copies for table activity)
- Packets of words and pictures for retelling the story of changes in transportation (for table activity)

Children's Literature
Delf, B., & Platt, R. (1995). *In the Beginning*. New York: Dorling Kindersley.

Kalman, B. (1992). *Early Travel*. New York: Crabtree.

Wood, R. (Consulting Ed.). (1995). *Great Inventions*. Victoria, Australia: Weldon Owen PTY Limited, Time Life Books.

General Comments
The intent of this lesson is to develop a sense of wonder and interest in how people and goods have been transported over time. Students will step back in time and look at pictures and narratives that express the evolution of transportation. They will come to realize how much easier it is to get from one place to another today and how most people, especially in America, enjoy a broad range of transportation choices.

General Purposes and Goals
To develop an understanding and appreciation for how: (1) transportation has changed over time; and (2) modern technology has enhanced the variety of transportation means available to us.

Main Ideas to Develop
- People long ago had very limited means of transportation. Travel was slow and hard. Most goods went by boat. When people traveled, they went by horseback or in wagons or carts.
- Inventions have resulted in faster transportation by land, water, and air.

- Water transportation developed much faster than land transportation. Early civilizations developed along rivers and seacoasts. Boats and ships were built for use in commerce, warfare, and exploration.
- As wheeled transportation became more common, better roads were needed. As time went by, faster coaches and gigs (two-wheeled carriages drawn by a horse) were built, and new road systems were designed.
- Railroads brought speed to travel. Manufacturers could transport their products over land to be sold in faraway places.

Teaching Tips from Barbara

I suggest devoting two days to the time line lesson so that the ideas have a chance to really sink in. I do the Long, Long Ago part on the first day. Then I add Long Ago the second day. I only touch a bit on the Today part of the time line because we cover many of these ideas in later lessons. I find it valuable to focus on a variety of choices, speed, distance, and power during the class discussions. The assessment for this lesson is fun as a sponge activity or as a way to begin the next lesson.

TABLE 1   Changes in Transportation: Long, Long Ago; Long Ago; and Today

LONG, LONG AGO	LONG AGO	TODAY
Traveled by foot	Improvements in ship construction (e.g., sailboat)	A range of car makes and models
Traveled by foot with goods strapped to poles, often carried by two people	Horse-drawn wagons	Trucks
Donkey and oxen	Stagecoaches	Sport utility vehicles
Harness invented so animals could pull sledges	Conestoga wagons	Jet airplanes
Rafts of logs and reeds	Steam engines	Ocean liners
Inflated skins	Electric trains and streetcars	Bullet trains
Dugout canoe	Gasoline engine	Spaceships
Frame boat	First automobile	
Reed boat	First airplane	
Sailboat		
Wheel was invented		

Starting the Lesson

Share the results of the home assignment. Then begin with a montage of pictures and photos depicting transportation. Ask student volunteers to place them in a tentative sequence reflecting long, long ago; long ago; and today. Listen for conceptions and misconceptions. Post these and re-visit them at the conclusion of today's lesson. Use pictures and words to illustrate the key points in the narrative.

Suggested Class Discussion

Long, Long Ago (Cave People)   The cave people lived by hunting, fishing, and gathering wild plants. They had no beasts of burden, wheeled vehicles, or roads. They traveled by foot and carried their babies and belongings strapped to their backs or heads. Loads that were too heavy for one person to carry were strapped to a pole and carried by two people.

Soon, people learned that they could drag loads along the ground on sledges. Sledges were made from logs, poles, rawhide, or anything else that could hold a load and be dragged by one or more people. Later, the people began to build sledges with runners. These vehicles became the first sleds.

Later, people developed agriculture and began to settle down permanently. Trade between settlements started to develop and created a need for better means of transportation. The donkey and the ox, which had been domesticated, helped meet the need. People began to use donkeys and oxen as pack animals. Soon the harness was invented so that the animals could pull the sledges. The use of donkeys and oxen as beasts of burden allowed people to transport heavier loads than they could before.

People also began to develop water transportation during prehistoric times. They built rafts out of logs and reeds. All of these early means of water transportation were propelled by paddles or poles and were used on streams or lakes. They were too fragile for ocean travel.

Much later, the sailboat and the wheel were invented and these inventions revolutionized transportation. [Show pictures of early sailboats and vehicles with wheels.] The first wheels were made of solid wood. Later wheels were designed with a rim, hub, and spokes. The spokes provided smoother riding and they were lighter and faster. The first spoked wheels were probably made for chariots.

[Point out on the time line and locate places on the globe.] Beginning in the 1400s, Europeans built ships capable of making long ocean voyages.

During the late 1400s and 1500s, such explorers as Christopher Columbus, Ferdinand Magellan, and Sir Francis Drake made great ocean voyages. As a result, European civilization spread westward, including to North America. In spite of the improvements in ship construction, ocean travel remained extremely slow.

Overseas trade began to increase rapidly during the 1600s. Shipbuilders launched bigger and bigger cargo vessels to handle the growing trade [show picture]. The bigger ships had to have more sails and the added sails helped to increase speed.

Stagecoaches became widely used in Europe around 1700. In other parts of the world, such as China, people continued to use older forms of transportation.

By the 1600s, most people used horse-drawn wagons to haul goods locally, but they seldom used wagons for lengthy voyages because of the poor condition of the roads. Until the mid-1800s, horse-drawn boats and barges were the chief means of long-distance, inland transportation. The animals trudged along the banks of rivers and canals and pulled the vessels with ropes.

It wasn't until the mid-1800s that the first major United States highway, known as the National Road, was completed [show picture]. It was made of gravel. It ran from Cumberland, Maryland, to Vandalia, Illinois. Pioneers who wanted to go further west had to cross a wilderness without roads once they got past the Mississippi River. They drove their covered wagons along dirt paths originally created by the Native Americans.

In about 1730, the first stagecoaches began service in the American colonies [show a picture]. They were called *stagecoaches* because their passengers traveled in stages, stopping at scheduled places for changes of horses. Carrying mail, the coach traveled fifteen miles per day, which was considered a good speed in the 1750s. Pioneers headed west to the American frontier in Conestoga wagons. These distinctive vehicles had curved floors and high sides to stop their loads from shifting, and broad wheels to spread the weight so the wagons didn't dig ruts into the roads and bog down easily. Pulled by a team of horses or oxen, they could carry up to six tons.

The invention of the steam engine marked the beginning of the greatest change in transportation since the inventions of the wheel and the sailboat. As steamships and steam-powered trains came into service, speed increased and passenger fares and freight rates dropped. The lower costs encouraged travel and the growth of cities. In addition, many people became accustomed to fast movement and rapid change.

The first electric trains and streetcars were used in the United States in the late 1800s [show pictures]. Later, diesel engines replaced steam engines, and still later, the gasoline engine was invented. In 1903, two American bicycle makers, Orville and Wilbur Wright, used a gasoline engine to power a small airplane that they had built [show a picture]. The Wright Brothers became the first men to design an airplane that could lift a person into the air and fly successfully.

Automobiles became the chief means of passenger transportation in the United States during the 1920s. The automobile that made Henry

Ford rich and famous was the Model T [show picture], which was first produced in 1908 in a factory located in Detroit, Michigan. A feature of this plant a few years later was the use of mass-produced interchangeable parts. [Illustrate the importance of this innovation.]

The low price of the Model T and of later models that Ford developed made the automobile available to modest wage earners. However, learning to drive the vehicles and keeping them repaired were difficult at first. Because America's roads were very rough—not built for cars—accidents and breakdowns were common. As the number of automobile owners increased, so did the demand for more and better roads. The development of dependable cars and good roads led to the growth of suburbs around big cities. Many of the people living in the suburbs began depending on their cars for shopping, personal business, and going to and from work.

Later, commercial airplanes [show picture] were built and people were able to travel almost anywhere in the world in a very short time. Long journeys became routine. As the result of improvements in air travel, ocean shipping, and refrigeration, goods that were once available only in certain regions are now distributed worldwide.

Before the development of engine-powered vehicles, nearly all transportation involved the shipment of goods rather than the movement of people. Today, however, passenger transportation is an essential part of life, especially in developed parts of the world. Workers tend to live farther away from their work than they did in the past and they need dependable transportation to get back and forth every day. Families need transportation for errands and shopping, and often they travel great distances while on vacation.

Activity

Give each table a copy of Figure 5 and a packet of words and pictures. Ask each group to add the words and pictures to the correct column. During a large-group discussion, draw tentative conclusions (e.g., Long, long ago was a no-tech age. Few people worked in the transportation field, people couldn't travel very far, and travel was very slow.).

Summarize

- The changes in transportation over the years have been dramatic. As a result, it is much easier to travel.
- Many more choices regarding methods of transportation are available.
- We can move people and goods very quickly (for the most part), no matter where we live.
- We can even travel into outer space.

Assessment

Using a collection of scenarios that characterize changes in transportation across time, ask students to role-play each one. Allow time for class discussion after each enactment. [You, as the teacher, should model the first enactment.] Have students identify when each of the scenarios would have occurred by locating the period in history on the time line.

> *Scenario #1* Cave dweller traveling in search of food.
> *Scenario #2* Cave dwellers transporting their family members to a nearby cave.
> *Scenario #3* People transporting their goods by sledges.
> *Scenario #4* People building rafts out of logs and reeds and propelling the rafts by paddles or poles along streams or in lakes.
> *Scenario #5* A first grader preparing for a trip across the United States today (consider all of the transportation options available).
> *Scenario #6* A pioneer second grader moving from Michigan to California.

Encourage students to add and enact other scenarios (e.g., taking a ride in a Model T, traveling by barge down the Mississippi to visit relatives in New Orleans, a family traveling westward through the wilderness hoping to find gold in California, etc.).

Home Assignment

Encourage each student to have a conversation with his or her family about the changes that have occurred in transportation during the parents' and grandparents' lifetimes. Have the family write a paragraph describing these changes that could be shared during the next class session. If elderly individuals are available, involve them as additional resources who can provide personal testimony regarding changes in transportation over the years.

Dear Parents,

We are learning about changes in transportation over time. Please share and discuss with your child changes that have occurred during your family's lifetime. For example, when you were a child, your family might have had only one vehicle; your family couldn't have had an SUV because it wasn't available on the market; and so on. Please write a paragraph describing these changes that your child can share during our next class discussion.

If elderly relatives or neighbors are available, please ask them to share their experiences. Responses from them regarding changes in transportation over the years would be welcomed. Thank you!

Sincerely,

FIGURE 4   Model Letter to Parents

LONG, LONG AGO	LONG AGO	TODAY

FIGURE 5   Changes in Transportation: Long, Long Ago; Long Ago; and Today

Lesson 3

Types of Transportation

Resources

- *Transportation*. (1994). Chicago: World Book Inc.
- Land transportation pictures depicting engineless means (e.g., walking, carrying a load on one's back or head, animals carrying loads (beasts of burden), animals pulling carts, bicycles pulling carts)
- Land transportation pictures depicting engine-powered means (e.g., automobile, bus, motorcycle, train, truck)
- Water transportation pictures depicting rafts, boats, and ships, including cruising vessels
- Air transportation pictures depicting passenger planes, including the Concorde, helicopters, military transport planes, mail/cargo planes
- Pictures of engineless aircraft (e.g., gliders, hot-air balloons)
- Bulletin board for picture display of land, water, and air transportation
- Transportation Bingo
- Class scrapbook with categories identified
- Individual scrapbooks for individual student data gathering and spaces for journal entries
- Transportation Scrapbook Entry (Figure 7)

Children's Literature

Conrad, L. (1989). *All Aboard Trucks*. New York: Grosset & Dunlap.

Evans, F. (1994). *All Aboard Airplanes*. New York: Grosset & Dunlap.

Harding, M. (1989). *All Aboard Trains*. New York: Grossett & Dunlap.

Kentley, E. (1992). *Boats*. New York: Alfred A. Knopf.

Kirkwood, J. (1997). *Cutaway Trucks*. Brookfield, CT: Cooper Beech.

Little, K. (1987). *Finding Out About Things That Fly*. Tulsa, OK: EDC.

Lopez, D. (1995). *Flight*. San Francisco: Weldon Owen Group.

Oliver, S. (Photographer). (1991). *Eye Openers: Trains*. New York: Dorling Kindersley.

Otfinoski, S. (1997). *Behind the Wheel: Cars Now and Then*. New York: Benchmark.

Otfinoski, S. (1997). *Riding the Rails*. New York: Benchmark.

Relf, P. (1996). *Tonka, Big Book of Trucks*. New York: Scholastic.

Richards, J. (1998). *Cutaway Trains*. Brookfield, CT: Cooper Beech.

Royston, A. (1991). *Cars*. New York: Simon & Schuster.

Royston, A. (1998). *Eyewitness Readers: Truck Trouble*. New York: Dorling Kindersley.

Sandler, M. W. (1996). *Inventors*. New York: HarperCollins.

Weir, C. D. (1996). *All Aboard Cars*. New York: Grosset & Dunlap.

Wood, S. (1998). *See and Explore: Trains and Railroads*. London: Dorling Kindersley.

Thomas, A. (1987). *Finding Out About Things That Float*. Tulsa, OK: EDC.

General Comments

The focus for this lesson will be the main kinds of transportation: land, water, and air. Land transportation depends mainly on wheeled vehicles such as automobiles, trains, and trucks. The most important water vehicles are ships and boats. Air transportation depends almost entirely on airplanes. The intent is to pique students' interests regarding the multiplicity of types that exist in their community so that they will want to investigate the range of possibilities.

General Purposes or Goals

To help students understand and appreciate: (1) the three main kinds of transportation (land, water, and air); (2) the advantages and potential trade-offs of engine-powered or engineless transportation; (3) the advantages and potential trade-offs of land, water, and air transportation; and (4) the variables that must be considered when deciding what means and type to use (e.g., geography, economic conditions, time, etc.).

Main Ideas to Develop

- There are many kinds of transportation.
- The three major kinds of transportation are land, water, and air.
- Transportation means also can be classified as engine-powered or engineless.
- Engine-powered means of transportation have many advantages over engineless means (faster, more dependable, carry greater loads).
- Disadvantages of engine-powered means of transportation include the following: cost more, usually need supporting facilities, and are expensive to build and maintain. Every form of engine-powered transportation consumes fuel as a source of energy.
- The automobile is the most common means of transportation on land in the United States (In some places it is bicycles or oxcarts.)
- Trucks carry large loads from place to place.
- Before the invention of cars and trucks, we used trains to travel long distances. Some people still use trains to get about, and trains carry large loads of freight.

Teaching Tips from Barbara

This is one of the most crucial lessons in the unit. It provides two important things for the students. First, it generates a large number of types of transportation. Students will benefit in future lessons by having various modes of transportation to discuss and evaluate. This lesson also allows students to begin categorizing, sorting, and evaluating transportation types. As a follow-up, I had my students sort pictures of transportation into categories (eg., land, water, air, engineless and engine-powered).

Starting the Lesson

Share the results of the home assignment. Then pose these questions: What are the main types of transportation? How do people decide which type to use? Build on prior knowledge but also listen for misconceptions that will need to be addressed.

Suggested Lesson Discussion

There are three main kinds of transportation: land, water, and air. Land transportation depends mainly on wheeled vehicles; ships and boats are the most important water vehicles; and air transportation depends almost entirely on airplanes.

Each type of transportation can be further classified according to whether or not it is engine-powered. Most engine-powered vehicles have gas, diesel, or jet engines [show pictures]. The majority of the vehicles that do not have engines are powered by the muscles of animals or human beings or by natural forces such as wind or flowing water [show pictures].

Engine-powered means of transportation have many advantages over engineless means: they're faster, more dependable, and can carry greater loads [show pictures]. The disadvantages are that they require lots of money and usually need supporting facilities. For example, cars and trucks need roads; trains need tracks and train stations; ships need docks and ports; airplanes need airports. All of the facilities are expensive to build and maintain. Every form of engine-powered transportation also needs fuel as a source of energy. Therefore, the combined cost of the vehicles, supporting facilities such as train stations and airports, and energy make engine-powered transportation expensive.

Engine-powered vehicles are the main means of travel in developed countries and in some of the urban areas of the less developed countries [show pictures]. However, many people in less developed places, especially in rural areas, still rely on engineless means of transportation that their ancestors used hundreds of years ago [show pictures].

Land Transportation   Land transportation is the most common by far, and in many cases, it is the only suitable or available kind. Land transportation can be divided into two categories: engineless and engine-powered [show pictures].

Engineless   Walking is the most elementary means. Carrying a load on one's back or head or using animals is also very elementary and was the primary transportation means in the early days. Animals used for this purpose are called *beasts of burden* or *pack animals.* Camels, donkeys, horses, elephants, llamas, and oxen are often used for carrying things. People use pack animals in regions that lack modern roads. Such regions include many deserts, mountainous areas, and jungles. Sometimes these animals are used by people who cannot afford other means of transportation [show pictures].

People also use their own muscle power to move wheeled vehicles such as carts and bicycles [show picture]. These methods require fairly flat, smooth roads for efficient use.

Animal-drawn carts and wagons used to be a major means of transportation in America and are still used in rural areas of many developing countries. Carts may be pulled by dogs or horses. Wagons are large four-wheeled carts that can carry heavy loads. Oxen or draft horses are very strong and are needed to pull these heavy loads [show pictures].

Engine-Powered   Automobiles, buses, motorcycles, snowmobiles, trains, and trucks are the most common engine-powered land vehicles [show pictures]. Automobiles, buses, and trucks are the main modern road vehicles. Automobiles allow people to travel whenever and by whatever route they choose. Buses carry passengers along fixed routes and between cities. Trucks can provide door-to-door freight service. In some parts of the world, motorcycles are used to take people to and from work; however, in the United States, motorcycles are used mainly for recreation.

Trains are a kind of land transportation, but they need tracks to ride on. Because of this, they usually cannot provide door-to-door freight service; however, they can haul far heavier loads than trucks can. They can also carry more passengers than buses [show pictures].

Optional   Snowmobiles skim across ice and snow. They have skis on the front and a moving track at the rear. An engine powers the track that propels the vehicle.

Pipelines provide transportation but the pipes themselves do not move. Most pipelines are built across land but some span rivers or other bodies of water. Pipelines transport liquids and gases such as petroleum and natural gas [show a picture].

[Note: You as the teacher may want to select one or more means of land, water, and air transportation to focus on in the class. Encourage students to use library sources to learn more about the other means.]

Automobile [Optional: Read the books *Behind the Wheel: Cars Then and Now* by Steve Otfinoski. The illustrations are attractive and interesting. Key points drawn from the book are as follows:]

- The first car hit the road in 1885. That year, a German inventor by the name of Karl Benz put a gasoline engine on a tricycle and drove it through the streets of Mannheim, Germany. Other early cars ran on steam and electricity. Then, in 1908, Henry Ford began making the Model T in Detroit. It was a car that many people could afford.
- Over the years, the automobile has undergone a variety of changes. Unique shapes, a range of colors, a range of features (e.g., automatic transmission, four-wheel drive, convertibles) have been available to people who could afford them.

[As you show/discuss the illustrations, ask the students to think about the kind of car they think they will be driving when they are old enough to sit behind the wheel. Have *Cars* available for its illustrations and for the purpose of helping students acquire an appreciation for the variety of automobiles that have been developed.]

[Explain to the students that besides the popularity of cars for personal use, including driving to and from work (where parking is available), today some cars are built to do special jobs.] Most police cars start out as ordinary cars, but then they are equipped with lights and sirens used to warn other cars to get out of the way or pull over. Often there is a screen between the front and back seats to separate drivers from crime suspects.

The fire chief has another type of special car. It has lights and a siren so the chief can get to emergencies quickly [show a picture].

A taxicab takes people to places for a fee. A taxi usually has a meter that keeps track of how far it goes and shows the passenger how much to pay [show a picture].

A limousine is another type of car that takes people places for a fee. It is usually reserved for special occasions (e.g., weddings, parties, funerals) [show a picture].

An ambulance is still another type of special car. When someone is really sick or seriously hurt and needs to get to the hospital quickly, an ambulance is called (911) [show a picture]. Ambulances are specially equipped with stretchers, blankets, and other emergency equipment.

Jeeps are used in the military for helping soldiers carry supplies and move from place to place. They can go over rough, bumpy ground that would stop other cars. This all-purpose vehicle can even be used as an ambulance in an emergency. Jeeps inspired all-terrain vehicles, dune buggies, and four-wheel drive cars and trucks [show a picture].

Some cars are built just to go fast. Race cars are made to be driven by specially trained drivers on specially built tracks. Automobile racing is one of the most dangerous sports in the world. Drivers need to wear lots of protective clothing to avoid being injured if their vehicles crash/collide [show a picture].

Car companies are always trying to build better cars—cars that use less gasoline, cars that are safer, and cars that are better for the environment. Obviously the automobile (engine-powered means of transportation) goes faster and is more dependable than engineless means. Another advantage is that the vehicle is for personal use. It can take its occupants much farther in an hour or a day than engineless vehicles can, and the individuals can travel in comfort.

Disadvantages of the engine-powered automobile include the costs of the vehicles themselves, costs for gasoline, and costs for maintaining cars (e.g., oil change, repairs, insurance, etc.), as well as the pollution that results from emissions, old tires, old batteries, and so on.

Trucks   [If any student's parent is a truck driver, you might want to invite him or her to visit the class and serve as a resource. Read the book *Eyewitness Readers: Truck Trouble*. Encourage the students to listen and decide whether they might or might not like to be truck drivers when they grow up. They should be prepared to give reasons for their responses.]

[After reading and discussing the story and trade-offs associated with being a truck driver, explain to the class that John (in the story) was driving a semi tractor-trailer carrying cargo from one place to another.] Tractor-trailers carry everything from toys to turkeys. There are other types of trucks on the highways: a tow truck hauls broken-down vehicles to the repair shop; transporters take new cars from the factory to car dealers across the country. [Use the book *Tonka, Big Book of Trucks* to describe and discuss the many types of trucks.] Trucks are used in building houses, building roads, observed on the highway, or used around town, in the city, on the farm, at a seaport, at the state fair, at a fire, and at a space shuttle launch.

[Skim through the entire book with the class, emphasizing types of trucks found primarily in one or two places. For example, you might concentrate on trucks seen mostly on the highways.] A tractor-trailer is a two-part truck with the tractor at the front that has a powerful engine, and the trailer that carries the load. Tractor-trailers are also called semi-trailers, or "semis" for short. Some semis have a special compartment with a bed where one driver can sleep while the other drives—or where a lone driver sleeps after he pulls off at a truck stop. A tanker trailer carries liquids such as milk, oil, or gasoline. A tow truck rescues cars that cannot move by themselves (the driver hooks a cable to the front of the car and a powerful winch winds the cable until it lifts the front end of the car off the ground so the truck can pull it to a repair shop). A car transport is a special tractor-trailer that delivers new cars to the dealers who sell them.

Trucks seen mostly in the city might include a moving van (a truck that holds everything from a house or an apartment), or a cherry picker (a truck that gets its name from the way it lifts a worker high in the air—high enough to pick cherries at the top of a tree). In the city, a cherry picker lifts a worker up to repair electric wires or streetlights. The worker climbs into the bucket and uses the controls inside to move the bucket in any direction. A street cleaner picks up dirt and litter in the streets. Its big turning brushes whisk the dirt into the truck's big tank. A spray of water helps to keep the dust from flying in the air. At some point the truck will empty the dirt at a garbage dump.

There are also trucks for other important jobs. For example, they can mix concrete, carry logs, plow snow, and so on. Trucks come in all sizes and shapes.

Trains   Before the arrival of cars and trucks, people used trains to travel from place to place. The puffing steam engines that once pulled the trains have been replaced by powerful diesel engines and very fast electric locomotives.

It takes a lot of work to build a railroad. Sometimes railroads have been built through forests, so trees had to be cut down. If they come across obstacles such as lakes or rivers, the railroad builders have to construct bridges. Another way to cross lakes and rivers and even mountains is to dig tunnels beneath or through them [show a picture].

Trains carry both goods and people. A train that carries goods is called a freight train. Some freight trains have flat cars to carry containers. Others have special cars that carry automobiles. Some trains carry livestock (animals) while others carry packaged cargo such as computers. Some trains carry fruits and vegetables. The food is kept in refrigerator cars so that it will not spoil on the way to the supermarket. Often, freight trains consist of many different kinds of products. The caboose is the very last car on most freight trains. This serves as the train crew's home and the conductor's office. From the cupola or roof lookout, the conductor can check for signals from the crew at the front of the train (modern trains use videos, phones, and other electronic equipment) [show a picture].

Passenger trains carry people and their luggage. Some trains travel only from suburbs to the city and back again. These are referred to as commuter trains for people who commute to their jobs or schools. Other trains travel across the country. Sometimes they are referred to as intercity trains. Many passenger trains are pulled by electric locomotives. Electric locomotives do not produce their own power. They get their power from a power plant, often many miles away [show a picture].

Passengers sit in cars called coaches. Most short-distance commuter trains have only coach cars but some long-distance intercity trains provide services such as a dining car and sleeping cars. Some trains feature double-decker coach cars and observation cars.

Some passenger trains run at very high speeds (e.g., bullet trains in Japan); some run on tracks in underground tunnels while others run on tracks above the street [show a picture].

Today, there are several choices for transporting goods and people. Time available and costs associated with each means of transportation must be considered. The rising costs of fuel and the awareness of car and truck pollution continue to make trains a viable option.

Water Transportation   This depends mainly on boats, ships, and rafts. People use boats mainly on rivers, canals, and lakes. A ship is a larger vessel sturdy enough for ocean travel. A raft is a floating platform constructed out of materials such as logs or barrels [show a picture].

Nearly all ships and many boats are powered by engines. Most ships specialize in carrying cargo on ocean waters and on bodies of water linked to the oceans. Few ships specialize in transporting passengers. Those that do are often referred to as cruise ships.

The biggest passenger ship in use is the *Queen Elizabeth II* or *QE2*. It is like a small city with shops, restaurants, movies, and even a hospital. This cruise ship has four swimming pools, a health club, and a garage for passenger's cars. It even prints its own newspaper.

There are various types of motorboats that carry passengers locally. Motorboats are very often used for pleasure. There are some engine-powered boats, especially tugboats used for hauling freight. Tugboats have powerful engines that enable them to tow heavily loaded barges. Barges are used mainly to haul freight along inland waterways [show a picture].

In general, ships and boats are the slowest engine-powered vehicles; however, some very fast ones have been developed (e.g., hydrofoils skim across the water on skids or runners).

Engineless water vehicles include dugouts, canoes, rowboats, sail-boats, and rafts. People use paddles or oars to propel dugouts, canoes, and rowboats. Sailboats are powered by the wind [show a picture].

People take to the water for many reasons: to explore, trade, fish, and have fun. Numerous types of water transportation have been developed to serve each purpose. For thousands of years, people have been developing new ways to make travel on the water easier, safer, and faster. The earliest craft were simple rafts and floats. Then the hollowed log was invented. This was the first boat, an invention as important as the wheel. The wooden boat is the ancestor of the great sailing ships and the huge ferries and container ships of today. There are now hundreds of different types of boats and ships made from almost every material imaginable—reeds, animal skins, plastic, fiberglass, iron, and steel [show pictures].

[Show students a variety of pictures depicting the range of water transportation and underscoring their uses. Then select one or two to focus on. Encourage the students to learn more about others that are of particular interest to them. For the class, you might select the cruise ship as described earlier because some students might have some familiarity with cruise vacations.]

[Another one that might hold high interest for the students is the submarine.] Submarines travel under the sea. They are powered by diesel engines or nuclear-powered turbines. Nuclear submarines can work for years without needing to be refueled and can stay underwater for as long as two years without coming to the surface. Submarines play an important role in our national defense program [show a picture].

Air Transportation For thousands of years, people all over the world dreamed of flying. But less than one hundred years ago, someone actually invented a machine that could carry people through the air. The first flight only lasted twelve seconds and went only 120 feet. The first airplanes were powered by propellers. Propellers have blades that spin very fast. The blades push air behind the propeller and make the airplane go forward. Many planes still use propellers.

Another kind of airplane is the jetliner. Powerful jet engines make it possible to fly very far at very high speeds. An example is the jumbo jet known as the Boeing 747. It can carry five hundred passengers. It has six kitchens and twelve bathrooms [show a picture].

Airplanes provide the world's fastest practical method of transporting passengers and freight. Most airliners primarily carry passengers. Even the biggest airplanes can carry only a fraction of the freight that a ship or train can haul. As a result, it is very expensive to send things by air, especially things that weigh a lot. Perishables, fresh flowers, mail, emergency medical supplies, lightweight electronic equipment, or other supplies that need to reach a place in a hurry are typically sent by air [show a picture].

[There are many types of aircraft that could be included as a part of the lesson. We suggest that you show students the variety that exists, select a couple to emphasize in the lesson, and encourage individual students to learn more about other types of particular interest.]

The Concorde is a supersonic transport jet. It goes faster than the speed of sound. It is the fastest passenger plane in the world. It can fly all the way from New York to London in three hours. The Concorde is very expensive to operate, seats only one hundred passengers, and is banned from many cities because of its sonic boom [show a picture].

Helicopters are another kind of aircraft [show a picture]. A rotor on top of the helicopter spins like a propeller to lift the aircraft straight up. Helicopters are slower than airplanes and harder to fly, but they can be very useful. For example, they can take off and land in small spaces. They can hover—hang in the air—in one place. A helicopter is often used in wartime. It is also very useful during emergency situations, rescuing people from sinking ships or burning buildings by dropping the victims a line, then pulling them up. Helicopters can fly slowly. In big cities, radio and television reporters sometimes fly helicopters over highways to warn drivers about any traffic jams they see. They also can lift or carry things that are too big or heavy for other vehicles to move. Sometimes the U.S. Army uses helicopters called skycranes to carry planes, tanks, trucks, and even small buildings.

There are many other kinds of engine-powered aircraft. Included are many kinds of military planes as well as spacecraft. Additionally, there are some engineless vehicles such as gliders and hot-air balloons. These are used mainly for recreation [show a picture].

Activity

Use Transportation Bingo to determine students' understanding of types and variables associated with the types. (The bingo cards could be a project for an adult volunteer. Have cards with sixteen pictures or sketches of types of transportation. Sticker books, workbooks, and picture dictionaries are excellent sources.) During the activity, the teacher reads a description and the student looks for a good match. The first student to complete a "run"—horizontal, vertical, or diagonal—calls "Bingo!"

Summarize

- There are three main kinds of transportation: land, water, and air.
- Land transportation depends mainly on wheeled vehicles such as automobiles, trains, and trucks.
- The most important water vehicles are ships and boats.
- Air transportation depends almost entirely on planes.

Assessment

Throughout the unit, have the students participate in the development of a class or individual scrapbook that displays writing, thinking, drawing, computer graphics, categorizing, and so on to reveal major understandings. At the conclusion of this lesson, have the students collect and display pictures associated with the three types of transportation and explain what geographic and economic considerations are associated with each example. Encourage a wide range of examples. This activity will be expanded into the home assignment.

Examples:

> I want to take a ride in an engineless vehicle that floats through the
> air. It has wings. (Glider)
>
> I want to go to the store for a loaf of bread. I want to use an
> engineless means of travel. I will travel by myself, although I
> could have a passenger. I need to wear a helmet. (Bicycle)

Home Assignment

Encourage each student to work with his or her family on a transportation
scrapbook. The emphasis for the entry associated with this lesson will be
on the types of transportation (land, water, air) the family has used, for
what reason(s), and types the family has not used and why. Send home a
copy of Figure 7 for families to use when creating their scrapbook entry.

Dear Parents,

As you know, we are studying about transportation. Your child
will be creating a scrapbook as a means of displaying writing,
thinking, drawing, and illustrations done on a computer. Please
spend a few minutes with your child discussing the types of
transportation (land, water, air) your family has used, for what
reasons, and types of transportation your family has not used
and why (e.g., perhaps your family does not use bus
transportation because you own a car or do not live near a bus
route). Together, create an entry for the scrapbook that reflects
your discussion. A form has been enclosed to help you with
creating the entry.

Sincerely,

FIGURE 6   Model Letter to Parents

TYPE OF TRANSPORTATION	REASON USED	REASON NOT USED
1.	1.	1.
2.	2.	2.
3.	3.	3.
4.	4.	4.
5.	5.	5.
6.	6.	6.
7.	7.	7.
8.	8.	8.
9.	9.	9.
10.	10.	10.

FIGURE 7   Transportation Scrapbook Entry

Lesson 4

....

Passenger Transportation

Resources

- Word cards: Personal and Public
- Pictures of personal and public transportation around the world
- Pictures illustrating various travel and parking conditions around the world
- Photos of local means of public transportation
- Photos of local bus stop, taxi stand, train station, airport
- Telephone directory
- Telephone (play) for role-play
- Pictures and word cards of local means of transportation (for table activity)
- Figure 9: Student Response Form: Passenger Transportation

Children's Literature

Bingham, C. (1994). *The Big Book of Things That Go.* New York: Dorling Kindersley.

General Comments

The intent of this lesson is to develop a sense of wonder and interest in how people travel. Students will have an opportunity to reflect on the types of private and public means of travel they have experienced personally as well as to observe other types that are available in their own communities. They will also be exposed to the idea that in rural areas of developing countries, many people still rely on age-old transportation methods.

General Purposes or Goals

To develop: (1) an understanding and appreciation for the personal and public transportation types that are available in their community and the trade-offs associated with these types that people might consider in deciding which ones to use; (2) a sense of curiosity about developing countries and the age-old methods of transportation still in use; and (3) appreciation for why rural areas in these places still use these methods.

Main Ideas to Develop

- There are two main types of passenger transportation: personal and public.
- People who use personal transportation operate their own vehicles.

- Those who use public transportation pay to ride on vehicles owned and operated by companies or the government.
- Mass transportation was invented to carry large numbers of people at a time.
- People decide which means of transportation to use based on time, money, personal preferences, what types are available, and so on.

Teaching Tips from Barbara

Once again, pictures are the keys to helping make this lesson memorable. Use pictures from previous lessons for simplicity. To make the content more meaningful for my students, I shared my own plans for a trip. The students helped me to decide between renting a car and taking a taxi. I was surprised to find that after my trip, the students couldn't wait to find out what transportation I had used. Even after the unit was done, whenever I went on a trip, they asked those same questions.

Starting the Lesson

Discuss the responses from the home assignment. Then ask students what types of passenger transportation exist in the local area. What is the difference between public and personal transportation?

Suggested Lesson Discussion

There are two main types of passenger transportation: personal and public transportation. People who use personal transportation operate their own vehicles. Those who use public transportation pay to ride on vehicles owned and operated by private companies or the government. [Place large word cards on a bulletin board labeled "Personal" and "Public." As you introduce and describe local examples, place their pictures in the appropriate column.]

Personal Transportation   [Begin by describing the personal means of transportation that you or your family use.] I drive a maroon van that you see in our school parking lot. My husband drives a white Honda. We drive our van and car ourselves. These are called *personal* means of transportation. In our community, most people travel chiefly by car or truck or van. Our roads are good; we have plenty of space for parking our vehicles; and most adults have enough money to acquire one. In our family, we also own bicycles and my husband has a motorcycle. These too are personal means of transportation. We drive/ride them ourselves. A few people in the community also have personal airplanes. They are quite expensive and are not as convenient for most things that people in our community do. Also, there are fewer places where personal airplanes can be parked. [Place pictures of each of these means of personal transportation in the appropriate column.]

In rural areas in developing parts of the world, people often still travel by foot, bicycle, camel, and other engineless means because the roads are not as good and the people can't afford automobiles. There are also many parts of the world that have very large numbers of people but not many places to park vehicles. Few people use cars in these areas. {Show pictures to illustrate these various conditions. Place the pictures in the appropriate column—personal.}

Public Transportation   {Refer to word and column on bulletin/white board.} Public transportation is transportation that people pay for in order to ride in vehicles owned and operated by companies or the government. In our local community we have taxis. {Place a picture of a taxi in the public transportation column.} People hire taxis to take them wherever they want to go in the city. When taxis are waiting for passengers to call in and ask to be picked up, they display a "for hire" light on the roof. A taxi has a meter inside that indicates how many miles the ride is so that the driver knows how much to charge the passenger.

In some countries, rickshaws {show a picture} are used as taxis. There are even places where water taxis (boats) {show a picture} are used to transport people. Often, these are used in places where the people have less money and the roads are not good. In some places, the streets are so crowded that it is faster to go from one part of the city to another by boat. {Show photos illustrating the range of ways people are transported depending on the existing conditions.}

Less common, but available in our city, are limousines {show a picture}. They are another means of public transportation. People use these for special occasions (e.g., weddings, funerals, proms, etc.).

Buses are the chief mass transit vehicles {show a picture}. School systems usually own school buses that they use to transport students who live some distance from the school back and forth from home. These buses are also used to transport students to and from special events (e.g., band festivals, football and basketball games, etc.). Buses and the costs associated with gas and insurance are paid for through school taxes.

Cities usually have a bus system to transport people around the local area. You probably have observed bus stops—places where people are picked up and dropped off. People pay a set amount of money every time they ride the bus. They either have purchased bus passes or tokens, or they buy a ticket when they board. {Elicit students' observations regarding other public means of mass transit that are found in the local area (if any). Encourage them to bring photographs to add to the bulletin board.} Many people who live in cities do not have cars, so they depend on public transportation to get them to their jobs or schools, to shopping centers, or to sports and entertainment events. Also, some people who do own cars nevertheless take a bus or commuter train to work because it is cheaper and easier than dealing with the hassle of rush hour commutes in a crowded city and paying high fees to park their car near their office building.

Many very large cities such as New York and Chicago also have subways. A subway train speeds along tunnels built under the city's streets. Elevated trains run on tracks above the streets. [Show pictures of these.]

Public transportation between cities is called intercity service. Intercity service is provided mainly by airplanes, buses, and trains. In some areas, riverboats and ferryboats carry some intercity passengers. [Show pictures of all of these means of transportation. Add them to the bulletin board display.]

When people need public transportation, they go to the telephone directory and look up the number of the company that provides that type of service. [Ask students to name the local cab companies. Locate them in the telephone directory. Model by using the telephone directory and dialing the number. You tell the operator where you live, the time you need the cab to pick you up, and the city or state where you are going.]

If you need a bus, you find out the schedule (usually posted) and go to the nearest bus stop and wait [show a bus schedule and a close-up of a familiar bus stop]. If you plan to take a train or an airplane to another city, you go to the train station or airport. It is best to make reservations and buy your tickets in advance because there are a limited number of seats available. [Show photos of local means of public transportation and the sites where you go to get a ride, ticket, etc.]

Activity

Provide each table with a picture and/or word card identifying one means of transportation (public or personal) that is provided locally. Have the group determine what the passenger would need to consider before using it (e.g., cost, time, etc.). In other words, what are the advantages and disadvantages for selecting it? Allow class time for minipresentations and discussion.

Summarize

* There are two types of passenger transportation: personal and public.
* People who use personal transportation operate their own cars or trucks.
* People who use public transportation pay to ride in vehicles owned by companies or the government (some need to do so because they do not own cars; others do so because they find it cheaper or easier than driving).
* Mass transportation has been invented to transport large numbers of people at a time.

- Mass transportation is owned by private companies or by the government.

Assessment

Present scenarios to the class and on a predeveloped form and have the students identify what means of transportation would be the best choice on copies of Figure 9. Is it personal or public? Encourage students to use the bulletin board displaying pictures and words as cues for selecting responses. During the follow-up discussion, the students will have the opportunity to share their reasons for their choices. Underscore the idea that there can be more than one choice. Reasons are important.

Scenario #1 My family needs to go to the supermarket to buy groceries for the week.

Scenario #2 My mother has a business trip planned to a city 150 miles away. She needs to be there by 8:00 A.M. and she will return to our home in the late afternoon.

Scenario #3 An elderly woman lives in an apartment downtown. She no longer drives, but she needs to go to the mall.

Scenario #4 My father has a three-day business trip planned to New York City.

Scenario #5 My neighbor is planning a sightseeing trip through the Rocky Mountains. Time is not a consideration. Seeing the sights is the most important.

Scenario #6 The family is planning a vacation to California. It is traveling by air but doesn't want to leave the car at the airport.

Scenario #7 The high school basketball team has a game tonight in a town fifty miles away.

Scenario #8 The family wants to go to the baseball game this evening.

After students have independently identified the means and determined if it is personal or public, discuss the reasoning behind the selection. Note that in many cases there is more than one good choice (e.g., #3: The elderly woman might take a public bus or a taxi to the mall. The bus would be cheaper, but she would need to walk to the bus stop. Then when she is finished shopping, she would need to walk to the bus stop located at the mall. If it's difficult for her to walk or she is on a tight schedule and doesn't have time to wait, the more expensive taxi might be a better choice.).

Home Assignment

Have each student share with her or his family what she or he has learned about public and personal passenger transportation. Encourage the family to list all the means that its members have used. Have them discuss and list the trade-offs associated with each. Finally, encourage the family to talk about a memorable experience it can recall that is associated with transportation (e.g., the taxi driver who took us to the wrong hotel; the limo that had a flat tire, almost making us late to our cousin's wedding; the bus strike in our town that caused thousands of people to miss work, etc.).

Dear Parents,

Our class is continuing to learn about transportation. The current topic is public and personal transportation. As a family, please list all the means of transportation you have used and the trade-offs associated with each. If possible, share stories about memorable experiences associated with public or personal transportation that your family recalls. For example, a taxi driver might have taken you to the wrong hotel or your family might have overslept and missed a flight. Your child will have an opportunity to share during our next social studies lesson. Thank you!

Sincerely,

FIGURE 8   Model Letter to Parents

MEANS	PUBLIC OR PERSONAL	REASON
1.		
2.		
3.		
4.		
5.		
6.		
7.		
8.		
9.		
10.		

FIGURE 9   Student Response Form: Passenger Transportation

Lesson 5

. . . .

Emergency Vehicles

Resources
- Emergency vehicle and resource person (to describe the functions of the vehicle and show the special equipment)
- Pictures and photos of emergency vehicles

Children's Literature

Bikes, Cars, Trucks, and Trains. (1995). New York: Scholastic.

Bingham, C. (1994). *The Big Book of Things That Go.* New York: Dorling Kindersley Publishing.

Wolhart, D. (1991). *Emergency Vehicles.* Mankato, MN: Capstone.

General Comments

Accidents and disasters are unpleasant, so we don't like to think about them. However, despite how careful people are, they do occur. It is important to know that there are people trained to help people in trouble and take them to where they need to go. Rescuers use special vehicles that carry a lot of equipment and help the rescuers do their jobs. Among emergency vehicles are police cars and motorcycles, ambulances, police boats, rescue helicopters, lifeboats, tow trucks, and more.

General Purposes or Goals

To help students understand and appreciate: (1) types of emergency vehicles available; (2) who uses them; and (3) what they do for people.

Main Ideas to Develop
- Emergency vehicles (police cars, ambulances, lifeboats, etc.) provide help for people who have experienced an accident or a disaster.
- Emergency vehicles carry a lot of equipment to help rescuers do their jobs.
- When an emergency vehicle has its sirens screaming and lights flashing, it has the "right of way," which means that other cars and trucks on the road have to pull over and stop.
- Emergency vehicles are built with extra-strong materials and are well taken care of so that they can go very fast and will not break down during an emergency run.

Teaching Tips from Barbara

As part of this lesson, I invited a police officer parent to bring his cruiser to school. The key to success was making sure that we focused on the *transpor-*

tation aspects of emergency vehicles (students sometimes tried to turn the conversation to other aspects of emergency jobs). To help, I posted the following question: How is an emergency vehicle different from other vehicles?

Starting the Lesson

Begin by discussing family responses to the home assignment. Then ask if any of the students and/or members of their families have had recent experiences with emergency vehicles. Listen for prior knowledge and misconceptions.

Suggested Lesson Discussion

These vehicles are needed when there has been an accident or a disaster, when someone is very ill and needs to be taken to the hospital in a hurry, when a car or truck breaks down on a highway, and when there are other emergencies. [Ask students to think about the emergency vehicles they have observed. List them on the white board.]

There are land, water, and air emergency vehicles. [Describe the land types that are visible in the local community.] [This lesson provides an opportunity to draw on local members of the community who are associated with emergency vehicles. If one exists, ask him or her to bring the vehicle to the school grounds and explain its use, special equipment, etc.]

[Using pictures and explanations, describe emergency vehicles and their functions.]

Police Car   Another name for a police car is a *squad car.* A shield may be painted on the door with the word *police.* Flashing lights are mounted on a bar on top of the car. The police car radio is used for communicating messages to the police station. The police car is equipped with a computer for getting information about the driver of any car that the police stop. Sometimes police cars are equipped with screens between the front and back seats to keep the driver safe from people who have been picked up and are being taken to the police station for questioning. Squad cars need to be equipped with heavy tires for driving on all kinds of roads as well as a loud siren, and they must be built to go very fast. Police use squad cars to do all kinds of things: stop cars whose drivers are driving unsafely, arrest criminals, bring home lost children, and so on.

Ambulance   Ambulances are used for rushing people to hospitals. Ambulance drivers give medical care to people who are suddenly very sick or hurt. Most of the people who work with ambulances are emergency medical technicians or paramedics. When they arrive, they first decide what is wrong with the patient and make sure it is safe to move him or her. Then they use the ambulance to take the patient to the hospital.

Ambulances carry all sorts of special medical equipment: oxygen bottles, neck and back collars, splints, bandages, heart monitors, stretchers, and much more. They are equipped with radios and cellular phones so that the paramedics can talk to doctors and nurses at hospitals.

Fire Trucks Firefighters not only are skilled at putting out fires, but they answer many other kinds of emergency calls. They are trained to handle medical matters and to give first aid while an ambulance is on its way. Firefighters might help clean up a chemical spill or rescue someone who is trapped in a crashed car. They are trained to help people start breathing again (CPR).

Rescue Helicopter Planes and helicopters also move sick and hurt people to hospitals. They are used at sea, over mountains, and when a patient has a long way to travel. Sometimes they are used when a regular ambulance can't get through (e.g., in the case of a bad traffic jam). Medical aircraft are equipped with the same types of medical supplies as ambulances. Medical aircraft cost a lot of money to buy and to operate, so it is very expensive for patients to use aircraft for medical transportation.

Emergency Boats Emergency watercraft are used in oceans as well as on rivers and lakes. For example, a lifeboat would head out to sea in stormy weather to rescue people in trouble. Radar equipment helps the crew find the people quickly. (Their trouble might be caused by a fire on board, a storm, a collision of two boats, or engine failure.) Emergency boats are equipped with lights, sirens, radios, cellular phones, medical supplies, and so on.

Tow Trucks Not everybody would think of a tow truck as an emergency vehicle because it usually doesn't have sirens and it doesn't have medical supplies on board. It is not used to save people's lives. Instead, tow trucks are equipped with special hoists that lift disabled cars onto special frames. They hold the car's front wheels so it can be taken to the repair shop. Tow trucks are equipped with two-way radios and cellular phones so that they can communicate with the driver. Tow trucks must be very strong so that they can manage the stranded cars and trucks.

Snowplow Snowplows are also considered to be emergency vehicles, because they clear snow from roads so that other emergency vehicles can get through. A snowplow has a wide steel blade on the front to shovel snow off the road. Some snowplows are tractors with big buckets in front. The bucket scoops up the snow and dumps it in a pile—or in some cases, puts the snow in a dump truck to be hauled away. Snowplow drivers work very hard in bad, snowy weather. Usually their equipment has flashing lights for warning other drivers and good heaters and blowers for keeping ice and snow off their windows. Snowplows have very powerful engines so they can withstand the heavy weight of the snow.

All of these vehicles are especially built to do their special transportation jobs.

Activity

At the conclusion of the interactive session focusing on emergency vehicles, ask students to close their eyes and think about the vehicles described. Students should be prepared to share which one they found most interesting and explain why.

Summarize

- There are many types of emergency vehicles for helping people in times of accidents, disasters, bad weather, and so on.
- Emergency vehicles are built specifically to do their special transportation jobs.

Assessment

Using pictures of emergency vehicles, have each team of students draw a picture of an emergency vehicle out of a hat and then discuss among themselves the key points regarding what it is, why it is important, and when it is used. After five minutes, have a spokesperson share the group's collective ideas with the class. If time permits, have each group explain why it would or would not want to operate the vehicle it drew.

Home Assignment

Encourage families to discuss their experiences with emergency vehicles. Have them list the key points from the discussion so they can be shared in class (e.g., The garage caught on fire and the fire department was called. Two fire trucks were sent to the scene. Red lights flashed en route to our house. During last winter's ice storm, my older brother slid off the highway. A tow truck had to pull our car out of the ditch.).

Dear Parents,

We have been talking about emergency vehicles and how important they are for helping people in times of accidents, disasters, bad weather, and so on. Please spend a few minutes with your child sharing the experiences that your family has had with emergency vehicles. Your child will have the opportunity to share the results of your discussion with his or her classmates. Thank you!

Sincerely,

FIGURE 10   Model Letter to Parents

Lesson 6

Mass Production

Resources
- Pictures of modern-day assembly lines
- Picture of early assembly line (Henry Ford days)
- Video depicting a vehicle assembly line (optional)
- Pictures depicting steps in building a school bus
- Cutouts representing the parts of a school bus (to be used in the simulation of an assembly line)
- Bulletin or flannel board for displaying the steps/pictures in building a vehicle
- Assembly line worker (optional)

Children's Literature
Sadler, M. (1996). *Inventors*. New York: HarperCollins.

General Comments
This lesson is designed to give students a flavor for the assembly line and what it has come to mean in our country. It was invented about two hundred years ago by an American inventor named Eli Whitney. Henry Ford used it at his Highland Park factory in Michigan, and as a result, he could produce more automobiles in 1914 than all of his competitors combined. [If a parent works in a vehicle plant or other factory, this would be an ideal opportunity for the person to serve as a resource to the class and explain what an assembly line is, how it works, and the challenges associated with it.]

General Purposes or Goals
To help students understand and appreciate: (1) how a vehicle is assembled; and (2) how mass-produced interchangeable parts speed up the manufacturing process.

Main Ideas to Develop
- An assembly line is a line of factory workers and equipment on which the product being assembled passes consecutively from operation to operation until completed.
- Vehicles (cars, trucks, and buses) are made in factories where every worker specializes in a specific job, doing it over and over many times a day so that many of the same products can be made in a short time period.

- The manufacturing process for vehicles such as automobiles and school buses features mass-produced interchangeable parts.

Teaching Tips from Barbara

I start the lesson with the assembly line to "build" school buses. I then weave the information that I want my students to know into the discussion as they choose jobs and watch the assembly line. For this lesson, I also contacted a General Motors plant in our area. They provided a video tour for us to watch.

Starting the Lesson

Encourage students to share the responses from the home assignment. Then ask students what they think an assembly line is. List their responses. [Show a picture of an assembly line.] [As an attention-getter, simulate an assembly line by "building a school bus" out of simple cutout parts. Elaboration will occur during the activity.]

Suggested Lesson Discussion

An assembly line is a line of factory workers and equipment on which the product being assembled passes consecutively from operation to operation until it is completed. In 1913, when most cars were made by hand, Henry Ford's Highland Park factory was manufacturing one hundred cars a day on an assembly line [show a picture]. Workers did each of these steps over and over, assembling the car as it moved down the line. Most cars and trucks are still mass-produced in factories, although many of the dangerous or tedious jobs are done by mechanical devices called *robots*. [See *Bikes, Cars, Trucks, and Trains.*]

One of the reasons most vehicles can be mass-produced is that they use interchangeable parts [show photo]. A worker on the assembly line might be responsible for adding the engine or wheels to the metal body, known as the *chassis,* or a worker might be responsible for installing the seats or adding the car's dashboard. The worker does the same job over and over, many times every day. The same size wheels or dashboards are installed in many cars. If the type changes for a different model or set of specifications, the information is put into the computer so that the workers who supply the line with parts bring the right type and color. Because assembly plant workers become so familiar with a given part and because they do the same task over and over, they become very skillful and very quick. [Discuss the trade-offs associated with working on an assembly line (e.g., lack of variety, boredom, may begin daydreaming and forget to be as precise as is expected, etc.). If a parent works on an assembly line, this would be an optimum time to elicit his or her expertise. A visit to a local vehicle manufacturing plant or a CD-ROM depicting the assembly line process, if scaffolded appropriately, could provide other powerful learning opportunities.]

Activity

Have the students experience an assembly line and the use of interchangeable parts. To prepare for this simulation, explain to the class that you are going to tell the story of how a school bus is made. Display pictures of the steps and accompanying words on the bulletin or flannel board. Indicate that after telling the picture story describing how the bus is made, you will set up a simple assembly line so that they can get a firsthand experience.

Include the following in the picture story:

1. Each bus begins with a set of plans. A worker uses a computer and screen to examine the plans.
2. Workers build the bus frame and wrap the frame in sheets of steel.
3. The bus is spray painted yellow. (All school buses are painted yellow.)
4. The seats are made of foam padding and wood.
5. The seats are bolted to the floor.
6. A stop sign is put on the left side of the bus.
7. Mirrors are put on the left side and the right side. They help the driver to see behind the bus.
8. Lights are put on the front and the back of the bus.
9. Windshield wipers are put on and tested.
10. Workers put the engine in the bus.
11. The body of the bus is water tested for leaks.
12. The bus leaves the factory and is ready for schoolchildren to ride in it.

After completing the picture story and posting the pictures and words describing how a bus is made in a factory on an assembly line, ask the class to study the picture story carefully and be ready to explain which of the assembly line tasks would be the most difficult and why. Elicit student responses.

Then conduct a simple simulation.

First, have each student build a bus with simple paper cutouts. Parts that could be included are chassis, wheels, steering column, dashboard, and seats.

Time the process. Then create an assembly line. "Train" each student to do one process, such as making the wheels and attaching them to the chassis, creating interchangeable parts and doing the same process over and over. Time the "manufacture" of a bus using the assembly line. Add a person to serve as quality controller. Compare the time it takes for one individual to "build a bus" to the time it takes when an assembly line is used.

Discuss the key points associated with mass production. What are the trade-offs?

Summarize

- Vehicles are mass-produced in factories and, as a result, many can be built quickly and up to a specific standard.
- Every worker specializes in a specific task, doing it over and over many times a day.
- The manufacturing process for vehicles features mass-produced interchangeable parts.

Assessment

Ask each student to write a journal entry describing how a school bus is built. Prior to the actual writing, allow students to work in pairs to talk about their ideas.

After the students have completed their journal entries, have them share with the class. Then, as a total group, discuss how building a school bus would be different if the parts were not mass-produced. Responses such as excessive time, lack of standardization, untrained workers, and excessive costs might be included.

Home Assignment

Encourage each student to share with family members his or her journal entry describing manufacturing a school bus. Then have them compile a list of positives and negatives associated with manufacturing a product on an assembly line.

Optional If a parent works on an assembly line, encourage him or her to allow the child to observe the assembly line in action. Photographs could be shared with the class.

Dear Parents,

We are learning about mass production. Your child is bringing home his or her journal entry to share before you discuss the positives and negatives associated with manufacturing a product on an assembly line. Please compile a list of your responses and send it with your child tomorrow so it can be incorporated into our class discussion. Thank you!

Sincerely,

FIGURE 11   Model Letter to Parents

Lesson 7

. . . .

Transportation: Necessary Regulations

Resources
- Driver's license
- Proof of insurance and/or registration
- License plate
- Pictures depicting inside/outside of car to illustrate lights, seat belts
- Traffic lights
- Traffic signs
- Photos of parking meter or parking sign
- Picture of a gas station

Children's Literature
Kalman, B., & Hughes, S. (1986). *I Live in a City*. New York: Crabtree.

General Comments
This lesson is intended to raise students' level of concern regarding the role of rules and laws within the transportation industry. Students will begin to realize that regulations are necessary for safety and responsible decision making (e.g., traffic lights, speed limits, load limits, etc.).

General Purposes and Goals
To help students understand and appreciate: (1) the importance of transportation regulations; and (2) how they affect people's personal lives.

Main Ideas to Develop
- Rules and laws are a necessary part of the transportation industry.
- Rules and laws are regulations that are needed for safety and responsible decision making.

Teaching Tips from Barbara
The role-play helps to make this lesson meaningful to students. It also would be easy to create a simple video instead of a role-play to show these rules and laws. Either way, this is a good lesson to draw out from the students what they already know about transportation-related rules and laws. I was surprised at how much my students could tell me just from being observers, not drivers.

Starting the Lesson
Share and discuss the home assignment. Then begin this new lesson by explaining that many government regulations apply to the transportation

industry and to the operation of vehicles. Elicit responses from students regarding the meaning of regulations. Listen for prior knowledge and any misconceptions that the students may have.

Suggested Lesson Discussion

Transportation has lots of government regulations associated with it. While we don't usually think a lot about them, these regulations are needed for safety and responsible decision making. [Using pictures, artifacts, and words (e.g., driver's license, license plates), describe and role-play a simple trip to school via car or the school bus.]

1. First, the parent and child get into the car. [Mention that the vehicle has been built to safety specifications so that it will be safe on the highway.]
2. The parent needs to have a valid driver's license.
3. They must fasten their seat belts. In our state, it is the law (if appropriate).
4. The parent needs to be able to show that he or she has insurance (and/or registration, if applicable) in case there is an accident.
5. The car must have lights that are operational.
6. The driver must use the turn signals to let other drivers know when he or she is intending to turn right or left.
7. The driver must respond to the traffic lights and signs. For example, if the traffic light is red, the driver must stop and let the vehicles who have the green light go. In some instances, there are signs that indicate the driver can turn right on red when the lane has cleared.
8. The driver must watch the speed limit.
9. Parking restrictions are other considerations for the driver. For example, meters indicate the length of parking time allowed. There are often signs posted on side streets that tell drivers how long—if at all—they are able to park.
10. Every vehicle must have a current license plate from the state. The state has a record of who owns the car. The money that the driver pays for the license plate is used to repair the roads.

[Show pictures of a city with an emphasis on transportation.] Because there are a great many people living and working close together in cities, they need to cooperate, take responsibility, and practice good citizenship. [Show pictures from *I Live in a City*. Focus on the regulations associated with transportation for the purpose of keeping ourselves safe in the streets.] We need to cross the road at an intersection or crosswalk when the sign indicates it is safe to cross. Never cross a road between two parked cars. Never chase a ball that has rolled into the street.

Drivers also need to follow certain regulations. Each needs to have a valid driver's license. Drivers need to obey the speed limit as posted.

Drivers need to yield to emergency vehicles. They need to signal when turning right or left, etc. All of these regulations and many more are needed for our safety. These rules help people make responsible decisions.

There are also people who help enforce the laws (i.e., police officers). Judges decide if people have broken the laws, and if so, what their punishments should be. [Use the pictures on pp. 10–11 in *I Live in a City* to stimulate discussion about rules associated with transportation and how these rules help us.]

Activity

Have students (in pairs) talk about one safety rule associated with transportation that they think is very important and why. Allow time for whole-class discussion.

Optional   Go on a field trip to an airport or train station. Focus on the regulations (rules and laws) associated with that form of transportation and how these regulations influence safety and responsible decision making.

Summarize

- Rules and laws are a necessary part of the transportation industry.
- Regulations are needed for safety and responsible decision making.
- Police officers help to enforce the rules and laws.
- If people break laws, judges decide the punishments.

Assessment

Have students complete open-ended statements focusing on transportation regulations. Examples:

1. Regulations are necessary for transportation because _____.
2. One safety regulation is _____.
3. We need speed limits because _____.
4. People must be a certain age to drive because _____.
5. In order to drive a car, the driver needs a driver's license because

   _____.

6. I make better decisions when I _____.

Home Assignment

Have each student, with the guidance of an older sibling or an adult, list all of the forms of transportation he or she has observed in the community. Then, have the student select one (or more) and discuss and list the rules and laws (regulations) associated with it. Encourage the students to share their responses with their classmates during an upcoming social studies lesson.

Dear Parents,

As we continue learning about transportation, we would encourage you to spend a few minutes with your child listing all the forms of transportation that you observe in your community. Then select one (or more) and discuss and list the rules and laws (regulations) associated with it (e.g., regulations concerning manufacturing specifications, safety features, licensing of the vehicle and driver, traffic laws, etc.). Your child will be encouraged to share his or her responses with classmates.

Sincerely,

FIGURE 12   Model Letter to Parents

Lesson 8
....

Maps: Tools for Transportation

Resources

- Maps to represent family trip scenario (these will depend on your location)
- Word cards
- Sample address to illustrate
- Map of local area
- Legend, key
- Scale of miles
- Street map
- Telephone directory (street map section)
- Polaroid camera, film
- Desktop display including miniature vehicle, buildings, and so on for demonstrating mapping
- Variety of map types (street, road, weather, blueprint of vehicle)
- Activity sheet
- Single street map of local area with legend
- Wrapped packages with names/addresses (to be delivered by UPS truck driver)
- Table 2: Maps: Tools Used for Transportation

Children's Literature

Broekel, R. (1983). *A True Book: Maps and Globes*. Chicago: Children's Press.

Cutting, B., & Cutting, J. (1996). *The Map Book*. Bothell, WA: The Wright Group.

Noonan, D. (1995). *Amazing Maps*. Bothell, WA: The Wright Group.

Taylor, B. (1992). *Maps and Mapping*. New York: Kingfisher.

Wilson, A. (1996). *The Weather Chart*. Bothell, WA: The Wright Group.

General Comments

This lesson is intended to heighten the students' interest in maps and teach them about their usefulness in people's lives and about the kinds of maps employed in careers associated with transportation (e.g., truck drivers, pilots, ship captains, etc.).

Main Ideas to Develop

- A map is a medium for locating places—even places where we have never been before. It is a drawing of a place.

- Shipping brought about increased use of maps.

- Mapmakers use symbols or signs and colors so they can get plenty of information in a small space. A symbol is a figure that stands for something else.

- A map has a key or legend. It shows the symbols and colors used on the map.

- On the map, the main directions are cardinal—north, south, east, west.

- Maps are useful for people employed in careers associated with transportation, as well as for people who privately make decisions related to transportation.

Teaching Tips from Barbara

We do a separate unit on map skills in our district, so I incorporated those objectives into this lesson. Therefore, we did some work on map skills and spent extra time on this lesson. However, it's important to keep in mind that you want students to see the main ideas that maps are tools to be used by people who are transporting themselves or goods.

Starting the Lesson

Discuss the responses from the home assignment and then present a scenario about a family planning a vacation. The family has decided it can take eight days and seven nights and that it will drive. Some of the nights will be spent in motels; however, the children have convinced their parents that the family should camp out at least three nights. After lengthy family meetings, it has been decided that the family will spend two days and nights in a metropolitan area, shopping and visiting a museum and a zoo, then go to a popular campground for three days of camping, and then spend the final two nights in a motel close to a beach on a lake. (You will probably need to tailor this scenario to your area and what's available in neighboring states.) Consider the tools that the family can use to plan the trip.

Suggested Lesson Discussion

[Show a street map of the local area, a road map of the state, a city map of the metropolitan area, a road map of the state in which the campground is located, and a road map of the state where the beach is. Each map will be helpful in planning the trip (e.g., museum, hotels, etc.). A weather map could also come in handy for learning about camping conditions. An alternative is to get the local weather report on the radio.]

A map is like a picture showing where things are. [Stand on a stool above a desktop that has been set up with a special arrangement that could be mapped.] A map is made by taking a picture from above and then making it smaller using lines and colors to communicate locations to users. [Demonstrate this process. Expand the discussion by encouraging students to share stories about the kinds of maps their families use when they plan a vacation or go to a new place. Give students an opportunity to examine the collection of maps.]

[Take a Polaroid photograph of the desktop with such items as a model truck, a drawing of a truck stop, a model of a bridge, and a model of a railroad crossing specifically situated. Demonstrate the making of a map by using the photograph to draw a map on the board. Explain that the key or legend shows the symbols used on the map.]

We are going to imagine a truck driver who has just taken a new job with UPS. [Show the packages labeled with local street addresses. Using a local city map, demonstrate to the class how the driver will be able to locate the right addresses using the appropriate map tools.]

[Show a road map.] The key has symbols for such things as highways, towns, cities, and a scale of miles. A new driver has been hired by (local supermarket) to take products from (large city in your state) to (large city in your state). The driver will use the map to figure out direction, distance, how long the trip will take, and so on. The driver will also need directions and a street map to locate the supermarket facility in (second city) [Demonstrate].

Optional   Other scenarios could be explained and demonstrated if time is available. Among the types of transportation workers who rely heavily on maps are the following:

Tour bus operator	Ambulance driver
Moving van operator	Garbage truck driver
Taxicab driver	Careers of parents that are associ-
Mail truck driver	ated with transportation
Car carrier driver	

Activity

Provide each table with a collection of maps and an activity sheet with the following questions and a blank version of Table 2 to fill in.

1. What kinds of maps would a tour bus operator need if the tour bus went from your school to [major metropolis]? _____

   _____

2. What kinds of maps would be needed by an ambulance driver transporting a patient from your city to the capitol city in your state?

   _____

3. Imagine you are a UPS driver and you need to take packages to the following addresses:
   Mark each address on the local map you have been provided. Then, as a class, complete the following chart.

TABLE 2   Maps: Tools Used for Transportation

MAP TYPE	SAMPLE CAREER	HOW INDIVIDUALS USE THE MAP
Road map	Truck driver	Decided what route to take
Street map		Decide how long it should take to make the trip
Weather map		

In reviewing the chart as a class, underscore the idea that maps are helpful in acquiring information that can be used in planning and making decisions associated with transportation.

Summarize

- Maps are essential tools for transportation.
- Maps are drawings that help people locate other people and places.
- Maps are helpful to people in planning and making decisions associated with transportation.

Assessment

Have students pair up and talk about maps as tools for transportation. After they have had the opportunity to share their ideas verbally, have them write individual journal entries addressing the following question: How do maps help people make transportation decisions? Encourage students to share their entries with their peers.

Home Assignment

Encourage each student to read his or her journal entry with a family member and then with the assistance of the family member, expand the entry to include more ideas. Then, as a family, have them list and talk about all of the ways that maps are used in their household. If possible, have the family members share examples of map types they use. Map reading as a family activity would be a great addition.

> Dear Parents,
>
> Attached is your child's journal entry that was provided as a response to the question: How do maps help people make transportation decisions? We encourage you, as a family, to expand the response as you converse with your child about the uses of maps. If possible, share one or more maps that you use (or have used in the past). As a bonus, do some simple map-reading activities with your child. Thank you!
>
> Sincerely,

FIGURE 13   Model Letter to Parents

Lesson 9

. . . .

Human Designs and Construction Facilitate Travel

Resources
- Pictures: trails, early roads, superhighway, railroad track, subway, monorail, canal, bridges (see pp. 50–55 of *Trains and Railroads*)
- Photo of an early transportation system in local area
- Photo and map of Miami, Florida
- Photo and map of Florence, Italy
- Photos and pictures of local human designs and construction that facilitate travel
- Pictures from *Transportation and Communication* (see pp. 14–17)
- Globe
- Figure 16: Human Designs and Construction Chart (overlay, or photocopy)

Children's Literature
Coster, P. (1997). *Transportation and Communication*. Danbury, CT: Franklin Watts Children's Press.

Gallimard, J. (1995). *Bikes, Cars, Trucks, and Trains*. New York: Scholastic.

Wood, S. (1998). *Trains and Railroads*. London: Dorling Kindersley.

General Purposes and Goals
To develop an awareness of, curiosity about, and understanding of the range of designs and structures that humans build to make transportation easier and places more accessible.

Main Ideas to Develop
- Human designs and construction facilitate travel.
- Different types of transportation need different types of roads.
- When roads and railways come up against obstacles like mountains and rivers, engineers need to design tunnels and bridges so that vehicles can reach their destinations.
- Railways are special overland roads for trains to travel on.
- Canals are human-made waterways that shorten routes between larger bodies of water.

Teaching Tips from Barbara
I found that this lesson worked well as a thematic web. All four of the major human designs (railways, highways, bridges, and canals) are roads with special purposes. By using a web (see Figure 14) and having students brain-

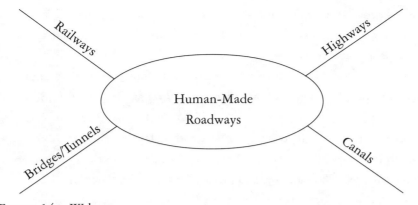

FIGURE 14   Web

storm, I was able to organize the information and compare similar aspects of all four. I used the main idea (listed above) to help me decide which information to talk about within each category. I suggest inviting older children or parent volunteers to help students complete the assessment.

Starting the Lesson

Share and discuss the home assignment. Show students a series of pictures that illustrate trails, early roads, superhighways, railroad tracks, canals, bridges, and so on. Elicit comments as students study the pictures and drawings.

Suggested Lesson Discussion

Roads often developed along paths that had been created by constant foot and hoof traffic. Many of the early roads in America were built along the Native American trails and later along the routes set by stagecoaches and pioneers. [Show picture of early roads; see *Transportation and Communication*, pp. 10–17.] [Show photo of early transportation system in the local area. The local historical society can be a great resource.]

Different types of transportation need different types of roads. [Show students a photo and a map of Miami.] Miami is one of several cities that has been designed on a grid system for people who want to travel by car. The straight, wide roads enable traffic to move through the city quickly and easily. Cities like Miami have grown up over the last one hundred years. [Show a photo and a map of Florence, Italy.] Cities like Florence were built hundreds of years ago before cars were invented. The short, narrow streets were designed for people traveling on foot or horseback.

[Show the students a picture of a superhighway. Reference all explanations to the local area.] Today we have very modern highways in many parts of the world—special limited-access roads on which cars and trucks can travel fast.

Railways are special roads—tracks created for trains to travel on. [Show a picture or a photograph.] Sometimes it is difficult to build railroad tracks through cities, so they are often put underground. This way, people can use subways to travel around town quickly, avoiding traffic jams on the streets above.

When roads and railways come up against obstacles like mountains or rivers, people design and build structures that facilitate travel. [Show students the pictures on pp. 14–15 in *Transportation and Communication*.] Some bridges are built to carry traffic across valleys. Road tunnels are sometimes built to carry traffic through mountains or under cities, rivers, and even seas. [Show photos and pictures of local structures that have been built to facilitate travel.]

Since the very earliest times, people have transported goods and passengers along rivers using boats. In fact, the earliest towns were usually built along rivers. However, rivers did not always go where people needed or wanted them to go, so engineers dug channels called *canals*. These usually ran from one town to another so that goods could be transported back and forth. [See pp. 16–17 in *Transportation and Communication*.] Some very famous canals such as the Panama Canal are human-made waterways that shorten the routes between large bodies of water. [Using a globe, demonstrate how a ship passes through the Panama Canal in Central America instead of having to sail around the continent of South America.] The canal saves thousands of miles of travel.

Optional [To help students develop an awareness and curiosity about the human designs and structures built to facilitate travel in their own community, show a photo of a bridge, a tunnel, and so on and tell their stories.]

Activity

Table Talk—Have students discuss transportation experiences that they have had that included human designs and construction that facilitated their family travel (e.g., "We rode the train to Chicago. A railroad track was built to make travel easier between our city and Chicago." "A bridge has been built in our city so we can travel across the river that runs through the area."). Use a photocopy of Figure 16 for capturing student responses during a group discussion.

HUMAN DESIGN AND CONSTRUCTION	LOCATION	HOW IT ASSISTED ME
1. Underpass	South Pennsylvania Ave., Lansing, Michigan	My family drives on the road at the same time a train needs to pass by.
2. Mackinac Bridge	Northern Michigan connecting the upper and lower peninsulas	Allows my family to take its car from the lower peninsula to the upper one.

Summarize

- Human designs and construction help make travel easier, sometimes faster, often safer.
- They allow us to go places we might not be able to reach otherwise.

Assessment

Have students use words and drawings to complete a journal entry focusing on designs and construction that help us move people and goods. (Upper-elementary student mentors might be helpful for successful completion of this assignment.)

Railways are special tracks that _____
_____.

Highways are special roads that _____
_____.

Bridges are _____
_____.

Canals are human-made waterways that _____
_____.

Home Assignment

Encourage students to share their journal entries with their families. Then as a family, have them discuss human designs and construction that they have used to aid them in their travel. Encourage them to look for local examples first. Send home copies of Figure 16 so that the information can be shared easily during an upcoming social studies class.

Dear Parents,

Our class has been discussing human designs and constructions that aid in travel. Please encourage your child to share his or her journal entry and then continue the conversation by talking about designs and constructions that have aided your family travel. Please use the enclosed Human Designs and Construction Chart so that the information can easily be shared during an upcoming social studies class. Thank you!

Sincerely,

FIGURE 15   Model Letter to Parents

As a family, discuss the human designs and constructions that have aided you in your travels. List them below. Tell where they are located and how they assisted you.

HUMAN DESIGN AND CONSTRUCTION	LOCATION	HOW IT ASSISTED ME
1. Underpass	South Pennsylvania Ave., Lansing, Michigan	My family drives on the road at the same time a train needs to pass by.
2. Mackinac Bridge	Northern Michigan connecting the upper and lower peninsulas	Allows my family to take its car from the lower peninsula to the upper one.
3.		
4.		
5.		
6.		
7.		
8.		

FIGURE 16   Human Designs and Construction Chart

Lesson 10

. . . .

Transportation Around the World: More Alike Than Different

Resources
- Globe
- World map
- Map of the United States
- Pictures and photographs: local modern means of transportation; tundra/dogsled; rickshaw in Singapore; elephant in Thailand; camel in Egypt; baby being carried by African woman; tuk tuk in Thailand; modern trains/aircraft in Thailand, Egypt, and Africa; Amish horse and buggy; performer riding an elephant at a circus; horse-drawn carriages in Central Park; trolleys in San Francisco; special modes of transportation for unique geographic features and climatic conditions
- A word card for every student: Side #1—More Alike, Side #2— More Different

Children's Literature
Morris, A. (1990). *On the Go*. New York: Lothrop, Lee, and Shepard.
Noonan, D. (1994). *From Camel Cart to Canoe*. Bothell, WA: The Wright Group.

General Comments
To set the stage for this lesson, collect pictures and photographs of unique types of transportation throughout the world as well as visuals that illustrate the similarities among types of transportation that are enjoyed by people and places across the globe. As a result of this lesson, students should come to understand that availability of resources, religious beliefs and customs, climate, local geographic features, and unique circumstances such as tourist attractions are among the factors that contribute to differences.

General Purposes and Goals
To help students understand and appreciate: (1) why transportation across the globe is generally more alike than different; and (2) how we can account for differences that exist.

Main Ideas to Develop
- In general, transportation across the globe is more alike than different. For example, every continent has access to airplanes and ships.

- Availability of economic resources, religious beliefs and customs, climatic conditions, local geographic features, and unique circumstances such as tourist attractions are among the factors that contribute to and explain the differences that exist.

Teaching Tips from Barbara

This lesson will help you see why the building blocks from the first few lessons were important. As we talked about transportation around the world, we used the same terms and sorted in the same ways. Here again, pictures of the types of transportation were helpful, especially unfamiliar ones.

Starting the Lesson

Share responses from the home assignment. Then pose the following question to the class: "Is transportation in countries around the world more alike or more different?" Provide each student with a two-sided card labeled "More Alike" on Side #1 and "More Different" on Side #2. At the outset, have each student place his or her response side up. Count the number of Side #1 opinions and Side #2 opinions. Post the tally on the white board. Discuss. Underscore the importance of listening carefully so that they will be able to explain their answers and illustrate with examples.

Suggested Lesson Discussion

Today we are going to examine our local area and later take an imaginary trip around the globe to see if we can answer this question: Is transportation around the world more alike or more different from what we have? [Begin by showing pictures and photographs of local means of transportation (e.g., bicycles, motorcycles, cars, sport vehicles, trucks, trains, airplanes, boats, etc.). Students should be encouraged to add other examples.]

[Show a map of the United States and one of the world.] The kinds of transportation that people use depend on many factors. For example, an individual's personal resources often are the deciding factor. Many people around here own cars or trucks because they have good jobs and can make the monthly payments. Many students borrow money from their families and/or work part time to make the payments. There are people, however, in the United States who either cannot afford a car or choose not to spend money on a vehicle. They ride bicycles, take trains or buses, or walk. For many people who live in large cities, finding parking places presents problems and traffic is very congested, so some choose not to have vehicles and use public transportation instead.

There are other people who have money to purchase a car but their religious beliefs prohibit it. For example, the Amish people still use a horse and buggy [show a photo]. Their beliefs revolve around a simple life, free of technology. Climate is another factor that influences transportation choices. For example, snowmobiles are only used when it's cold and we have snow; sailboats and motorboats are used when it's mild and require bodies of water.

Geographic features are another consideration. For example, while you can travel by boat in America, you need to go to a place where there is water, and the size and depth of the body of water dictate the type of boat you can use. For example, to take a trip by ocean liner, you would need to go to a seaport to board it, then cruise through waters that are deep enough to support its weight.

Sometimes special circumstances such as tourist attractions are reasons for maintaining simple modes of transportation in areas that are generally very modern. For example, in Central Park in New York City, you will find horse-drawn carriages [show photo]. Tourists pay money to enjoy the sights using this mode. In San Francisco, another very modern American city, there are cable cars for the tourists. [Include other examples that would be familiar to students (e.g., elephant at a circus) and show pictures.]

Today in America, we have a range of transportation modes. Most are modern, but there are examples of less modern modes that are used under special circumstances. Personal resources, religious beliefs, climate, geographic features, and tourist attractions are among the factors that account for the types of transportation used. Time and the purpose of the trip must also be taken into consideration. For example, a businessperson in New York would probably not take the horse and buggy to work.

Now, we are going to leave our local city by airplane and travel to Alaska [show on the globe]. Obviously Alaska has airplanes because we are landing there and we can leave from there. It also has cars, trucks, and so on. Alaska also has some unique types of transportation because of its climate and physical features (e.g., kayak, dogsled, etc.). [Show pictures and explain why these unique forms of transportation exist.] In the continental United States, we sled for pleasure, but some people in very cold, snowy places need sleds to aid them in their search for food. Geography and climate are the key factors that contribute to the use of dogsleds in some of the remote places in Alaska [show photos].

[Using the globe, photographs, and pictures, have the class visit China, Thailand, Egypt, West Africa, and so on.] All major cities of all of these places, even in developing parts of the world, have all the types of transportation that we have. However, not all people can afford these modern means. For example, in China and Thailand, and in many parts of Africa, many cannot afford automobiles or trucks.

Also, many people in these countries prefer to take public modes of transportation even though they have adequate financial resources because the traffic is very congested, especially during rush hours. It can take several hours to drive a car to work or to school. In some of these parts of the world, we find a mix of modern transportation and modes of the past. For example, on the busiest street in Bangkok, Thailand, you might find a family riding an elephant next to cars and trucks [show a photo]. You might find a man driving a camel cart next to a line of cars on the busiest streets in Cairo, Egypt [show a photo]. You would also find that tourist attractions account for some use of elephants as transportation in Thailand and camels as transportation in Egypt [show photos to illustrate].

Modern types of transportation are not the choices enjoyed by everyone because of their financial situation, their beliefs and customs, the time they have available for travel, the convenience, the local geographic factors, and so on.

While the world today is closely connected by modern means of transportation, there are remote areas where good roads have not been built (e.g., jungles, deserts, the far north), where people cannot afford private vehicles and have to depend on public transportation, where people cannot afford expensive tickets to ride on sleek buses so they go by old buses, tuk tuk, bacha, rickshaw, and other less modern means. There are also parts of the world where people want to hang onto their traditions and values or where people maintain outmoded means of transportation in order to attract tourists.

Activity

At the end of the interactive lesson, pose the question again: "Is transportation around the world more similar or more different?" Ask for a show of cards for the response. Tally. Record. Discuss. What are the reasons behind each response?

Optional Read and show the pictures in *From Camel Cart to Canoe* after locating India and Nepal on the globe and showing photos of modern transportation there. The book illustrates the contrasts in types of transportation found there and the modes frequently selected because of lack of resources, climatic conditions, and so on.

Summarize

- Means of transportation are more alike than different.
- Climate, geographic conditions, financial resources, customs, beliefs, tourist attractions, and personal preferences are among the factors that account for transportation choices.

Assessment

Have students complete open-ended statements with pictures and/or words. For example:

1. Transportation around the world is more alike than different. Here is a picture to illustrate this.

2. Ways people travel who don't have much money are by _____ and _____ .

3. When it is very cold and there's lots of snow, people might go by
   _____ .

4. If you wanted to travel by water and go a long distance, you might travel by _____ .

5. If you are a tourist in an American city, you might travel in an un-usual way such as by _____ .

6. In the United States, there are people who do not have cars because of their religious beliefs. The Amish people are one example. They usually travel by _____ .

Home Assignment

Encourage the family members to examine transportation around the world, focusing on similarities and differences. Have the student share his or her picture story (assessment). Then, as a family, have them find pictures/information about similarities and differences in transportation around the world. Ask students to bring the results to class to be included in a bulletin board display.

Dear Parents,

Please spend a few minutes with your child as he or she shares his or her picture story. Then as a family, look for pictures, drawings, and information about similarities and differences in transportation around the world. Students will be asked to bring the results to be included in the bulletin board display that has as its caption:

> "In general, transportation across the globe is more alike than different. Availability of economic resources, religious beliefs and customs, climatic conditions, local geographic features, and unique circumstances such as tourist attractions are among the factors that contribute to and explain the differences that exist."

Thank you!

Sincerely,

FIGURE 17   Model Letter to Parents

Lesson 11

A Visit to a Local Transportation Facility: Train Station, Airport, or Harbor

Resources
- Parental permission slips
- Parent volunteers
- City map with symbols identifying major transportation facilities
- Tickets (e.g., bus, airline, train, etc.)
- Telephone directory and calendar
- Pictures of train stations, airports, and harbors (Optional: trucking facilities, bus depots)
- Photos of local train station, bus station, airport, harbor, etc. (if these facilities exist in your local area)

Children's Literature Sources
Dupasquier, P. (1984). *A Busy Day at the Airport*. Cambridge, MA: Candlewick.

Dupasquier, P. (1984). *A Busy Day at the Harbor*. Cambridge, MA: Candlewick.

Dupasquier, P. (1984). *A Busy Day at the Train Station*. Cambridge, MA: Candlewick.

General Comments
Bus depots, train stations, airports, and harbors are where buses, trains, airplanes, and boats arrive and depart. They are the places where passengers and freight are put aboard if they are beginning their trip and where they get off if completing their trip. These facilities are marked on the city map. Often they have restaurants, restrooms, ticket counters, and so on. to provide services to their customers. It is recommended that the class visit at least one local transportation facility to learn about the people involved and the roles they play in servicing the customers.

Main Ideas to Develop
- Transportation facilities provide places for goods and passengers to arrive and depart.
- The primary function of local transportation facilities is to serve customers—people who want/need to travel or send goods to another place.

Teaching Tips from Barbara
We prepared for the field trip by reading *A Busy Day at the Airport*. We also created a list of things to look for at the airport. I was able to pass

that on to the parent volunteers to help them focus discussions during the trip. It was very helpful for students to have goals in mind to look for. We also had the students brainstorm a list on the way to the airport of the types of transportation they saw on the streets.

Starting the Lesson

Share and discuss the results from the home assignment. Begin this new topic by asking students what they know about the local transportation facilities. Have they ever been to the airport? Train station? Harbor? Who goes there? For what purposes? The focus will depend on where your school is located.

Establish the need for a family to get tickets and board a train for a long weekend in Chicago or for an auto manufacturer to send cars via rail to California. You might want to discuss the trade-offs associated with various kinds of freight transportation that are available locally.

Suggested Lesson Discussion

The cheapest way to move cargo is by water. Rail transportation costs three times as much as water transportation, and truck transportation costs ten times as much. Air transportation is by far the most expensive way to move freight. It costs nearly forty times as much as water transportation. Because air transportation is so costly, cargo planes usually carry only expensive, lightweight, or perishable merchandise. Time is a major consideration when considering how freight should be transported. [Revisit which transportation facilities are available locally. If a harbor is not nearby, for example, then goods must be shipped to your area by truck, rail, or air.]

Passenger travel choice depends on cost, time available, purpose (e.g., scenic or otherwise), and convenience of transportation facilities in local areas as well as at destinations. [Role-play a scenario establishing the purpose for the passenger or cargo to travel and talk about going to the local facility to purchase a ticket, check baggage, board the train, bus or airplane, etc. As a part of the role-play, use the telephone directory and calendar to make a reservation and the map to locate the local facility.]

[Read the appropriate transportation book depending on the site of the planned field trip.]

> *A Busy Day at the Airport*
> *A Busy Day at the Train Station*
> *A Busy Day at the Harbor*

[One challenge is for the students to determine the similarities and differences between the actual train station and what is portrayed in the story. The field trip emphasis should be on where the facility is located, what it provides for the traveler, who works there and what jobs they do, the importance of a centralized location, the importance of a time schedule, etc.]

[As children ride to the field trip site, have simple maps available so they can follow the route. Arrange in advance for someone to show them the facilities, underscoring the goals of the lesson. If the field trip is to the local train station, arrange for them to meet a ticket counter employee, a conductor, and an engineer. If possible, have students board a train to note and discuss the facilities provided.]

[If the students visit the airport, make sure they meet a counter attendant who provides the ticket, punches in the frequent flier mileage, weighs the luggage, and checks it through to its destination (marking the bag accordingly); the security workers who inspect the luggage and check the passengers; the boarding agent; control tower employees; etc. If possible, arrange for the students to board the aircraft and meet the pilot and flight attendants.]

Activity

At the conclusion of the field trip, have the students discuss with their seatmates what they learned about the train station, airport, or whatever facility they visited. Upon returning to the classroom, have each student draw the most important thing she or he learned about the transportation facility. Use volunteers or upper-grade mentors to write the captions for the students. Encourage all students to share their responses with the class.

Summarize

- Bus depots, train stations, airports, and harbors are examples of common transportation facilities that provide services to their customers. They are the sites designated for passengers and goods to arrive and depart.
- The size (population) of the local area and its physical features determine the facility types available.

Assessment

Provide each student with a sheet numbered 1–10. Read off each question in the following list and have each student place a *T* or an *F* beside the number. Then have the students, in pairs, make the false statements true.

True or False Quiz

1. F   The main purpose of the train station is to store many, many trains.
2. F   The purpose of the airport is to store airplanes.
3. T   Train stations, harbors, bus stations, and airports provide places for people to secure tickets for their trips.

4. T Telling time is a very important skill for people who work at transportation facilities.

5. F Most types of mass transportation such as airplanes, trains, and buses, arrange to pick up and drop off passengers wherever they say.

6. T It takes many different kinds of workers to run an airport, train station, or bus depot.

7. T The main purpose of an airport or train station is to provide services for its customers.

8. T Most city maps have map keys that help the readers locate major transportation facilities in the local area.

9. T Usually, the size and geography of the local area determine whether or not the specific transportation facilities are available.

10. T Before you can board a type of public transport such as a train, you must buy a ticket.

Home Assignment

Encourage each student to share with family members his or her picture and narrative describing what he or she learned during the field trip about transportation facilities in the local area. Then, as a family, have them locate on the map the other local transportation facilities that they have visited and tell why (e.g., bus depot to pick up Uncle Joe who came here to visit, bus depot to pick up a large package of candles sent here from a neighboring city, train station to board a train to a nearby city, etc.).

Dear Parents,

Today we visited the _____ . Please take a few minutes to talk with your child about what she or he learned. She or he has a picture story to share with you, too. Then as a family, locate on a map other local transportation facilities you have visited and talk about why (e.g., bus depot to pick up Uncle Joe who came here to visit, bus depot to pick up a large package of candles sent here from a neighboring city, train station to board a train to a nearby city, etc.).

   We will discuss your responses during our next social studies class. Thank you!

                                        Sincerely,

FIGURE 18   Model Letter to Parents

Lesson 12

....

Decision Making: Which Mode? Which Means?

Resources
- United States map
- Travel brochures (e.g., hotels, restaurants)
- Travel schedules (e.g., air, land, water if possible)
- List of prices from a travel agency
- December calendar
- World map
- Situation cards
- Decision-Making Chart (Figure 20)

General Comments

On a day-to-day basis, families often do not think about the variables that impact travel decisions because most of their local travel is probably done by car or truck. This lesson is intended to open students' eyes to the many decisions associated with modes and means of transportation.

General Purposes and Goals

To: (1) develop an awareness of how people make decisions related to transportation—personal and professional preferences, time, money, convenience, geographic features, personal values (leisure, science trip, etc.); and (2) evaluate their family's decisions associated with travel (become wise consumers of means of transportation).

Main Ideas to Develop

- Individuals and businesses make decisions about how goods and people should be transported.
- Preference, convenience, money, time, geographic features (physical), and personal values are variables that need to be considered when making decisions regarding what mode and means of transportation to use.

Teaching Tips from Barbara

This whole lesson is a terrific assessment tool to help you see which students are both understanding and using the information taught so far. The kids really enjoy the scenarios and role-playing. I often have them work in groups or teams to make a decision for each scenario. Be sure to have students give their thinking and reasoning behind their decisions.

Starting the Lesson

Discuss responses from the home assignment. Explain that every person, family, and business has many things to think about when traveling or when sending goods or providing services. There are many considerations to be addressed before making a decision.

Suggested Lesson Discussion

[Introduce students to a role-playing scenario with you as the key player, describing a family planning its one-week vacation. For this and subsequent scenarios, adjust the locations involved to suit your geographical location.] The family has one week (December 17–25) and it plans to go from Michigan to Denver. What is the best mode and means of transportation? [Using a United States map, determine number of miles to travel. Price out a list of items that will be considered (e.g., gas price per gallon, hotel costs, average price of meals per day on the train).] If an automobile is used, we need to determine travel time required (and the time available to spend in Denver), the costs involved (hotel costs, gasoline, train fare, taxi, airplane, etc.), and any other relevant considerations for choosing between flying, driving, or taking trains. [Use the white board or flip chart for recording calculations, etc.]

[Select role-playing scenarios from the following situations for enactments and discussion. Remember, you will need to be a key player/facilitator.]

- Family is moving to Switzerland for a three-year assignment. Father insists on taking his new automobile.
- Family is attending a reunion in a neighboring town.
- Older brother going from Michigan to New York to go to college. He needs to transport his belongings.
- Family is going to Chicago from Michigan to attend a wedding.
- The family has plenty of time and wants to take a leisurely and scenic trip through the Rocky Mountains. (The family will depart from Lansing, Michigan.)
- The supermarket manager in Lansing has just realized the milk supply is low. He calls the Grand Rapids dairy company and requests a delivery this afternoon.
- The farm family is selling livestock to a meatpacking plant in Chicago. How should the animals be transported from Lansing to Chicago?
- The family has ordered a new dining room table and chairs from a famous furniture maker in Amana, Iowa. What means and mode should be arranged for it to be sent to Lansing?

Activity

Table Talk—Have students discuss what they learned about transportation decision making, then have each child complete an open-ended statement that begins with "The most important thing I learned about making transportation decisions is _____. My family needs to know this because _____." Have students share among peers at each table and then with the whole class.

Summarize

- Individuals and businesses make decisions about how people and goods should be transported.
- Preference, convenience, money, time, geographical features, and personal values all need to be considered when making transportation decisions.

Assessment

Using situation cards, ask students to listen as you read the condition and then decide what mode and means of transportation should probably be used and why. Students should signal by putting a finger on their foreheads when they are ready to respond. When all are ready, ask students to pair/share their responses and discuss reasons for their decisions. Then, randomly select students to share their ideas with the whole class.

SITUATION CARDS
[Have local, state, national, and world maps/pictures available. Adjust geographical locations in these situations to suit your local area.]

1. The major supermarket's warehouse in a nearby city needs to bring canned goods to the local grocery store. What's the best means and type of transportation?
2. The supermarket has ordered bananas from Central America. What's the best way to send bananas?
3. Fall collections of children's clothes from the main store in a nearby city need to be sent to the local clothing store. How should the clothes be sent?
4. A man in a local hospital needs a special medicine that is manufactured in Minnesota. Local pharmacies do not carry it. How should the medicine be sent?
5. Your sister is moving into the dormitory at a university several hundred miles away. What's the best means and type of transportation for the family to transport her belongings?
6. Your family has decided not to drive to New York City for an upcoming family reunion. What are other possible means of transportation they could use during their week's stay?

7. Your grandparents are planning the trip of a lifetime. Time and money are not major considerations. They don't get around very well, yet they want to travel to at least three continents. What major means of transportation should they take?

8. Your father needs to make a very quick business trip to California. How should he go?

9. Your family is planning a day at the zoo in a nearby city. How should you go?

10. The family car is in the repair shop and your older brother has been asked to go to a local supermarket to purchase bread and milk. What type of transportation should he use?

11. Your family in lower Michigan wants to take the shortest route to Wisconsin to visit relatives. What means and types should it use? Is there more than one possibility?

12. You and your grandfather are planning a fishing trip to northern Michigan. What means and types of transportation will you probably use?

13. Your family is building a new barn. It has ordered a load of lumber from a company a couple of hundred miles away. How do you expect the lumber to arrive?

14. A replacement part needed for a current car model is manufactured in Europe. What means and types of transportation should be used to make sure it arrives at the factory in a timely manner?

15. Your family has ordered new lawn furniture from a company in North Carolina. How will you expect it to be sent to your home?

Home Assignment

Have students take home a set of transportation situation cards to stimulate a family discussion regarding variables to consider when making traveling choices.

Then ask families to select one mode and means such as land/truck. Have them brainstorm ideas/situations regarding trucks as the best choice. Then, have them discuss when trucks would be an inappropriate choice. Send home copies of Figure 20 for recording their responses. Have students bring their responses to class for group sharing.

Dear Parents,

Your child is bringing home a set of "transportation situation cards" to stimulate a family discussion regarding variables to consider when making transportation choices. After discussing the cards, please select at least one mode and means of transportation and discuss the trade-offs involved (given the transportation need presented). A Decision-Making Chart has been provided for recording responses. An example has been included to get you started. Please send the chart back with your child for group sharing. Thank you!

Sincerely,

FIGURE 19   Model Letter to Parents

MODE	MEANS	WHEN A GOOD CHOICE	WHEN A BAD CHOICE
Land	Truck	Lots of freight; when a big truck is available; when you don't need to cross a body of water; when you have an experienced driver	When you have a very small amount of freight; when a big truck isn't available; when you have to cross water and the bridge is under repair; when you can't find a driver with a license

Figure 20   Decision-Making Chart

Lesson 13

Careers in Transportation

Resources
- Photos and pictures of a range of careers associated with transportation
- Interview schedule for eliciting responses regarding careers related to transportation
- Identification cards describing transportation resource guests (assessment activity)
- Guests from the community who work in the transportation industry
- Careers in Transportation Worksheet (Figure 22)
- Transportation Hunt Activity Sheet (Figure 23)

Children's Literature
Raatma, L. (1999). *Safety on the School Bus*. Mankato, MN: Capstone.

Royston, A. (1998). *Truck Trouble*. New York: Dorling Kindersley.

General Comments
For this lesson, students will have an opportunity to visit with a school bus driver, a local city bus driver, a postal delivery worker or UPS driver, a taxi driver, or a semi-truck driver. Transportation workers will be selected based on availability and resources in the local community. Probably at least one parent works in a transportation career (e.g., driver, scheduler, air traffic controller, travel agent, etc.). The students will act as reporters. Accompanied by adult volunteers, they might work in small groups and audiotape or videotape the interviews and take photos.

General Purposes or Goals
To develop: (1) understanding and appreciation of the diversity of career opportunities associated with transportation; (2) understanding of the roles of people who work in transportation and the costs associated with their work; and (3) a sense of efficacy regarding the possibilities for pursuing careers in transportation or even creating new ones.

Main Ideas to Develop
- We depend on many people to move goods and people.
- People are responsible for personal and mass transportation.
- We pay for the services that these people provide to us.

Teaching Tips from Barbara
This lesson was particularly interesting and meaningful to my students. The families chose to interview and discuss a wonderful variety of careers. We

had a mountain of information to review as children shared the interviews with each other. The Transportation Hunt is a great activity, and I suggest sending it home early in the unit, so families have lots of time to work on it.

Starting the Lesson

Share and discuss the responses from the home assignment. Then, begin by explaining to students that reporters are people who work at radio stations, television stations, and newspapers whose responsibility is to get information and write it up for reading, paraphrasing, and/or telling other people what they have learned. One technique that a reporter uses is the interview. Recall the interviewing that students did in their school with people who spend a lot of time working in the area of communication.

Suggested Lesson Discussion

Sometimes a reporter prepares questions in advance. Other times she or he asks questions as they come to mind. The reporter takes notes, uses a video camera or a tape recorder (if the story will be used in a news program on television or radio), and/or takes photographs to use if the story will be presented in a newspaper or a magazine. Today you get to be reporters. [Model the reporter role by interviewing a school bus driver.]

[Give each student an interview protocol—or have the class generate questions—to gather information from people in their community who have careers related to transportation.] Sample questions that might be used:

1. What is your name?
2. What is your job?
3. Describe your major responsibilities.
4. Describe your typical workday.
5. What do you like most about your work?
6. What is the most frustrating part of your work?
7. What type(s) of education and training do you have and how does it help you in your work?
8. What other interesting things can you tell us about your work?

[After you have modeled by interviewing the school bus driver, ask one or more students to reenact the situation. Discuss. Then have students take turns questioning, in groups with one student as recorder. Interview several other members of the local community who work in transportation who have come to the classroom to serve as resources. Each group will interview one individual. One plan would be for each group to have an upper-grade mentor serve as the scribe. Mentors could also record the conversations (on audiotape or videotape) as well as serve as the photographer. For literacy, have your students with their upper-grade mentors write up and present their stories. Another option is for the interviewees to assist in the write-ups. Share the major points of the interviews as an entire class.]

Activity

Have each interview group return to the person the group interviewed and share the two most important things it learned.

Summarize

- We depend on many people to move goods and services.
- Many transportation workers connect to places around the globe.
- Transportation workers need special skills and are paid by the company they are associated with.
- Transportation workers provide us with a range of services that impact our daily lives.

Assessment

Using identification cards describing the transportation resource guests, have students select a card and describe the transportation career opportunity they learned about during the interviews/follow-up class discussion. Ask each student to explain whether it would be a career that he or she might like to explore someday, and why or why not. Encourage students to pose questions about these careers (what else they would like to learn). They might be able to get their questions asked as part of the home assignment.

Home Assignment

Encourage the students to talk with their family members about the services and people they have experienced in the transportation field, and to talk with friends, neighbors, and relatives engaged in work related to transportation—some aspect of moving goods and people. Send home copies of Figure 22 for recording highlights of the interviews/discussions. As an option, you can also send home copies of Figure 23 for further exploration of transportation-related careers.

Dear Parents,

We have been discussing careers in transportation. During the next several days, please take some time to assist your child in talking with someone who has a career in transportation. A Careers in Transportation Worksheet has been included for recording responses. Your child will have a chance to share this information with our class. (Optional: We also have enclosed a Transportation Hunt Activity Sheet to provide additional opportunities for you to discuss transportation-related jobs with your child as you observe these jobs being carried out in your neighborhood. An example has been provided to help you get started.) Thank you!

Sincerely,

FIGURE 21   Model Letters to Parents

Name _____

I talked with _____ about transportation.

His/her jobs include _____

_____

_____

_____

_____

The special skills needed to do a good job include _____

_____

_____

_____

_____

This work is important because _____

_____

_____

_____

_____

I would/would not like to do this job someday because _____

_____

_____

_____

_____

FIGURE 22   Careers in Transportation Worksheet

During out-of-school hours, you go many places and observe many things. During the next week, list every type of transportation vehicle that you see. Identify where you saw the vehicle, what it is used for, and why or why not you'd like to have a job associated with it.

TYPE OF TRANSPORTATION	SITE WHERE OBSERVED	VEHICLE'S USE	WHY I WOULD/WOULD NOT LIKE A JOB ASSOCIATED WITH IT
UPS delivery truck	In front of our house	Deliver packages	I would not want to spend most of my workday in a truck.

FIGURE 23   Transportation Hunt Activity Sheet

Lesson 14

. . . .

Transportation: Being a Responsible Citizen

Resources
- White board and markers
- Training wheels
- Helmet, appropriate clothing such as bicycle pants, training wheels, and so on.
- Pictures depicting bicycle safety
- Pictures and drawings illustrating bicycle rules and laws
- Pictures of traffic signs

Children's Literature
Brown, M. (1993). *D. W. Rides Again*. Boston: Little, Brown & Co.

Holub, J. (1998). *Red, Yellow, Green—What Do Signs Mean?* New York: Scholastic.

General Comments
This lesson is intended to sensitize students to the responsibilities bicyclists have to themselves as well as to others.

General Purposes and Goals
To help students understand and appreciate the importance of following the laws associated with bicycling in order to protect themselves as well as other people on the road.

Main Ideas to Develop
- There are many responsibilities associated with transportation (e.g., helmets, safety belts, traffic laws, conservation of resources, ecological pollution matters, etc.).

Teaching Tips from Barbara
The book *D. W. Rides Again* is a key part of making this lesson successful. The students were able to relate the ideas in the book to their own lives. I also was able to get additional safety information from a local bicycle association. I had students keep a seat belt log over the course of a week to focus on another area of safety.

Starting the Lesson
Share and discuss the results of the home assignment. Then ask students if they've ever thought about their responsibilities to themselves and others when they ride bicycles. Listen for their experiences and misconceptions.

Using pictures and props (helmet, appropriate clothing such as bicycle pants, training wheels, etc.), ask students what they need to know and be able to do *before* they begin riding a bicycle. Why? List their responses on the white board. Do one's actions/behaviors associated with biking affect other people? If so, how?

Suggested Lesson Discussion

D. W. Rides Again is a fictional story that makes some very important points about responsibilities—to yourselves and others. Listen and think about additional responsibilities you might add. Points emphasized in the story are: Make sure you always wear a helmet; while riding with traffic, watch out for holes and always stay alert; use hand signals indicating what you plan to do (e.g., stop, turn right, turn left, etc.); never show off—even adults can have accidents if they don't pay attention.

SUGGESTED QUESTIONS FOR GUIDED DISCOURSE AFTER THE STORY

What are some of the rules for riding a bicycle?

Why is it important that you know the rules and follow them?

Who makes bicycle rules?

How could you hurt other people if you don't follow those rules?

If you hold your left hand out and down, what are you telling the people on the road behind you?

Left hand out and up means what?

Left hand out means what?

What could happen if you "clown around" or don't pay attention while riding your bicycle?

Why do kids need to use training wheels before they ride their bicycles on roads?

When you follow the bicycle rules and laws, how are you practicing good citizenship?

In the story, D. W.'s father landed in the water. Why?

What lesson did both he and D. W. learn?

What new things did you learn about bicycle safety?

What new information could you provide to D. W.?

What are the advantages of an adult using a bicycle instead of a car or a truck? Disadvantages?

How is a bicyclist conserving natural resources?

Summarize

• There are many responsibilities associated with bicycling.

Activity

Have each student create a visual that responds to this question: How can I practice responsible citizenship as a bicyclist? Share and discuss with the class. Create a billboard or bulletin board for display in the hallway of the school.

Assessment

As a class, prepare a letter to parents explaining what it means to be a responsible bicyclist.

Home Assignment

Encourage family members to discuss bicycling rules and laws and how citizenship is practiced as a result of being a responsible bicyclist. Have them use the class letter as the stimulant for the conversation.

Then, as a family, have them discuss and list other ways citizenship can be linked to transportation issues (e.g., Drivers make sure their vehicle windows are free of snow, ice, etc. when driving so that they have clear visibility. All passengers wear seat belts. Children in car seats ride in the back seat. People riding motorcycles, snowmobiles, etc. wear the proper safety equipment and follow the laws for speed. Passengers in school buses are seated when vehicles are moving. Drivers do not exceed the speed limit.). Encourage the student to bring the list to an upcoming social studies class.

Dear Parents,

Enclosed is a letter that our class prepared to inform you about what it has learned about being a responsible bicyclist. Please use it as a stimulant for a conversation with your child. Then, as a family, discuss and list other ways citizenship can be linked to transportation issues (e.g., Drivers make sure their vehicle windows are free of snow, ice, etc. when driving so that they have clear visibility. All passengers wear seat belts. Children in car seats ride in the back seat. People riding motorcycles, snowmobiles, etc. wear the proper safety equipment and follow the laws for speed. Passengers in school buses are seated when vehicles are moving. Drivers do not exceed the speed limit.)

Please send your response to school so it can be shared in an upcoming class discussion. Thank you!

Sincerely,

Figure 24   Model Letter to Parents

Lesson 15

. . . .

Transportation: An Authentic Assessment

Resources:
- See Table 3: Suggested Artifacts for Review
- Local transportation workers (eg., school bus drivers, truck driver)

General Comments

For this lesson, students will have the opportunity to revisit the entire transportation unit and review the big ideas. Select one artifact (bulletin board, poster, chart, time line, copy of student work, etc.) from each lesson for the discussion/assessment. In the spirit of authentic assessment, invite two or three individuals from the community who work in the transportation area (e.g., school bus driver, school transportation business manager, local truck driver) to come to the classroom and listen to students share what they have learned about transportation. If time permits, ask the guests to give feedback, ask questions, and share some key ideas about their transportation careers. To ensure that this attempt at authentic assessment is beneficial, you will need to engage in careful planning with the guests. Concern for appropriate level of difficulty will be very important.

General Purposes and Goals

To: (1) draw on prior knowledge, understanding, appreciation, and applications conducted at home and at school to enhance meaningfulness and continued curiosity in learning about transportation; (2) revisit and reflect on the big ideas developed about transportation; and (3) engage in an "elementary" version of authentic assessment and practice communicating with individuals in the community who have special interest and expertise in transportation.

Main Ideas to Develop
- Transportation is the movement of people and things from one place to another.
- People move from one place to another for many reasons: to work, go to school, shop, go to the post office, go to the doctor or dentist, visit relatives, worship, attend recreational events, and so on.
- Goods are moved from one place to another for many reasons: raw materials must be carried to factories to be processed; products from farms and factories must be carried to different places (e.g., markets and stores to be sold).
- People long ago had very limited means of transportation. Travel was slow and hard. Most goods went by boat. When people traveled, they went by horseback or in wagons or carts.

- Inventions have resulted in faster transportation by land, water, and air.
- As wheeled transportation became common, better roads were needed. As time went by and faster and faster coaches and gigs, or two-wheeled carriages drawn by horses, were built, new road systems were designed.
- Railroads brought speed to travel. Also, trains could carry large loads and heavy types of freight, so manufacturers could transport their products over land to be sold in faraway places.
- Water transportation developed much faster than land transportation. Early civilizations developed along rivers and other larger waterways. Boats and ships were built for use in commerce, warfare, and exploration.
- There are many main kinds of transportation.
- The three major kinds of transportation are land, water, and air.
- Transportation means also can be classified as engine-powered or engineless.
- Engine-powered means of transportation have many advantages over engineless (faster, more dependable, carry greater loads).
- Disadvantages of engine-powered means of transportation include: they cost more, they usually need supporting facilities, and they are expensive to build and maintain. Every form of engine-powered transportation also needs a source of energy.
- The automobile is the most common means of transportation on land.
- Trucks carry large loads from place to place.
- Before the arrival of cars and trucks, we used trains to travel from place to place. We still use trains to get about or to carry large loads of freight.
- There are two main types of passenger transportation: personal and public.
- People who use personal transportation operate their own vehicles.
- Those who use public transportation pay to ride on vehicles owned and operated by companies or the government.
- Mass transportation was invented to carry large numbers of people at a time.
- We depend on many people to move goods and people. We pay for the services that these people provide to us.
- People decide which means of transportation to use based on time, money, personal preferences, what types are available and other considerations.
- Emergency vehicles (police cars, ambulances, lifeboats, etc.) provide help for people who have experienced an accident or a disaster.

- Emergency vehicles carry a lot of equipment to help rescuers do their jobs.
- When an emergency vehicle has its sirens screaming and lights flashing, it has the "right of way," which means that other cars and trucks have to pull over and get out of the way.
- Emergency vehicles need to go very fast, need to be built with extra-strong materials, and need to be well taken care of so that they will not break down during an emergency run.
- Vehicles such as automobiles and school buses feature a manufacturing process that uses mass-produced interchangeable parts.
- Vehicles (cars, trucks, and buses) are made in factories where every worker specializes in a specific job, doing it over and over many times a day so that many of the same products can be made in a short time period.
- An assembly line is a line of factory workers and equipment on which the product being assembled passes consecutively from operation to operation until completed.
- Rules and laws are a necessary part of the transportation industry.
- Rules and laws are regulations that are needed for planning, safety, and decision making.
- A map is a medium for locating places—even places where we have never been before. It is a drawing of a place.
- Shipping brought about the use of maps.
- Mapmakers use symbols and colors so we can get plenty of information in a small space. A symbol is a figure that stands for something else.
- A map has a key or legend. It shows the symbols and colors used on the map.
- On the map, the main directions are cardinal—north, south, east, west.
- Maps are used by people employed in careers associated with transportation, as well as people who privately make decisions related to transportation.
- Human designs and construction facilitate travel.
- Different types of transportation need different types of roads.
- Bridges are structures that provide passage over a waterway, railway, or other obstacle.
- When roads and railroad cars come up against obstacles like mountains and rivers, engineers need to design tunnels, bridges, and so on so that vehicles can reach their destinations.
- Railways are special overland roads for locomotives to travel on.

- Canals are human-made waterways that shorten routes between larger bodies of water.
- Cultural diffusion via transportation has become faster and more comprehensive, shifting and homogenizing the world.
- Availability of resources, local geographic features, tourism, cultural beliefs, and customs are among the factors that explain transportation differences.
- Transportation facilities provide places for goods and passengers to arrive and depart. They serve as central depositories.
- The primary function of local transportation facilities is to serve customers—people who want/need to travel and people or companies that need to send goods to another place.
- Individuals and businesses make decisions about how goods and people should be transported.
- Preference, convenience, money, time, geographic features (physical), and personal values are variables that need to be considered when deciding what means of transportation to use.
- There are many responsibilities associated with transportation (e.g., helmets, safety belts, traffic laws, conservation of resources, ecological pollution matters, and so on).

We recommend that after each lesson the teacher decide what "artifacts" will be used for the authentic assessment. This planning/preparation should begin at the outset and be an established expectation. Extend a written invitation to each of the guests early in the unit.

Teaching Tips from Barbara

I find it very helpful to revisit the list of main ideas before I begin the review lesson. This particular review lesson suggests using the journal entries, posters, charts, and other artifacts created during the unit to review each topic.

Starting the Lesson

Discuss the home assignment. Remind the students that today they will have a chance to showcase what they have learned by sharing their ideas with guests who are associated with transportation.

Suggested Lesson Discussion

[Each pair of students will be assigned a number that corresponds to the unit lessons. The resource people will take turns pulling out a number from the hat. The students assigned to that lesson will share what they have learned. The resource people will have a list of the main ideas from the lessons so they will be in a position to ask clarifying questions.]

TABLE 3   Suggested Artifacts for Review

LESSON	SUGESTED ARTIFACTS
Lesson 1 Transportation: What Is It? Why Is It Important?	• Bulletin board display of modes and means of transportation
Lesson 2 Changes in Transportation over Time	• Time line
Lesson 3 Types of Transportation	• Class or individual scrapbook
Lesson 4 Passenger Transportation	• Passenger transportation chart
Lesson 5 Emergency Vehicles	• Collection of pictures and photos representing the various types of emergency vehicles
Lesson 6 Mass Production	• Bulletin board display: "Steps in Building a Vehicle"
Lesson 7 Transportation: Necessary Regulations	• Student open-ended statements and responses
Lesson 8 Maps: Tools for Transportation	• Maps: Tools Used for Transportation (Table 2)
Lesson 9 Human Designs and Construction Facilitate Travel	• Human Designs and Construction Chart (Figure 16)
Lesson 10 Transportation Around the World: More Alike Than Different	• Collection of pictures/photos (home assignment representing transportation around the world)
Lesson 11 A Visit to a Local Transportation Facility: Train Station, Airport, or Harbor	• True/false quiz
Lesson 12 Decision Making: Which Mode? Which Means?	• Situation cards
Lesson 13 Careers in Transportation	• Careers in Transportation Worksheet (Figure 22)
Lesson 14 Transportation: Being a Responsible Citizen	• Letter to parents prepared by class to explain responsibilities of a bicyclist

Large-Group Discussion and Activity

After every lesson has been reviewed and the resource people (transportation guests) have completed their questioning and commenting, return to the large group and write a letter to the families summarizing the highlights of the unit and thanking them for helping with the home assignments. Also, prepare a thank-you letter to the transportation guests.

Unit 3: Family Living

Introduction

To help you think about family living as a cultural universal and begin to plan your teaching, we have provided a list of questions that address some of the big ideas developed in our unit plans (see Figure 1). The questions focus on what we believe to be the most important ideas for children to learn about family living. These include: the nature and functioning of families; kinship relationships; how and why families change over time; what it means to get married or divorced and why people do so; changes in family size and everyday living patterns that have occurred over time, particularly those related to shifts from the rural life of agrarian societies to the city and suburban life of modern societies; cultural differences in family living patterns; comparisons across rural, small-town, and large-city settings; reasons that families sometimes move within or even across countries, and the adjustments that such moves require of family members; the roles of families and of schools in teaching children what they need to learn; the need for families to have rules; the help available to families in emergencies; and ways that families can help other families and their communities at large.

To find out what primary-grade students know (or think they know) about these questions, we interviewed ninety-six students in Grades K–3. You may want to use some or all of these questions during preunit or prelesson assessments of your students' prior knowledge. For now, though, we recommend that you jot down your own answers before going on to read about the answers that we elicited in our interviews. This will sharpen your awareness of ways in which adults' knowledge about family living differs from children's knowledge, as well as reduce the likelihood that you will assume that your students already know certain things that seem obvious to you but may need to be spelled out for them.

If you want to use some of these questions to assess your students' prior knowledge before beginning the unit, you can do this either by interviewing selected students individually or by asking the class as a whole to respond to the questions and recording their answers for future reference. If you take the latter approach, an option would be to embed it within the KWL technique by initially questioning students to determine what they know and what they want to find out, then later revisiting their answers and recording what they learned. An alternative to preassessing your students' knowledge about topics developed in the unit as a whole would be to conduct separate preassessments prior to each lesson, using only the questions that apply to that lesson (and perhaps adding others of your own choosing).

The students' responses to the family living interview displayed many of the same patterns seen in earlier interviews. They knew much more about family living here and now than in the past or in other cultures, and the sophistication of responses was related much more closely to age (grade level) and personal experiences than to achievement level or gender. There were frequent indications of chauvinism in talking about other cultures and presentism in talking about the past (i.e., viewing people in the past as less intelligent or creative than we are because they lacked modern inventions).

The initial questions asked the students to define families and talk about why most people live in them. Most of the students were able to define or describe a family but found it more difficult to explain why people live in families. About a third couldn't respond, and most of the rest suggested reasons such as wanting to get their basic needs met, wanting to live with others (i.e., not alone), or loving/wanting to take care of or help one another. Only twenty-one students spoke of couples wanting to get married/have children.

Knowledge about kinship relationships developed gradually across the age range studied, with younger students primarily emphasizing social ties among the people involved (e.g., family members love one another) and older students beginning to learn about genealogical or legal ties (e.g., family members are related by blood and marriage). Overall, students found it easiest to define grandparents, somewhat more difficult to define aunts and uncles or cousins, and most difficult to define stepbrothers and stepsisters. Legal relationships were even more difficult and confusing for the students than genealogical ones. Unless they could speak from direct experience, the students had difficulty talking about adoptive or stepsibling relationships.

1. Today we're going to talk about families. What is a family? [Probe for whatever the student can say about the composition and nature or functioning of a family.]

2. Why do most people live in families?

3. Families include grandparents, aunts and uncles, and cousins. What are grandparents? . . . What are aunts and uncles? . . . What are cousins? . . . What are stepbrothers and stepsisters? [Probe to see if student can define these relatives in terms of relationships to his or her parents, if necessary using examples from the student's own family. For example, "OK, you have an Aunt Missy. What makes Missy your Aunt? . . . How is Missy related to you?"]

4. The number of people in a family can change over time. Sometimes families get bigger. How might a family get bigger? . . . What is another way that a family might get bigger? . . . How do families' needs change when they get bigger?

5. Sometimes families get smaller. How might a family get smaller? . . . What is another way that a family might get smaller? . . . How do families' needs change when they get smaller?

6. What is marriage? [If necessary] What does it mean to get married?

7. What is divorce? [If necessary] What does it mean to get divorced?

8. How are families these days different from families in the past? . . . What are some other differences? . . . Any others?

9. In what ways are families these days the same as families in the past? . . . How else are families the same as they always were?

10. In the past, most parents wanted a lot of children, but these days most parents want only a few. Why is that?

11. Everyday life has changed for mothers, fathers, and children. What do mothers do? What did mothers in the past do? [Continue to probe until student can no longer respond to the original question, then ask the following more specific probes.] What did mothers in the past spend a lot of time doing that today's mothers don't do? . . . What do today's mothers spend a lot of time doing that mothers didn't do in the past?

12. What do fathers do? What did fathers in the past do? [Continue to probe until student can no longer respond to the original question, then ask the following specific probes.] What did fathers in the past spend a lot of time doing that today's fathers don't do? . . . What do today's fathers spend a lot of time doing that fathers didn't do in the past?

Continues

FIGURE 1   Starter Questions

13. What do children spend their time doing? What did children in the past spend their time doing? [Continue to probe until student can no longer respond to the original question, then ask the following specific probes.] What did children in the past spend a lot of time doing that today's children don't do? . . . What do today's children spend a lot of time doing that children didn't do in the past?

14. These days, most kids live with just parents and brothers or sisters, but in the past, they often lived with their grandparents, aunts, uncles, and cousins, too. Why did things change?

15. In some other countries, even these days, most kids live not only with parents and brothers and sisters but also with their grandparents, aunts, uncles, and cousins. Why is that?

16. When have kids spent more time with their parents—these days or in the past? Why?

17. People all over the world live in families, but different countries have different customs. Do you know of a country where families do things differently than we do here? [If yes, probe for explanation.]

18. What about Japan—do Japanese families do things differently than American families? [If student talks about differences in physical characteristics, say, "OK, so they look different. But what about everyday family life at home? Is that any different?"]

19. Is family life different for people living on farms than for other people? [If yes, probe for explanation.]

20. How is family life different for people who live in small towns than for people who live in big cities?

21. Your ancestors came to America from somewhere else. Do you know where they came from? [If yes] Where? . . . Why did they decide to come here? [If necessary, define *ancestors*: "Your ancestors were your relatives back in time—your grandparents, great-grandparents, and so on."]

22. Families sometimes move to a different house or even a different city. Why do families move from one place to another? . . . Any other reasons?

23. Sometimes families move here from another country where they don't speak English. Why do they do that?

24. How does family life change when a family moves to a new country?

25. In the past, most kids went to school for just a few years, but these days most go for a lot longer. Why is that?

26. Kids learn things from their families. What are some things that most kids learn at home from their families? . . . What else?

27. Why do families need rules? What would happen to a family if it didn't have rules?

28. If families have a fire, a flood, or some other emergency, who can they turn to for help? . . . Who else?

29. What can families do to help other families?

30. What can families do to help their communities?

Figure 1 (Continued)

225

Perhaps the key idea to teach about kinship relationships is that there are two general categories: genealogical relations (blood relatives of one's biological parents) and step-relations (blood relatives of one's step-parents). The former relationships persist through changes in marital relationships or households, but the latter relationships can be severed through divorce or separation (although personal friendships and a subjective sense of kinship may persist).

Most students found it easy to talk about reasons that families might get larger or smaller, and the explanations they gave generally paralleled those likely to be given by adults, except for the students' frequent mention of pets and occasional descriptions of traumatic departures (a family member runs away, wanders off and gets lost, or discovers that he or she is in the wrong family because of a mix-up in identity). However, the students were unable to generate many ideas about how family needs would change following an increase or decrease in family size, except for the most obvious answer that needs for food, clothing, and other resources would increase or decrease. No student noted, for example, that there might need to be a redistribution of chores and responsibilities, that a new baby might mean a change in working hours for one or both parents or a need to arrange for child care during part of the day, or that the departure of a breadwinner might bring financial pressures. Thus, the students lacked an adult perspective on these questions.

Most of the students were able to respond to questions about what it means to get married or divorced, and what they said was generally accurate and free of misconceptions. The most common responses were that a couple likes/loves each other and therefore wants to live together as the reason for marriage, and that the couple has grown apart or had a fight as the reason for divorce. Few students mentioned either the legal papers or the ceremonies involved in marriage or divorce or the desire to have children and raise them within a family as a motive for marriage. Only eleven made reference to the marriage ceremony itself, and none described the marriage vows. Some responses focused on the child's rather than the adult's point of view, making reference to things such as the formal clothing, kissing, or cake involved in a wedding or the shuttling between homes or loss of contact with stepsiblings following a divorce.

No student specifically said that actions of the children were the reason for divorce, although a few of them hinted that they had something like this in mind. Few students mentioned court proceedings and none distinguished between being formally married and informally living together. The students' responses suggested that they would benefit from instruction on the vows that people make as the heart of the marriage ceremony, some of the legal ramifications of marriage and divorce, and the idea that growing apart/incompatibility is the usual reason for separation or divorce (rather than hostility, violence, the desire to marry someone else, or actions of the children).

The next series of questions asked the students to make past versus present comparisons concerning family life in general and the roles/activities of fathers, mothers, and children. There was extreme variance in the students' ability to respond to these questions. Almost all of them responded readily when asked about today's families, but most had difficulty when asked about families in the past or when asked to draw comparisons. Few if any of them were aware of the sweeping changes in family living that accompanied the industrial revolution and the shift from extended families living together on farms to nuclear families living separately in cities or suburbs.

Repeating a pattern seen in our earlier interviews, the students' images of the past were noteworthy for what historians call *presentism:* the tendency to judge the past from today's perspective instead of viewing the time and place in question through the eyes of the people who lived there. Presentism is pervasive in young children's views of the past, leading them to view past life as drab and past people as stupid (or at least, limited in creativity) because contemporary technology and conveniences had not yet been invented. Many of the students viewed people of the past as sitting around idly with little to do whenever they were not engaged in daily chores, or else as having little time to do much else other than their chores.

Although they did not talk about a shift from extended families functioning as economic and social units on farms to contemporary nuclear families living in cities and suburbs with breadwinners working at modern jobs, some students did identify general shifts between the past and today: More mothers now work outside the home, fathers are more likely to work in offices than to be farmers or blacksmiths, and children go to school for most of the year throughout childhood and adolescence. Many more consumer products are available now, and most people buy the things they need at stores rather than grow or make them at home. In responding to these questions, some students kept coming back to certain themes: In the past, there was slavery or restrictions on opportunities for black people to marry and enjoy family life, but things are different today; families in the past rarely left their farms because their means of transportation were limited or they couldn't find baby-sitters to watch their children; people didn't buy as much then because they didn't have today's well-stocked stores and/or because they didn't have much money; they grew most of their food and made most of their clothes; they didn't have access to modern medicine and hospitals; the population was sparse so they felt a need to increase it and therefore tended to have large families; people then were hardworking and responsible, whereas today we are spoiled and lazy; childrearing and schooling have become more humane; and gender roles now overlap more than in the past. Most of these themes were accurate as far as they went, although often tinged with presentism.

Even though these children were relatively young and lived in modest but pleasant communities, their comments about family living in general and their own families in particular were characterized more by realism (sometimes even cynicism) than by romanticism or idealism. There were frequent references to conflict between the parents or between one or both parents and the child, as well as intimations that one or both parents (but typically the father) did little but sit around all day and watch television. Some of these students not only did not look up to their parents as role models but held them in contempt.

Some of the rare and unique responses were notable for their precocity: Modern grandparents love you but nevertheless often move away (e.g., to Florida); relatives are obligated to take you in if you become destitute; modern parents tend to focus on quality rather than quantity in raising children, although some are too busy with careers or other things to have much time for their children; it is nice to be able to buy lots of things but this complicates our lives; modern jobs involve more pleasant work done in more pleasant surroundings, but they take parents away from their children and require them to make child care arrangements; women do not passively wait for male attention but planfully pursue desired men; conflict often arises between men and women because men like to drink and go to bars; in the past, children played games that involved little or no equipment, but today they play with computers and complicated toys; large families present opportunities to take advantage of economies of scale; and modern sports and recreation opportunities are nice, but sometimes parents (again, especially fathers) are more involved in these activities than in their families.

The next set of questions asked students to draw contrasts in the family living circumstances or activities of people living in different geographical areas or types of communities. First, they were asked about family living customs in other countries in general, and in Japan specifically, that differ from our own. Many of the students were unable to respond to these questions, and most of the rest drew comparisons between countries but did not focus on family living. Furthermore, much of what they said was rife with stereotyping or chauvinism. Some of the responses featured stereotypes that have some basis in fact, or at least did in the past (e.g., the English ride subways, the French drink wine, the Chinese eat with chopsticks, and Africans live in huts). However, there also were numerous confusions and misconceptions (e.g., there is less night in Mexico, there are no schools in Africa, the Belgians speak Spanish, the Egyptians live in pyramids, Australia is full of headhunters who use bows and arrows, Germans celebrate Hanukkah instead of Christmas).

There also were frequent instances of chauvinism. Often these were displayed in the disparaging way that the students talked about "different" customs, but sometimes they were expressed more directly through comments such as "they talk weird." To counter the students' tendencies toward presentism in thinking about the past and chauvinism in thinking about contemporary life in other cultures, it is important to teach them about life in the past or in other cultures in ways that enable them to empathize with the people being studied. In particular, it is important to help students to view these people in the context of their time and place, so that their goals and motives become understandable and their behavior is seen as intelligent adaptation (and not as weird, bizarre, or evidence of deficits in intelligence or creativity). As anthropologists like to say, it is important to teach about cultures in ways that "make the strange familiar" and "make the familiar strange."

The students' responses to questions about life in other countries also were notable for their focus on child-oriented things such as holiday celebrations and Santa Claus, toys and games, bath times, and parades. We believe that this tendency is due not only to age-related interests but to the ways that other cultures are often taught at school or conveyed in books and television programs written for children. These treatments often pay disproportionate attention to aspects of culture that are particularly striking or interesting to children, especially celebrations. Consequently, they often create stereotypes and leave the false impression that the people being portrayed are more different from than similar to us.

Along with frequent chauvinistic characterizations of life in other countries, there were occasional statements critical of American society. One student said that the Japanese people dress "fancier" than we do and another said that the Japanese people spend a lot of time improving their neighborhoods whereas Americans are prone to sitting and watching television. There also were occasional ironies reflecting cultural diffusion. One student noted that the Japanese do not use piñatas to celebrate birthdays like we do. This student clearly thought of piñatas as an American (i.e., not Mexican) custom. We observed parallel responses during our food interviews, when several students drew contrasts between prototypical Asian foods and "American" foods such as spaghetti, pizza, or tacos.

The students also were asked to draw contrasts between family life on farms, in small towns, and in large cities. Here again, most students either were unable to respond or (more typically) drew contrasts between the communities involved but did not focus specifically on family life. The students' views of life on farms were generally negative, depicting it as difficult (i.e., involving more work) and less desirable than city or suburban living. This was surprising both because these negative images of farm life did not appear in responses to our earlier food interview (which included a series of questions on farming) and because the students lived in one of the outlying suburbs in a modestly sized metro area that is surrounded for many miles in all directions by hundreds of farms. Even though there were farms located immediately adjacent to (and in a few cases, still within) their community, it was clear that most of these students had little or no experience with farm life, and many of them harbored major misconceptions about it.

In their view, farmers or farm families have to work most of the time and have little time for anything else, must endure unpleasant smells coming from pigs and other animals, must live in small houses that often lack amenities found elsewhere, and generally don't have much and "don't know how to live like real people do." Some students even believed that farm children do not go to school and are illiterate, that farm families live in barns (which must be painted red), or that farmers do not have children (or if they do, it is only because they want someone to carry on the family's farming tradition). Such responses indicate that city and suburban children with little or no direct experience with farms or farm life stand to benefit from instruction not only on land-to-hand relationships in food production and other processes and technical aspects of farming but also on the motives of farm families, the satisfactions they derive from their work and their lives generally, the fact that their children go to similar schools and learn similar things as city and suburban children do, and so on. In short, city and suburban children need to learn that farm people are much more similar to than different from themselves and their families.

Stereotyping and misconceptions were also evident in the students' comparisons between small towns and big cities, although to a lesser degree. Many students depicted small towns as quiet backwaters, and some of them embellished this with misconceptions (e.g., danger from bears, people hunting and gathering for food, many people lacking cars or electricity, or people eating poorly because they don't have enough stores). Other students expressed misconceptions about cities, including several seen previously in responses to our shelter interview (e.g., thinking that the space in cities is all taken up so that one cannot build a house there, confusing apartments with hotel rooms). Some students drew valid contrasts, although usually not about family living (e.g., small-town people are more likely to live closer to their relatives, there are more sidewalks in cities, money is concentrated in cities, there is a greater amount and variety of shopping and jobs in cities, city life tends to run at a quicker pace, and apartment building owners often do not allow tenants to have pets).

The next set of questions addressed students' thinking about family moves (local) and migrations (to a new country). The questions focused on what might motivate families to move/migrate and what might be the effects of the move/migration on family living.

We began by asking the students if they knew where their ancestors had come from and why they had emigrated to America. Only a handful of the students had any specific knowledge about their ancestors' national origins, and most of them were unable to say why their ancestors emigrated. This lack of "family story" information suggests the value of genealogical activities in early social studies (e.g., asking students to interview their parents about their ancestors and perhaps developing a family tree chart).

The next questions asked about why families might move or migrate. Most of what the students had to say in response to these questions was sensible and free of misconceptions, although frequently limited to the child's point of view. Thus, most explanations of why a family might move emphasized that the family had gotten tired of its old house, had gotten larger and needed a larger house, or wanted to leave a deteriorating house or neighborhood. Few of them talked about a change in job or a desire to move to a better school district.

More than two-thirds of the students were unable to respond to the question about why people might move from a non-English-speaking country to the United States. Those who were mostly guessed (e.g., that the people wanted to learn English or to escape oppression) or generated relatively vague responses (e.g., they were seeking something that was lacking in their country of origin). Only a few students mentioned a desire for economic betterment in talking about migration, whereas most adults would mention this first (perhaps along with a desire to escape oppression). Almost half of the students could not respond to the follow-up question about how family life changes when a family moves to a new country, although the remaining students mostly produced responses that reflected empathy with the people (e.g., understanding that they would miss their old friends, have difficulty communicating in an unfamiliar language, or feel strange or out of place when dealing with new social experiences and customs).

Overall, most responses to this series of questions were micro-level ones focusing on the familys' satisfaction with its house or neighborhood, rather than macro-level ones focusing on economic opportunities or political climates in the countries involved. Few of these students had yet acquired images of the United States as a nation of immigrants, a land of opportunity, or a haven for people seeking freedom and democracy.

We asked the students why children today go to school longer than they did in the past, to see if they would say anything about child labor laws, mandatory schooling laws, or related legislation designed to protect children from exploitation and guarantee their educations. Most of the students were unable to respond to this question, and most of the rest guessed that schooling was less available in the past (i.e., there were fewer schools or fewer grades at the schools) or that there was less to learn in the past. Only one student clearly articulated the idea that in the past most people were farmers so most students received only a basic education because they were needed to work on the farm, although three other students gave responses that incorporated part of this idea.

The next question asked about what things children learn at home from their families, and follow-up probes asked about what is learned specifically from mothers or female relatives versus from fathers or male relatives. The students' responses to these questions emphasized academic skills (primarily reading, writing, and arithmetic), manners and morals, self-care skills and responsibilities, health and safety rules, and sports and physical skills. Most students gave relatively generic responses (e.g., how to act) rather than highly specific ones (e.g., how to pick up the dog).

The students mentioned generally similar things in talking about what is learned from mothers versus fathers, with two main exceptions. First, there were seventeen mentions of traditional male role behaviors (e.g., acting masculine, assembling or repairing things, using machines, playing traditionally masculine sports) and twenty two mentions of traditional female role behaviors (e.g., caring for children, acting female, cooking and other domestic arts). The students generally spoke of learning male role behaviors from fathers and female role behaviors from mothers, although four of them did mention female role behaviors that they had learned from their fathers.

The second exception concerns the relative frequencies of responses coded in certain categories. Specifically, the students talked about learning academic skills, manners and morals, self-care skills and responsibilities, and health and safety rules about twice as often when talking about learning from mothers as when talking about learning from fathers. However, most if not all of this difference is likely explained by the presence versus absence of a father (or father figure) in the home. We suspect that children with both parents living in the home would report that these "gender neutral" behaviors are learned as much from fathers as from mothers.

Some responses to these questions were consistent with the traditional ideal of a happily married couple raising children who admire and identify with them. However, a significant minority of the responses included negative comments about one or both parents (but typically the father). These comments expressed contempt for the parents' failures to carry out their personal or parental responsibilities appropriately or resentment for their harsh or neglectful treatment of the child. They are worrisome, especially when one considers that they were made in response to questions about what is learned from parents, not questions about parental behaviors that made the students angry or unhappy. Like some of the responses to the earlier questions about family life in the past and present, these comments are characterized more by realism (and sometimes cynicism) than by romanticism or idealism.

The next question asked about why families need rules, to see if students understood that rules are not just constrictions on individual freedom but mechanisms to make it possible for groups of people to live together in harmony. The students' responses were generally accurate and free of misconceptions, emphasizing that rules help keep you healthy or safe, guide you in treating other people fairly, clarify your responsibilities, and prevent chaos (i.e., without them, family life would get wild, crazy, or out of control). Thus, almost all of the students understood that rules are needed to promote harmonious living in the group context, and one even had the insight that a lack of rules might mean that your family doesn't love you.

The next question asked whom families can turn to in an emergency such as a fire or a flood, to see if students were aware of the public services and "safety nets" available in their communities. All of the students had something to say in response to this question, and the vast majority of their responses were sensible (e.g., call the police, the fire department, 911, or relatives, neighbors, or friends). However, a few of the younger students spoke of getting help from Superman, the FBI, or God. Only one student specifically mentioned the Red Cross, and none mentioned the Salvation Army or other social agencies. Thus, K–3 students have not yet acquired specific knowledge about these agencies. The police were mentioned more often than even the fire department, 911, or relatives and friends, indicating that these suburban children had a benign view of the police as helpful public servants, not as authority figures to be feared or avoided. Minority/inner-city students might respond differently to this question.

When asked how families might help other families, most of the students talked about providing the families with whatever help they needed (ranging from helping free a car stuck in snow to taking in people who were at least temporarily homeless). However, the students found it much more difficult to respond to the last question about how families might help their communities. A majority were unable to respond, and many of the others spoke only about avoiding littering or pollution. However, some students produced inspiring responses: Several were potential neighborhood activists or office holders, one had been inspired by Martin Luther King, and one generated a noteworthy list of ways that people could improve their neighborhood through volunteerism and political activism.

Overview of Family Living Unit
—Barbara Knighton

If you are considering exploring the idea of using cultural universals, the family living unit is a good one to begin with. Most school districts require that one of the early grades deals with this topic as part of the social studies curriculum. Therefore, this is a good place to begin looking at social studies with a different focus and an emphasis on big ideas.

Another benefit to beginning with this unit is the availability of resources. There are several books to go with the lessons in this unit. However, if you don't already have these books, libraries often have the books available. You might have other, equally appropriate books that can be used successfully. Other artifacts and props for the lessons are usually easy to find, such as pictures, maps, games, clothes, and food. Your students' families can help by sending in many of these things ahead of time.

The topic of families has become and continues to be controversial. To prevent any problems, I carefully planned my focus for the unit and kept my parents well informed of my plans. I also planned a Family Night for students to share their learning with the families after the unit was over.

During the lessons, I focused on families in general terms, and then asked students to apply what they learned to their own families. I often used my family as an example. In doing so, I tried to show that the topics and terms we were discussing were nonjudgmental, and I maintained a matter-of-fact as opposed to an emotional tone. I encouraged my students to have discussions and ask questions at home as well. Finally, I provided time during recess and lunch for questions and information sharing with individuals who might have been uncomfortable speaking in front of the whole group.

Parent involvement in this unit should start before you even begin teaching. You will want to address parent concerns right from the beginning. I sent a letter sharing some of the big ideas to my students' families a week before I was scheduled to start the unit. This provided an opportunity for parents to share concerns and ask questions.

At the end of this unit, we held a wonderful Family Night. Throughout the lessons, I had students save their journal entries, time lines, and papers in a portfolio. Then we invited parents, siblings, grandparents, and other family members to join us in a celebration of our learning. I displayed charts, time lines, and other artifacts from the unit. Students became tour guides for their families. We even had some special traditional family treats to eat at the open house celebration.

Lesson 1

What Is a Family?

Resources
- Strips of paper for writing questions related to family living that will be posted throughout the classroom
- Pictures and books in an interest center focusing on family living
- Bulletin board or large poster that has been started to depict the study of families, including their structures and functions
- Props to represent family life across time and space. Establish a "family living" corner or learning center. Include family-oriented games, family pictures, table, chairs, dishes, family trunk of mementos, and so on. The array of artifacts will expand as the unit unfolds. Encourage students to contribute family-oriented traditions, games, books, and more to the corner.

Children's Literature
Simon, N. (1976). *All Kinds of Families*. Morton Grove, IL: Albert Whitman & Co.

General Comments
To launch the unit, collect the instructional resources and display visual prompts to generate interest in the topic. Pose questions (written on wide strips of paper) around the room and on the bulletin board. Good questions might include the following:

What is a family?

Why do families change?

How do families change?

Why do families need rules?

What have you learned from your family?

How are families alike?

How are families different?

How has family life changed over time?

How can families help each other?

How can families help their community?

General Purposes or Goals
To: (1) stimulate curiosity and wonder about family living; and (2) help students understand and appreciate the meaning of family.

Main Ideas to Develop

- A child defines *family* on the basis of personal experience.
- The family is an important social organization in society.
- Families come in all sizes.
- Families come in all ages. (Young families have young children. Middle-aged families often have teen-age children, and older families often have grown-up children and grandchildren.)
- Most families are based on kinship—that is, the members belong to the family through birth, marriage, and adoption. However, some groups that are not based on kinship think of themselves as family because they share a home or feel ties of affection. For example, foster children and their foster parents are not related by adoption, birth, or marriage; however, they live together and consider themselves a family.

Teaching Tips from Barbara

It may be difficult at first to elicit questions about family living from students. I found that when I modeled a few questions first, the students were much more successful. At times, to help get things on track, I suggested the next topic to wonder about. Index cards are great to record the students' questions. When you create a bulletin board display from the questions, you can continue referring back to the questions as you find the answers during the unit. The book *All Kinds of Families* allows you to begin using a standard vocabulary and set of terms that you will use consistently throughout the unit. During the assessment, I used the "My family is special because" statement to begin celebrating the uniqueness of every family. This can be a sensitive topic, so beginning with this lesson, I try to set a matter-of-fact tone and establish the overall expectation that "of course families are different from each other."

Starting the Lesson

Stimulate curiosity and wonder by talking about the displayed family living pictures and by posing questions and eliciting questions from the students about family. Sample questions might include What is a family? How do families change? Why do families change? Why do families need rules? What have you learned from your family? How has family life changed over time? How are families alike? Different? How can families help each other and their community? Write students' questions on strips of paper and attach them to the bulletin board. Assure the class that these questions—and any others it might want to add later—will be discussed during the unit. Acknowledge the props around the room that relate to the topic. Encourage students to add to the collection.

Suggested Lesson Discussion

[Introduce and read the book *All Kinds of Families* by Norma Simon, emphasizing the following points in discussion.] Families are not all composed in the traditional way: a household of two parents and their children. Parents may not live in the same house; however, the family usually remains where children are provided their basic needs and receive love. Families celebrate happy times, but sometimes experience separations. All of us are part of a family and usually the family is a special part of our lives.

Activity

Have students share with a partner one new kind of family they learned about in the story. Then ask them to identify new questions they have about families. Write questions on strips and add to the bulletin board. Pose the new questions and encourage individuals to find information to share with the class. Make sure there are numerous library books available.

(Note: Set aside one or more language arts sessions for upper-grade mentors to come to the class. Using a collection of library books, have students work in pairs to find information regarding one or more questions.)

Summarize

- Families are not all composed in the traditional way: a household made up of two parents and their children.
- Many patterns of family life fit under the broad definition.
- A child defines *family* on the basis of personal experience.

Assessment

Have students work in pairs and discuss one kind of family that they learned about that is different from their family and why. When they have an idea to share, have them signal with "thumbs up." After sharing, ask them to individually write responses to a series of open-ended statements: A family is _____. Family members that live far away might include _____. My family is special because _____ _____. The people in my family include _____, _____, _____, _____, and _____.

Optional   Post words and phrases on cards to assist students with their written responses.

Home Assignment

Encourage students to share what they have already learned about families. Ask an adult or older brother or sister to help collect photos for their "This Is My Family" poster. If photos are not available, drawings can be substituted. Each student will have the opportunity to share his or her family poster with the class.

Dear Parents,

We are beginning a new unit titled Family Living. We hope you will actively participate in this unit by helping your child learn more about his or her family.

Please help your child create a poster titled "This Is My Family." If photos are not available, drawings can be substituted. We want your child to share his or her family poster with our class. The posters will be displayed in our classroom and returned to you at the conclusion of the unit. Thank you!

Sincerely,

FIGURE 2   Model Letter to Parents

Lesson 2

··

Many Kinds of Families

Resources
- Artifacts and photos that illustrate the kind of family the teacher represents
- Resource person to describe another kind of family
- Artifacts and photos that illustrate the kind of family the guest staff person represents
- Large word cards identifying kinds of families: nuclear, extended, adoptive, single-parent, blended, and foster
- Large piece of tagboard for constructing a graph
- Camera, film to take a photo of the graph
- Legal documents related to families (e.g., birth certificate, marriage certificate)

Children's Literature
Super, G. (1991). *What Kind of Family Do You Have?* Frederick, MD: Twenty-First Century Books.

General Comments
Many of the questions posted by you and elicited from the students will allow for a variety of responses. Students' own personal experiences will illustrate likenesses and differences among families. We encourage you to talk about your own family, using artifacts and photos to add interest and convey its specialness. Embedded in the "story" should be the supportive function of the family and the sense of belonging. The story will probably reveal happy and/or sad changes as well as the enduring values of your own family.

General Purposes or Goals
To help students understand and appreciate that: (1) family is defined by personal experience; (2) different kinds of families include nuclear, extended, adoptive, single-parent, blended, and foster; and families are more than just groups of people because they provide places for loving, supporting, and sharing one another's lives together.

Main Ideas to Develop
- Everyone you know is part of a family.
- There are many different kinds of families: nuclear, extended, adoptive, single-parent, blended, and foster.

• Families are more than groups of people. They consist of individuals who are related by birth or connected by a legal document such as a marriage certificate or adoption papers, and who share common values and provide love and support.
• Family members do not always live in the same home.

Teaching Tips from Barbara

There are two distinct parts to this lesson. I chose to separate them into two different days. The first part was my students' favorite because I shared my personal story, including all kinds of artifacts. In the second part, the students began to look at their own families. One of my goals for this lesson was to have my students practice the skill of making a decision and then supporting and explaining their choice. As part of the assessment, students created drawings of their families and then we created a graph together. When the students chose the type of family they belonged to, I was very accepting so long as they shared their thinking.

Starting the Lesson

Begin the lesson by sharing responses to the family poster home assignment. Share your family story, using pictures and artifacts (e.g., birth/marriage certificates) and adding interest and personal touches. Underscore the type of family you represent: nuclear, extended, adoptive, single-parent, blended, or foster family. (If time permits, invite another member of the school staff to share his or her story, especially one that represents a different type of family. For example, the principal's family might be a nuclear, blended family.) Underscore that families are much more than groups of people. Families provide places for loving, supporting, and sharing each other's lives together.

Suggested Lesson Discussion

[Introduce students to the book *What Kind of Family Do You Have?* by Gretchen Super. As you read the story, highlight the kinds of families by placing word cards on the bulletin board: "Nuclear," "Extended," "Adoptive," "Single-Parent," "Blended," and "Foster."]

Key points made in the story are that there are many different kinds of families and that the families in the story may be different from your family in some ways but like your family in other ways.

> *Nuclear family:* Mother, father, and their children live together.
> *Extended family:* Other relatives also live together in a family. These could include grandparents, aunts, uncles, and/or cousins.
> *Adoptive family:* The parents have a child they didn't give birth to. Probably the birth parents couldn't take care of their baby. They loved their baby and they wanted it to have a good home with somebody who would take care of it and love it.

Single-parent family: Only one parent lives with the children. Sometimes the other parent lives far away, but often he or she lives close by and the child visits. In some situations, the child lives half time with each parent (shared custody).

Blended family: When people live together who used to live in other families. A blended family is also called a stepfamily. Sometimes mom and dad get divorced. If they had children and dad gets remarried, the children might live with their dad, his new wife, and her children (if she has children).

Foster family: When a new set of parents takes care of a child for awhile. Sometimes parents aren't able to take care of their children, and until they solve their problems, a foster family will care for the children.

Activity

Ask students to share the most interesting ideas they learned from the discussion. Write the ideas on the board. Then ask each student to stand in front of the word card/label that best describes his or her kind of family. Indicate that you are making a "family" graph that tells the story of your class and the kinds of families represented. Take a photo of the family graph. Then lead the class in composing a story about the family graph, emphasizing that we all belong to families and share our lives with other family members.

Summarize

- Everyone you know lives in a family.
- A family is more than a group of people.
- Family members love and take care of one another.
- There are many different kinds of families: nuclear, extended, adoptive, single-parent, blended, and foster.

Assessment

Have each student draw a picture of his or her kind of family. Using the word cards that identify family types, ask them to label their picture accordingly. Then ask each student to share his or her picture with the class and explain the label. Again, underscore acceptance of all family types and the power of the family as a place of belonging and sharing lives together.

Home Assignment

Encourage students to talk about what they are learning in school about the many kinds of families. With help from family members themselves, each student should write a paragraph describing his or her kind of family, why it is special, how members provide love and support for one another, and specific things the family shares. Then students should bring the paragraphs to school as a means of informing the class about their families.

Dear Parents,

We are learning about the many different kinds of families: nuclear, extended, adoptive, single-parent, blended, and foster. Your child has learned about my family as well as the principal's family [or other staff member]. Our class wants to learn about your family. With the help of family members, I want to encourage your child to write a paragraph describing his or her kind of family, why it is special, how members provide love and support for one another, and specific things your family shares. Thank you!

Sincerely,

FIGURE 3   Model Letter to Parents

Lesson 3

. . . .

Families Change

Resources

- Photographs and artifacts depicting the changes that you, the teacher, have undergone across time (i.e., baby, toddler, teenager, young adult, mature adult)
- A collection of photos and pictures showing family changes across time
- Word cards listing family changes (e.g., death, divorce, arrival of foster child, new birth, marriage, adoption, grandparent moving in, etc.) (Have additional blank cards available for changes that the students might want to add.)
- Word cards listing emotions associated with family changes (e.g., anger, happiness, fear, sadness, etc.)
- Bulletin board—"Families Change"
- Our Family Changes photo guide (Figure 5)

Children's Literature

Rogers, F. (1996). *Let's Talk About It: Divorce*. New York: G. P. Putnam's Sons.

Other sources that you might use, depending on the composition of your class:

Girard, L. W. (1987). *At Daddy's on Saturdays*. Morton Grove, IL: Albert Whitman & Co.

Lash, M., Loughridge, S., & Fassler, D. (1990). *My Kind of Family: A Book for Kids in Single-Parent Homes*. Burlington, VT: Waterfront.

Mancini, R. (1992). *Everything You Need to Know About Living with a Single Parent*. New York: The Rosen Publishing Group, Inc.

Patrick, D. (1993). *Family Celebrations*. New York: Silver Moon Press.

General Comments

The lesson will focus on the changes that individuals and families experience across time, and on how the changes affect our needs and impact our emotions.

General Purposes or Goals

To help students: (1) develop an understanding of and appreciation for the types of changes that occur in families; (2) develop an appreciation for the types of feelings and emotions associated with these changes; and (3) realize that as families change, so do their needs.

Main Ideas to Develop

- A change is something that does not stay the same.
- Family members change (e.g., baby to teenager).
- Families change in size and composition.
- As families change, so do their needs. These changes may occur because of death, divorce, birth, marriage, adoption, and so on.

Teaching Tips from Barbara

This lesson was very meaningful to the students. They were easily able to think of ways in which their own families had changed. Often they would bring up these ideas in casual conversations long after the lesson and the unit were over. There also are many fictional stories that can support these ideas and stimulate class discussions.

Starting the Lesson

Begin the lesson by having the students share the results of the homework assignment. Make sure that as the teacher, you show evidence of doing yours. Then introduce the lesson by indicating that it will focus on change. Explain that all family members at one time were babies and that as the months and years passed, all of us changed in how we looked, our weight, our height, and other ways. Show your own baby picture. Talk about your very early childhood—what your parents relayed to you. Use artifacts if available (e.g., hospital ID bracelet, bonnet you wore home from the hospital, christening dress, etc.). Then show a sequence of photos depicting changes as you grew into a mature adult (e.g., first birthday, toddler, preschool, first day of school, junior high sporting event, teenager, high school and college graduations, marriage, etc.). Use artifacts and photos throughout to add interest and meaning to the "story."

Suggested Lesson Discussion

Individually and as family members, we change in how we look, what we can do, how we act, and what our likes and dislikes are. [Use personal examples to illustrate. Then indicate to students that they will have a chance to bring pictures to illustrate how they have changed.]

As individuals in families change, so do their needs. When you were a baby, you needed someone to feed you, change you, bathe you, and take care of you in other ways. As you got a little older, you needed someone to help you learn to walk and eat your food, but gradually, you started eating by yourself. Now you are able to fix your own cereal; however, you still depend on older family members to cook for you. Many of you select your own clothes for school; however, you need an adult to wash them for you as well as buy them for you. [Encourage students to share examples of how they have changed, and as a result, how their needs have changed.]

Families change in other ways, too. [Use a table, chairs, and place settings of dishes to represent and explain family changes.] Changes include the arrival of a newborn, divorce, death, a grandparent joining the household, or a young adult leaving the home after graduation. [Use pictures to represent people who leave or join the dining room table because of a family change: (1) mother, father, two children—older child goes off to college and only returns for the holidays; (2) grandfather comes to live with his son, daughter-in-law, and grandchild; (3) father, mother, and three children—one child dies in a car accident; (4) mother and daughter live together, then daughter gets married and son-in-law joins the family.]

[After a thorough explanation of family changes, ask for student volunteers to share examples of how their families have changed.] Changes affect family needs. For example, if a child graduates and moves into a dormitory or apartment, the family may not need as many bedrooms. It might redo a room into a study or decide to move to a smaller house. If a grandparent moves in, a bigger house might be needed. [Elicit other examples from students.]

With changes come feelings of anger, excitement, happiness, sadness, worry, and other emotions. [Post the word cards identifying these feelings and elicit examples of family changes that might be associated with each of them.] A child might be very happy to have a baby brother, or angry because she has to share her toys. A child might be happy that his sister is getting married or worried about not seeing her very often because she and her husband are moving far away.

Activity

At the conclusion of the picture-story presentation, have each student draw a picture to illustrate a change that his or her family has experienced recently and label the drawing with the feeling he or she experienced as a result of it. The student should be prepared to explain how the change affected family needs. Invite volunteers or upper-grade mentors to record the responses on the drawings. Display the drawings on a bulletin board labeled "Families Change."

Optional If time permits, share with the students an example of children's literature that illustrates a family change. One change children are familiar with because they or their friends have experienced it is divorce. *Let's Talk About It: Divorce* is a very thoughtful book about the subject. In it, Fred Rogers reminds children that although some things will change with divorce, some things stay the same. Children still have a family that loves them and that needs their love. The author explains that each family is different, each parent is different, and so is each child.

Summarize

- A change is something that does not stay the same.
- Family members change (e.g., baby, toddler, teenager, adult, etc.).
- Families may change in size and composition.
- As families change, so do their needs.
- With changes come feelings (e.g., happiness, sadness, fear, anger, etc.).

Assessment

Conclude the lesson with a large-group journal entry: "Change means
_____. As individuals, we have changed by
_____. Families change when
_____. When families change, needs may
change because _____."

Pair/Share—Have each student select a picture from a collection focusing on family changes, then describe the change to his or her partner and explain how the family might feel because of the change and why. If time allows, have each child explain how family needs might change as a result.

Home Assignment

Encourage each student to bring in photos depicting how she or he has changed and be prepared to describe the changes to the class. Also, encourage students to bring in at least one photo that describes how the family has changed and how needs have shifted as a result.

In preparation for the class discussion, family members should discuss the changes with their child. Send home copies of Figure 5 to help students and their families choose phographs for this assignment.

Dear Parents,

We have been learning about the changes that individuals and families experience across time and how these changes affect our needs and our emotions. We encourage you as a family to discuss these changes with your child and to send in photographs that illustrate some of them.

I have enclosed a discussion guide with an example to start the conversation. Thank you!

Sincerely

FIGURE 4   Model Letter to Parents

Example:

Picture #1   This is a picture of Molly at one week. She depends on her family to bathe her.

Picture #2   This is a picture of Molly at eight. She can bathe herself. She depends on her family to pay the water bill and buy the soap for her bath.

Picture #3   This is a picture of our family. Our family changed when Molly got a baby brother. Because of the change, our family needs to buy more food because we have one more member.

Your Turn:

Picture #1   This is a picture of _____ (child's name) at age _____. He or she depends on his or her family to _____ _____ _____.

Picture #2   This is a picture of _____ (child's name) that shows how she or he has changed. She or he now depends on the family to _____ _____ _____.

(The purpose is to show how, as the child grows up, she or he becomes more self-sufficient and independent.)

Picture #3   This is a picture of our family. Our family changed when _____ _____ _____.

Because of the change, our family needs more/less _____ _____

because _____ _____.

FIGURE 5   Our Family Changes Discussion Guide

Lesson 4

Family Life Has Changed over Time

Resources

- Time line on bulletin board
- Pictures and drawings to represent changes in family living over time
- Table 1: Family Life Has Changed over Time
- Globe
- Pictures of the Mayflower (interior and exterior)
- Pictures of Pilgrims and sailors on their way to America
- Bible box
- Trunk
- Calendar
- Foods typically eaten by Pilgrims (e.g., hard tack, jerky, cheese)
- Pictures of family living as experienced by the Pilgrims and pioneers (e.g., clearing the land, hunting, cooking, sewing, eating, celebrating)
- Picture of a wagon train
- Pictures of exterior and interior of covered wagon
- Pictures of landscape observed on journey westward
- Foods typically eaten by pioneers going westward (e.g., crackers, cornmeal, dried fruit, rice, beans, etc.)
- Pictures of family living as experienced by the pioneers moving westward (e.g., hunting, cooking, eating, repairing their wagons, etc.)
- Pictures of areas where pioneers settled in the West
- Pictures depicting family life today
- Potatoes—fresh (raw), baked, french fried, frozen, and canned (to illustrate the choices that today's families have)
- Articles of clothing—mass-produced, hand-knit dresses
- Variety of building material samples
- Pictures illustrating modern means of communication
- Pictures illustrating modern means of transportation
- Picture of Concorde airplane
- *World Book Encyclopedia*, Volume F. (1994). Chicago: World Book.
- Sample Interview Schedule (Figure 7)

Children's Literature

Alexander, B., & Alexander, C. (1985). *An Eskimo Family*. Minneapolis: Lerner.

Bial, R. (1995). *Portrait of a Farm Family*. Boston: Houghton Mifflin.

Browne, R. (1985). *An Aboriginal Family*. Minneapolis: Lerner.

Elkin, J. (1987). *A Family in Japan*. Minneapolis: Lerner.

Kalman, B. (1989). *Japan, the People*. New York: Crabtree.

Levin, E. (1986). *If You Traveled West in a Covered Wagon*. New York: Scholastic.

Margolies, B. (1990). *Rehema's Journey: A Visit to Tanzania*. New York: Scholastic.

McGovern, A. (1964). *If You Lived in Colonial Days*. New York: Scholastic.

McGovern, A. (1969). *If You Sailed on the Mayflower in 1620*. New York: Scholastic.

Rotner, S., & Kreisler, K. (1994). *Citybook*. New York: Orchard Books.

Rylent, C. (1982). *When I Was Young in the Mountains*. New York: Dutton Children's Books.

General Comments

This lesson describes how family living has changed over time. Long, long ago, families were self-sufficient and lived off the land. Everyone searched for food. As time passed, people developed weapons for hunting. Gradually, this led to the division of labor. Even so, families remained self-sufficient until the beginning of the Industrial Age. All family members worked and the family was the center of work, recreation, and education.

Families began to make decisions about changing their living conditions. For example, some very adventurous types left Europe to seek freedom and jobs in the New World; others traveled across North America in covered wagons seeking better land, gold, and other advantages.

Family living has changed dramatically in recent years with more family options but less togetherness and shared activities in the home.

General Purposes and Goals

To: (1) help students understand and appreciate the changes that have occurred in family living over time; (2) stimulate students' curiosity about these changes and realize the trade-offs associated with them; and (3) help students acquire a sense of efficacy that they can decide, at least in part, on the family lifestyle that they will adopt as adults (for example, recreating some of the past through family campfires, family games, family singing, etc.).

Main Ideas to Develop

- Family life has undergone a variety of changes over time. Early families were dependent on the land—their immediate surroundings—whereas today, families depend on people and places across the globe.
- Long ago, families raised their own food, built their own houses, and made their own clothing out of the local resources available.

- Before people used machines or modern means of transportation, they had fewer choices about what they ate, what their homes were made of, and what they wore.
- There was less standardization and more individual creativity involved in meeting family needs in the past (e.g., homemade cake, knitted dress, etc.).
- With modern technology, multiple career options, local and global availability of resources, multiple recreational options, multiple social options, modern means of transportation, and high-tech communication, modern family life has changed dramatically.

Teaching Tips from Barbara

As I shared the information from this time line, I tried to talk about similar facets of family life in each of the different times. I focused on ease of living, food, travel, shelter, recreation, and children's chores. These areas reflect cultural universals and therefore are a part of children's lives. My students were able to relate to them easily and draw comparisons to their own lives. Be sure to have students process the information through discussion and by re-creating the time line at the end. The home assignment encourages students to interview an older person about his or her family life as a child. I found that my students didn't necessarily need to find someone seventy years old to elicit contrasts with today's families.

Starting the Lesson

Discuss the results of the home assignment. Then begin the lesson by showing pictures of families long, long ago; long ago; and today. Place a few of these pictures on the time line and indicate that more will be added as the lesson unfolds.

Suggested Lesson Discussion

Long, Long Ago   Most people have always lived in families. One major reason is that infants need care, including food. The earliest prehistoric people lived in groups made up of several families. They moved from place to place, hunting animals and gathering wild plants for food. Everyone worked for the survival of the group by searching for food. At first, the early people hunted small animals. Later, they developed weapons to kill or capture large animals. This led to the division of labor, with men often being away on hunts and women staying at home with their families and caring for the children.

Long Ago   As time passed and animals were tamed, men began herding goats, sheep, and other animals. Women often did the farming—raised the crops. A family's wealth, however, depended on the herd because the animals provided a steady source of food and could be traded for other goods. Until the 1700s (the beginning of the Industrial Revolution), most families produced their own food and made their own clothing. The family served as the center for education, recreation, and religious training.

[Using props, pictures, and drama, tell the class the story of the first families who sailed for the New World in 1620, known as Pilgrims.] A Pilgrim is someone who goes on a long journey. The people on the Mayflower were leaving their homes to sail far away to a new land.

[Begin by showing a picture of the Mayflower and a picture of Pilgrims. Using a globe, explain that the Mayflower set sail from England on September 6, 1620, with sailors and 102 Pilgrims aboard. Use a calendar to dramatize the length of the voyage.]

These people decided to come to the New World for several reasons: religious freedom, work, and adventure. [Dramatize uncertainty, challenge, and wonder by showing a chest and explaining that all of a family's possessions allowed on board had to fit into this container.] Imagine, all of your family possessions had to fit into a small trunk! All other possessions had to be left behind. [Pause. Ask students to close their eyes and think about what their families would take if they were moving today and they could only take items that would fit into those containers. Elicit responses.] Today, a family would be able to buy what it needed once it arrived at its destination. In Pilgrim times, there were no stores in the New World. Today, you would take family keepsakes/treasures. Back then, while you would want to take your special things, the most important things put into the containers probably would have been cooking utensils and tools for building houses and working in gardens.

Now, imagine life on board the ship for two months. There was no privacy—you were forced to live as one big family. [Again, dramatize the challenges of a stormy sea, the potential for seasickness, and the repetition of every passing day.] Day after day you would eat the same foods: hard tack (dried biscuits), salted beef or pork, along with dried peas and beans (cooked in metal boxes during calm seas, but eaten cold at most meals). There was also some cheese to eat, but after a month or so, it would mold because there was no refrigeration. [Give students samples of the foods the Pilgrims ate while on board. Again, refer to the calendar and underscore that these foods were eaten every day for two months. Compare this with the variety they have in their diets today.]

Most of the people slept on the floor beneath the main deck. There was little light or fresh air. There were no bathrooms, and if you wanted to bathe, you would wash in salty water from the sea. You would wear the same clothes over and over. [Again, refer to the calendar as a means of dramatizing the time factor.] A family might have taken only one change of clothes—and only if there was room in the trunk. [Compare that to what a family today takes on vacation.] By the end of the very long journey—two months—the clothes were very dirty, maybe torn, and perhaps even outgrown.

During this long trip, people got sick; a few even died of high fevers. It was difficult to stay well in these very crowded conditions. You had poor diets and could not get much exercise.

On the Mayflower, fun was limited to playing with the couple of dogs and the cat that the sailors had on board, and reading and singing. The families on the Mayflower were very courageous. Their needs were met in very limited ways. These people paved the way for others to come to the New World to settle. Things today are dramatically different than they were in 1620—less than four hundred years ago.

[Periodically pause during this interactive lesson to elicit responses from the students that can be recorded on the chart comparing family life across three time periods (see Table 1).]

TABLE 1   Family Life Has Changed over Time

LONG, LONG AGO	LONG AGO	TODAY
1. Families were self-sufficient.	1. Families developed weapons and the division of labor came into being.	1. Families do different jobs.
2. All members searched for food.	2. They began to grow some of their own crops.	2. They buy goods and services.
3.	3.	3.
4.	4.	4.

As the Pilgrims and later the pioneers came to America, the whole family worked together to clear the land and plant, cultivate, and harvest the crops. People had to work very hard because almost everything they used they had to make themselves.

They built their own houses, and most people made all their own clothes. There was spinning, weaving, and knitting to be done. The spinning wheels and looms were handmade, too. Everyone in the family helped to make the clothes. For example, grandmothers might card the wool. Children gathered flowers and berries and roots, which were boiled in large pots to make dyes to color the yarn. Girls and women worked spinning the wool into yarn at the spinning wheel. Girls often learned to spin by the time they were six years old. Often men and boys would help weave the cloth on the loom. Then women would take the cloth (material) and make clothes for the whole family. All of the sewing was done by hand.

Making clothes was a continuous family job that family members worked on whenever they could. For example, when the boys took the sheep to the fields, they'd often take the looms along and weave cloth while they watched the sheep. When a woman would call on her neighbor, she'd often tie the spinning wheel to the back of her horse so she could spin yarn while she visited.

Families raised crops, hunted, fished, gathered berries, and prepared their own food. They planted beans, corn, pumpkins, and squash. They drew sap from maple trees and from the sap made maple sugar and syrup to sweeten their food. They planted vegetables and fruit using seeds brought over from Europe. Men and boys fished and hunted. To preserve their meats through the winter, they smoked, dried, or pickled them. They also dried fruits and vegetables so they would keep longer. They cooked stews, baked bread, churned butter, and made jams. All of these tasks took lots of time. Everyone in the family helped.

Eating a meal as a family was much different in colonial times than today. For example, when you sit down with your family today, you are allowed to laugh and talk. Often the television is on. In the colonial days, there was no radio or television, and children were not allowed to talk at mealtime. Pilgrim children could not even sit down. They had to stand up at the table throughout the meal. There was a printed book of manners. You were not to stuff your mouth to fill your cheeks or make noise while eating or drinking. In many homes, one big pot was put on the table. Everyone put his spoon or fingers into the pot to get the food. It was considered good manners to eat with your fingers.

Besides building their own homes, getting their own food, and making their own clothes, families had many other jobs to do—make dishes, beds, tables, chairs, brooms, buckets, and barrels. When these things got broken, they had to be fixed. They also had to make soap and candles. Boys and girls your age all helped with these family chores before school, after school, and at night. They were taught that work was good for them. Pilgrim and pioneer children did not have nearly as much time to play as you do. However, when they did, they had lots of fun. They played some of the same games you play today: tag, blind man's bluff, London Bridge is falling down, and here we go 'round the mulberry bush.

There were special days devoted mostly to fun (e.g., a special day to celebrate the good harvest). Sometimes families would get together to build a house and then have a party. Other families would get together to combine work and fun at corn husking bees and quilting bees.

As more and more people came to America, towns began to form and people began to open shops. Workers began to specialize in a kind of work. Other people who lived in towns began to pay for their goods and services. Early pioneer towns had cobblers, hatters, blacksmiths, pewterers, tanners, silversmiths, cabinet makers, clock makers, millers, wheelwrights, coopers, barbers, tailors, and so on.

Some of the people who came to America wanted to stay near where they landed. Others wanted to move farther westward. Many decided to move on when they realized that many new people, called immigrants, were coming there from other parts of the world.

[Dramatize the following events using a storylike, interactive format. Use props and pictures to enhance interest. Use questions and body language (e.g., close eyes to imagine key scenes).]

Imagine that you lived in pioneer days. You and your parents, along with your brother and sister, decided to move westward. [Point out the starting location and the site where you might end up if the trip is successful.] You had to leave behind everything you didn't really need because the oxen and horses had a difficult time just walking across the country. If the wagons were too heavy, the animals could die of exhaustion.

You had to figure out how much food you would need for the next six months. [Dramatize by showing the time span on a calendar.] There were no supermarkets, although families would be able to hunt and gather berries and some vegetables along the way. [Show foods you'd probably take, such as crackers, cornmeal, bacon, dried meat, dried fruit, potatoes, rice, brans, and a barrel of water.]

Families made and repaired their own clothing. They would need needles, pins, scissors, and pieces of leather to repair their shoes. They'd also need hammers, axes, string, knives, and nails to repair their wagons.

For daily chores, they would need soap, lanterns, wash bowls, and candles. They needed cooking utensils, as well as tents if they were going to sleep outside the wagons.

The trip usually was started after the spring rains because if you started too early, your wagon would get stuck in mud. Crossing rivers was a challenge. In some cases, you and your wagon would cross on large flat boats, while the horses, cows, and oxen were forced to swim across. If the river was not too deep, you might seal the wagon tightly with tar or candle wax, take the wheels off and push it across the river.

Often there were accidents with wagons. They tipped over and everything was lost or the river flowed so fast that the wagon was dragged away and you couldn't catch up with it.

Traveling in a covered wagon was slow. If it had been raining hard, you might only make a mile in a day. [Identify a local landmark to illustrate.] In a very good day, you might go ten miles [identify a local landmark ten miles from the school to illustrate]. Think about riding in a wagon—or walking alongside it—for six months to get where your family was going. Imagine being inside the wagon, feeling every bump as you moved across the prairie. There were no cushioned seats—just wooden boards, perhaps covered with a few blankets.

There was no radio, TV, computer games, or other electronics—only the sight of wild animals, a few other people traveling in wagon trains, too, and Native Americans (because most pioneer people traveling westward were passing through lands occupied by Native American tribes).

During this long trip, families were concerned about their children's education. If there were several children in the wagon train, they would get together for lessons when they stopped for meals. An older person would teach them, and some would then practice reading and arithmetic. Children learned new things every day—names of flowers and animals; how to fix things such as a broken wagon wheel; and a lot about cooking.

Families traveling together spent a lot of time together. They had to cooperate in every way—fixing things, doing chores such as milking cows, fetching water from a river, watching the cattle, cooking, collecting wood for the fire, and so on. Everyone worked together. Evenings were spent together, often around a campfire. Someone might play a harmonica or a fiddle and everyone else would gather around to sing and dance.

People usually went to bed early because every new day was filled with challenges. For example, crossing steep mountains [show pictures of the terrain] was very difficult. Sometimes the family had to lighten its load and leave some of its possessions along the way. Sometimes it had to cut down its wagon and be left with only a two-wheeled cart, because it was easier to take a cart over the mountains than a whole wagon. Imagine the excitement and joy when you finally reached the place where your family decided to stay and build a place to live!

You may wonder how we know about people who traveled west by covered wagon. We have diaries written by children and adults who recorded their experiences. [Show students an example of a diary.]

[Underscore the idea that many families did not travel westward, but rather settled in the eastern part of the country. Locate Appalachia on a map. Introduce and read the book titled *When I Was Young in the Mountains*. At the end of the story, ask the students to describe the colonial girl's family life in the mountains and compare it to that of a family who traveled by covered wagon. How were they alike? How were they different?]

Family life has continued to change. With the influx of modern transportation and high technology, today's family members have countless career choices, recreational choices, and social choices. Families have accelerated their wants, so a high percentage now relies on a two-person income. More people are getting more education and desire to join the work force. This is especially true among women.

Life today has changed dramatically since pioneer days. [Return to the chart (Table 1) and review the key points comparing family life long, long ago with family life long ago. Add the differences to the chart. Fill in the gaps with storylike narrative that characterizes family life today, yet points out that there are variances among families today.] Unlike families long ago, families today have multiple choices, such as choices about the kinds of food they will eat [illustrate by showing a raw potato, french fries, canned potatoes, frozen potatoes, dried potatoes, and a baked potato from a fast-food restaurant]. Pioneers had only the potatoes that they grew (if any). Modern processing techniques were not available and there were no fast-food restaurants.

Families today also have many choices about what to wear and where to get their clothes, whereas the pioneers had limited choices regarding fabrics, styles, and so on, and the women made the clothes by hand. Today, many women work at other jobs and have no time for sewing and knitting, but we have all kinds of clothing choices; most clothes are mass-produced in factories and then shipped to our stores, often from great distances. [Show a hand-knit dress and explain that this is rare today because hand knitting takes a lot of time and therefore costs a lot of money. Such a dress is highly prized because there wouldn't be many like it. Underscore the thought that in the past, women stayed at home and made all the clothes.]

In the past, families had little choice about the building materials used for their homes. Most of them had to use whatever was available locally that could be used to build a house suited to the climatic conditions. Today, because most families have at least one person working for money outside the home, and because modern transportation allows for materials in many parts of the world to be shipped anywhere for affordable prices, people have a range of choices.

Families today have many choices regarding how they will travel from one place to another, because all kinds of transportation have been invented and most are quite affordable (e.g., car, bus, train, airplane, boat, bicycle, etc.). Families can use faster means such as the airplane to visit a family member halfway across the world. In the past (pioneer days) it would take weeks—even months—to go by wagon train across the United States. Many pioneer families who decided to go westward never again saw the relatives they left behind. The early immigrants who came to America by boat said good-bye to family members for the last time. Today, if a family could afford to fly on the Concorde, for example, from New York [show a picture], they could visit their relatives in London in three hours—half of our school day!

Communication today is also very different for families. During pioneer times, a letter going by wagon train, for example, would take weeks or months. Today, a member of your family could communicate by electronic mail with a relative in California in a matter of seconds.

Family recreation has also changed dramatically. In the past, children had a few homemade toys, played physical games such as London Bridge or duck-duck-goose, and had very few books. They had singing and dancing, but had no television and no computers. Their recreational activities centered around the family and close neighbors. They had no electricity, no central heating, and limited or no indoor plumbing. Today's families have more choices than they can possibly exercise. Often, family members go their independent ways and there is almost no togetherness. Even if all family members are in the household at one time, they may be participating in different things such as watching TV, playing a video game, listening to a CD, surfing the Web, and so on. Families often have a range of technical equipment and many rooms in the house in which to use it, so there are fewer family conversations.

To complicate matters, family members have modern means of transportation and opportunities to participate in group sports of all kinds in the neighborhood/community (e.g., hockey, football, basketball, etc.). Many choices are available about any aspect of life.

[At the conclusion of this interactive conversation with the class about the changes in family life and the choices available, return to Table 1 and list features of family life today.]

Activity

Have the students participate in table talk. Designate tables by long, long ago; long ago; and today. Depending on the class size and/or student preferences, more than one table might be designated for each time period. The object of the exercise is for students to share ideas about their designated family life period and the challenges associated with it. Consider having upper-grade mentors or adult volunteers facilitate the table discussions. At the conclusion of the discussion, have each student write a paragraph describing his or her preferred family life period and why. (Post a range of words about the period to assist in idea generating and spelling. Remind the students that the chart comparing the time periods can also be used as a resource.)

Optional   Wherever we live, family choices are, for the most part, available. However, family life varies across culture and location. For example, if you lived in a city such as New York, your apartment would probably be surrounded by many other apartments, busy streets, and lots of stores. You could find a public playground nearby. Your chores would probably consist of keeping your room neat and perhaps helping with the dishes. You wouldn't have outdoor chores because your family wouldn't own any land surrounding your home. There would be lots of interesting sites for you and your family to see and experience. [Show the photos of *Citybook* by Rotner and Kreisler. Underscore the idea that family life (e.g., lifestyle, recreation, etc.) is influenced by your surroundings.]

[Then introduce other types of environments and family life associated with them. Suggested books with excellent photographs include *An Eskimo Family* by Alexander and Alexander, *An Aboriginal Family* by Browne, *A Family in Japan* by Elkin, *Portrait of a Farm Family* by Bial (the photographer portrays both a way of life and the individual lives of a midwestern farm family), and *Rehema's Journey: A Visit in Tanazania* by Margolies. These selections reveal family lifestyles that are influenced by culture and location. The availability of economic resources also becomes evident in the photos and can be brought into the conversation.]

[Following are major points to make as you share select segments of the books focusing on the diversity that exists among families even today.]

- Culture, location, and availability of economic resources are among the factors that influence family lifestyles even today.
- Families all over the world share some basic needs (e.g., food, shelter, clothing), but they meet them in different ways.
- Families in some parts of the world live very differently than we do because of their culture, location, and availability of resources.

Summarize

- Family life has changed in a variety of ways over time.
- Family life constants include these ideas: the family is still the basic social unit and the family remains one of the major support systems for its members.
- Families today have many more choices and make many more decisions about their lives. As a result, there is less togetherness and less dependence on other family members.
- Location and culture are dominant variables that influence family living.

Assessment

Have students describe in writing the most interesting thing they have learned regarding changes in family living over time and explain why. Pictures or line drawings should be added to illustrate and enhance meaningfulness.

Home Assignment

Encourage students to interview an older individual (preferably at least seventy years old) in an effort to get an in-depth and personalized appreciation for how family life has changed. (A family member should assist and be a part of this learning opportunity.) Send home copies of Figure 7 to help students with their interviews.

Dear Parents,

We have been learning about the changes that have occurred in family living over time and the trade-offs associated with these changes. I have enclosed a Sample Interview Schedule in hopes that your child, with your assistance, might interview an older individual (preferably at least seventy years old) in an effort to get an in-depth and personalized appreciation for how family life has changed.

After gathering the interview data, I hope you as a family will discuss this question: Is it easier or harder to be a functional family today than in the past? Your collective written response would really be helpful so we can incorporate it into our class discussion. Thank you!

Sincerely,

FIGURE 6   Model Letter to Parents

1. Describe a typical school day when you were a child _____

_____

_____

_____

2. Describe a typical evening when you were a child _____

_____

_____

_____

3. Describe a typical Saturday when you were a child _____

_____

_____

_____

4. Describe a typical dinner _____

_____

_____

_____

5. Describe your favorite recreational activities _____

_____

_____

_____

6. Describe some of the choices you had as a child compared to the choices I have as a child today _____

_____

_____

_____

Share your findings with your parents. Then discuss this question: Is it easier or harder to be a functional family today than in the past? Explain. Ask a parent to help you prepare a written response so it can be incorporated into the next class discussion.

FIGURE 7   Sample Interview Schedule

Lesson 5

. . . .

Geographic Influences on Family Life

Resources

- Globe
- U.S. map
- Photos of teacher's home
- Props—wood, brick, local and imported foods, items of clothing made in other parts of the world
- Pictures or photos from other parts of the world where life is heavily influenced by geographic factors (e.g., Greek Islands)
- Pictures or photos from an African village illustrating dependence on local resources and simplicity of family life
- Photos illustrating the teacher's family's jobs and types of recreation enjoyed
- Table 2: Geography Influences Family Living
- Geographic Influences Interview Schedule (Figure 9)

Children's Literature

Bailey, D. (1990). *Families*. Austin, TX: Steck-Vaughn.

General Comments

This lesson will emphasize the role that geography plays in family life. For example, physical features such as large bodies of water may influence what people do. However, the availability of personal resources often offsets geographic influences (e.g., in developed societies, almost any food or building material is available for a price).

General Purposes or Goals

To help students: (1) understand and appreciate geographic influences on family life; (2) understand and appreciate how personal resources often offset geographic impact; (3) acquire a curiosity about the influences of geography on their personal lives; and (4) realize their personal connections to the world.

Main Ideas to Develop

- Families often live far away from where their food or materials for their shelters are produced or where their clothes are manufactured.
- Climate and physical features influence family activities (e.g., recreation, available jobs, family decisions such as construction materials for shelters, local produce for eating, etc.).

- There are some places in the world where people still produce most of their own food, build their own houses out of materials produced locally, and make their own clothes. Usually, these places are found in developing parts of the world; however, some people, such as the Amish, choose this lifestyle based on their beliefs and values.

Teaching Tips from Barbara

This lesson was a good challenge for my students. I only spent one day on it, but I plan to do at least two days next time. Be sure to only pick one type of influence to review and discuss at a time. It can be confusing to try to talk about several different aspects all at once. In the home assignment, I chose to use the fourth question only. It focuses on products that families use and was easily accessible to the families. The other questions were more difficult for the families to answer.

Starting the Lesson

Discuss the results of the home assignment. Begin the lesson by locating the local area on a map of the United States. Then, using a globe, show it in relationship to the rest of the world. Explain that today you will describe how geography influences family life. (Use a storyboard, photos, props, and the globe for the interactive lesson.)

Suggested Learning Discussion

[You will need to tailor the following discussion to your local area.] Our families often live far away from where our food and materials for our shelters are produced and where our clothes are manufactured. [Show a piece of wood from a house, for example, and explain that the wood (lumber) came from the forests in northwestern United States.] The bricks were made from clay found in the southwestern United States, and the windows and doors were manufactured in the Midwest (Pella, Iowa). Because it gets very cold in this part of the country, sturdy building materials are needed. Climate influences our choices. While trees do grow here, there aren't enough to provide the amount of lumber needed for all of the wooden houses.

Geography influences our food choices. During the growing season, the family tends to eat a lot of locally grown fruits and vegetables. They are usually cheaper because they are plentiful, they don't have to be stored, and they don't have to be transported very far. However, at the end of our growing season, most of our fresh fruits and vegetables reach us by train or refrigerated trucks from warmer states. Some foods, such as bananas, are only grown in other parts of the world. Foods from other places tend to cost more; however, most are available to us for a price. If you have the money, you can have whatever food you want.

[Show a series of locally produced foods and foods from other places, underscoring the world connections our families have. Use the globe to show origins and travel routes.]

[Next, show a series of articles of clothing.] Because we live in a four-season climate, we need both warm and cool clothes. Often, the materials for our clothes come from other parts of the world (e.g., silk, cotton). Also, sometimes they are manufactured in faraway places because of cheap labor. [Examine the articles of clothing to identify their manufacturing locations (e.g., shoes from Spain, blouse from India, jacket from Hong Kong).]

[Show pictures from other parts of the world.] Some parts of the world are heavily influenced by local geographic factors. One example is Greece. [Locate the Greek Islands on the globe.] Greece has many islands, so a lot of Greek people own fishing boats and make their living by fishing or building fishing boats for others to buy.

Another example is Botswana. [Point out Botswana on the globe. Show a picture of women in Botswana.] These people have little money so they need to depend on the local resources. The women spend their time building houses out of mud and clay and the men tend the cattle. Often, the men have to leave their families for a part of the year to find land with good grazing for their cattle.

Sometimes people choose to do things simply—and with local materials—based on their beliefs and values. [Select a children's literature book about the Amish, Mennonites, or other subculture that has chosen a simple lifestyle. Your selection will depend on your community.]

[Tell your "story" about how geography influences family life, focusing on careers and recreational activities. Explain that your career/profession exists all over the world, but you'd need to settle in a place where English was the first language, where there would be enough people to have large schools, where there was an opening for an elementary teacher, and where other family members could find work. Show photos and provide examples underscoring how your family is influenced by geographic factors.]

[Describe the local area in terms of recreational activities available. Explain their connections to local physical features (e.g., lakes, rivers, hills and slopes) and to climatic conditions such as warm weather for hiking, fishing, boating, or swimming, and cold weather for snowmobiling, skiing, and so on.]

Climate and physical features influence family choices and decision making; however, people who have adequate financial resources can eat almost any food, purchase almost any building material, buy almost any type of clothing, and enjoy almost any type of recreation anywhere in the world. People from other places who have adequate resources can do likewise. That is why you may meet people from Germany at a nearby beach or people from Japan at the shopping mall.

Activity

At the conclusion of the "story," ask the class to collectively or individually complete the following open-ended statements, which serve to summarize the lesson.

"Some families depend on geographic features because _____

_____.

An example we learned about was _____

_____.

Families may live far away from where construction materials for their houses are produced because _____.

Our families get foods from _____ because

_____.

My family's clothing may come from _____ because _____.

Examples of how my family is connected to the world include _____

_____

_____."

Summarize

- Physical features and climatic conditions influence family life—the ways families do things and the choices they make.
- Families in our part of the world today (if they have adequate resources) can secure foods, articles of clothing, and building materials for their shelters from almost any part of the world.
- There are places in the world where families remain dependent on local resources for satisfying their basic needs. Sometimes this lifestyle is by necessity and other times it is due to choice.

Assessment

Have the class brainstorm the list of geographic factors (e.g., climate, physical features, location) that influence family living and the choices families make. The list should be recorded on the white board. Then ask each student to explain (by completing a chart) how these factors affect families around the world (see Table 2).

Optional After completing the chart, the students may choose to illustrate it.

TABLE 2 Geography Influences Family Living

GEOGRAPHIC FACTORS	HOW FAMILIES ARE AFFECTED
1. Climate	1. Families need to buy clothes suited to the climate.
2. Physical features	2.
3. Location	3.

Home Assignment

As a means of personalizing the lesson and making it more meaningful, have students interview their parents to determine how geography influences their family. Send home copies of Figure 9 to help students with their interview.

Dear Parents,

Our class is learning about how climate and geography affect the way we live. Please allow your child to interview you regarding geographic influences on your family life. We have enclosed an interview schedule for you to complete. The major ideas we are focusing on include the following:

- In our country, families often live far away from where their food or materials for their shelters are produced or where their clothes are manufactured; however, if these items are shipped long distances, they usually cost a lot more.
- Climate and physical features influence family activities (e.g., recreation, available jobs, family decisions such as construction materials for shelters, local produce for eating, etc.).
- There are some places in the world where people still produce most of their own food, build their own houses out of materials produced locally, and make their own clothes. Usually these places are found in developing parts of the world; however, some people, such as the Amish, choose this lifestyle based on their beliefs and values.

Thank you!

Sincerely,

FIGURE 8   Model Letter to Parents

1. How has the geography (climate/physical features, plains, hills, lakes, rivers, etc.) of our state influenced your family's choices about your jobs/careers?

_____

_____

_____

_____

2. How has the geography of our state influenced your family's choices about recreation? _____

_____

_____

_____

3. Describe other ways in which geography has influenced your family's lifestyle.

_____

_____

_____

_____

_____

4. What products does your family purchase from other states or countries? List and locate.

Product	Place of Origin
a. _____	_____
b. _____	_____
c. _____	_____
d. _____	_____

5. Explain why your family is able to get these products from around the world.

_____

_____

_____

_____

FIGURE 9   Geographic Influences Interview Schedule

Lesson 6

. . . .

Family Celebrations

Resources

- Globe
- Calendar
- Props depicting celebrations: birthday cake; tangerines; rice cakes; lucky money pocket; candy; flowers; carp kite; kimono; tobe; mideastern foods; traditional Thanksgiving foods; hanukkiya (Jewish candleholder also known as menorah); latkes (Jewish pancakes); green, black, red candles/holder for Kwanzaa
- Photo of local mosque

Children's Literature

Chocolate, D. (1992). *My First Kwanzaa Book*. Orange, NJ: Scholastic.

Kindersley, B., & Kindersley, A. (1997). *Celebrations: Children Just Like Me*. New York: Dorling Kindersley Publishing.

Kripke, D. (1997). *Let's Talk About the Jewish Holidays*. New York: Jonathan David.

Rendon, M. (1996). *Powwow Summer*. Minneapolis: Carolrhoda.

General Comments

The emphasis of this lesson is on family celebrations around the world. Families share languages, customs, traditions, and values, and it's often the sharing at special times that binds family members together. In this lesson, students will examine a select set of examples that illustrate family celebrations around the world. You might substitute other celebrations based on the composition of the class. The use of family and other local resources for this lesson is encouraged.

Point out that not all families of a given culture adhere to the same traditions and customs. Also, family circumstances sometimes prevent participation in celebrations.

General Purposes and Goals

To help students: (1) understand and appreciate that families share languages, customs, traditions, and values and that often these are made very visible through planned parties or celebrations; (2) understand that celebrations often bind family members together; (3) understand and appreciate their individual family customs, traditions, and values; and (4) develop respect for the diverse customs, traditions, and values of their classmates and other people who live in their community.

Main Ideas to Develop

- Families share languages, customs, traditions, and values. Often these are made visible through planned activities on special days.
- Families across the globe participate in celebrations. Some are similar to our celebrations while others are very different.
- Celebrations tend to bind families—provide a sense of connectedness/wholeness/ specialness.
- Respecting diversity results from learning about it and experiencing it.

Teaching Tips from Barbara

I found that creating a table comparing the different family celebrations helped to keep the information organized. I used a question to head each column: "What celebration?" "When?" "Who celebrates?" and "What do they do?" The resource book *Celebrations* was a particular favorite of my students. They often picked it to read and review on their own.

Starting the Lesson

Discuss the results of the home assignment. Begin the lesson by explaining that one celebration that many children throughout the world have in common is their birthday. Children in different cultures celebrate in different ways. Show photographs of your (teacher's) birthday celebrations growing up. (Optional: Bring in your favorite cake—the kind that your family always provided because it was your favorite. After the lesson, provide samples.) Sing "Happy Birthday" and tell stories about your parties, opening gifts, and other traditions. Elicit input from the students about their birthdays—how they celebrate, what they eat, and so on.

Suggested Lesson Discussion

Even in the United States, birthday celebrations are not all alike (e.g., different types of cakes, different activities or games). Some children have sleepovers; some go skating; some go swimming; some may not be able to have a party because of other family responsibilities, and so on. There are places in the world, however, where people are not educated about time in the same way we are. In these places, children may not know the specific day they were born, so birthdays are not celebrated.

Some children who live in the United States celebrate the way their families did when they lived in other places. For example, Juan's parents are from Mexico. [Locate on the globe.] At his party, children break a piñata. Candy and toys fall out of the piñata and the children at the party receive them as treats. People in Denmark hang flags outside their homes on their birthdays. In Russia, people celebrate with a birthday pie. In Japan, the third, fifth, and seventh birthdays are the most important. On those birthdays children often wear their native kimonos as a part of the celebration. [Show photographs from *Celebrations: Children Just Like Me* (pp. 4–5) of how children all over the world celebrate birthdays.] They may wear their native costumes for the special day, and most eat snacks, play games, and sing to celebrate the day.

[Continue showing pictures from *Celebrations: Children Just Like Me.*] For one year the photographer and writer team Barnabas and Anabel Kindersley traveled around the world meeting children and talking to them about family celebrations and festivals that they enjoy. [See pp. 60–64, "Meet the Authors."] They share these in four sections of the book categorized by the seasons of the year. We are going to look at one or two from each season. [Based on the composition of your class, you may want to add or delete accordingly.]

Chinese New Year (pp. 8–9)   Man Po is nine years old and lives in Hong Kong [locate on the globe]. One of the world's most colorful celebrations starts on the first day of the Chinese New Year, usually in February, and lasts for fifteen days. One of the traditions is that Chinese families clean their houses thoroughly to rid them of last year's bad luck. A spectacular parade takes place, and usually there's lots of feasting and visiting of family and friends. Celebrations are based on bringing luck, happiness, health, and wealth during the upcoming year.

[Show students some tangerines.] Tangerines are considered the lucky fruits of the Chinese New Year because of their bright color. Odd numbers are unlucky, so the tangerines are always given in pairs. [Show them sticky rice cakes.] Sticky rice cakes called *lin gu* are a special treat that families usually share during this holiday celebration. [Show a replica of the lucky money pockets (red envelopes with good luck messages written in gold).] On New Year's morning, Man Po is given lucky money by her parents and grandparents. All Chinese children and people who are not married receive money in special red envelopes.

Mother's Day (pp. 20–21)   [Show a picture of seven-year-old Matthew from England and locate on globe.] Often English children make special cards and buy their mothers flowers to celebrate the day. They give their mothers boxes of chocolates. In some parts of the world, this is called Mothering Sunday. In the past it was a time to relax the rigid rules of Lent and for working people to go home and visit their mothers. Mother's Day is a special day set aside for children to show appreciation for all the things their mothers do for them—provide love, cook food, wash/iron clothing, and so on. [Show items that are traditionally a part of Mother's Day celebrations (e.g., candy, flowers, cards.]

Kodomono-hi (pp. 30–31)   On the fifth day of May, Kazu and other Japanese boys celebrate Children's Day. [Locate Osaka, Japan, on the globe.] On this day, young boys fly streamers and enormous kites in the shape of a large fish (carp—known for determination and energy) from a large pole in the garden. Inside their homes, families display traditional warrior dolls and bathe their children in iris leaves. The main purpose of the festival is to demonstrate the qualities of strength and determination. On this day, boys wear kimonos—the traditional dress for both females and males. At birth, Japanese boys are given a set of samurai dolls [show picture]. The samurai were courageous Japanese warriors. The dolls represent strength and fearlessness. On Kodomono-hi, families display the warrior dolls.

Optional The girls also have a special day. Girl's Day occurs on March 3 and is known as Hine Matsuri. It is a day dedicated to dolls—either dolls brought especially for the girl or dolls that have been in the family for many years. They are considered too valuable to play with, so they are displayed in the best room of the house [see doll display, p. 17]. The dolls represent Japanese values such as calmness and dignity and are set as examples for young girls to follow. Some Japanese believe that a person's illness or bad luck can be transferred to a doll. They therefore hold a special ceremony each year on this Doll Day. Families that are worried about their children's health donate dolls to the shrine. Shinto priests offer special prayers and then throw the dolls onboard wooden ships that they destroy at sea [show pictures, pp. 16–17]. During Doll Day, stores and stalls sell small models of these dolls. Some contain delicious snacks such as tiny cakes [show sample]. Girls dress up in the traditional costume (kimono) as part of the celebration [show kimono/shoes].

[You should be aware of cultural diversity in your classroom and draw on parental resources and other community resources when available.] Not all people of a given cultural heritage (e.g., Japanese) participate in these celebrations or even hold the same beliefs and values. These traditions have long been a part of Japanese culture and learning about them helps us understand the behavior of men and women in Japan—the gender roles they play, and so on.

Ramadan (pp. 36–37) A celebration that occurs in the summer for Muslim families is Ramadan. Dalia lives in Jordan [locate on the globe and show pictures of her in her prayer clothes (p. 36) and in western clothes.] Most people around the world dress much as we do most of the time. However, they wear their native costumes on special days. For example, white robes are worn by Muslims to show that all are equal before their god. Muslims in America, maybe even some in your school, celebrate Ramadan; however, they might not wear their native costumes.

For Ramadan, Muslims fast (avoid food) between sunrise and sunset for one month. On the first day of the celebration, the family attends special prayers at the mosque. [Show a picture of the mosque in your community if one exists.] Females usually pray at home, but on this day women and girls go to the mosque. However, they use a different entrance than the men and boys.

At the end of the fasting period, Muslims have big family meals with lots of special foods. [Have children sample special foods enjoyed at the feast (e.g., labaneh—dried yogurt, or ma'moul—cookies).] During this celebration Muslims give food to the poor, visit relatives, and exchange cards and gifts.

Thanksgiving (pp. 46–47)   This celebration began in North America [locate on the globe]. It's one of our most important festivals. It marks the early settlers' first harvest—a time when they gave thanks for surviving in the new land for a year. [Show pictures of Thanksgiving in the Bronx, New York. Elicit input from students about their Thanksgiving celebrations, noting that not all people are able to celebrate because of family circumstances. Show examples of some of the traditional Thanksgiving foods (e.g., pumpkins, potatoes, squash, cranberries, apples, and turkey), explaining that these were the ones available to the early settlers. Have a sample of one of the traditional foods available for tasting.]

Many winter holidays and celebrations include gifts and candles. [Show picture of children around the world who take part in festivals that occur during the winter months (e.g., p. 48). Underscore the range of dress for the celebrations.] For the purposes of this lesson, we will focus on St. Nicholas Day, Hanukkah, Christmas, and Kwanzaa. [Note: You may want to emphasize other celebrations, based on the make-up of your class. Involve parents and other local resources, always underscoring the major understandings to be emphasized: (1) families share traditions, customs, and values; (2) families learn how to celebrate from each other; and (3) families across the globe celebrate the same things but celebrate in various ways.]

Hanukkah (pp. 52–53)   For many Jewish people, this is their favorite holiday because it represents religious freedom (2,100 years ago). [Show Israel on the globe.] As the story goes, when the Jews returned to their temple to put things back in order after the Syrians (their enemies) had destroyed many holy things inside, they found the Eternal Light no longer lit. It was supposed to burn all the time. The Jews looked for pure oil so they could light it again, but their enemies had also found the oil and spoiled it. Finally, after lots of searching, they found a little jug of unspoiled oil. They thought it was only enough to keep the lamp burning for a day. However, a wonderful thing happened: there was enough oil to burn for eight days, until more pure oil could be found. [Show the class the elaborate candlestick that is used to remind them of this miracle.] During this holiday, when families get together they light candles and recite special blessings before the evening meals. This elaborate candlestick is called the hanukkiya, or menorah. It holds nine candles, eight of which represent each night of Hannukkah. The ninth candle in the middle is used for lighting the others.

In some Jewish families children receive a small gift on each night of the festival. Other families give only one big gift on the first night of Hanukkah. Many people wrap their presents in blue and white paper, which are the colors of the Israeli flag. [Optional: Share latkes—potato cakes that Jewish people make for this celebration. These are made of grated potatoes, onions, flour, and eggs, and fried in sizzling olive oil. The oil represents the oil that burned in the temple lamp for eight days. Show picture of children celebrating Hanukkah.]

St. Nicholas Day (p. 54) This occurs on December 5 and is celebrated by families across eastern Europe [locate this area on the globe and show a picture of Matis, who lives in Slovakia (p. 54)]. Slovakian children including Matis believe that during the night St. Nicholas will come and fill children's boots with treats. Slovakian children carefully polish their boots and place them on the windowsill. They leave the window partly open so St. Nicholas can get in and leave chocolate treats. Coal, potatoes, onions, and devils are sometimes also left in the boot because the children have been naughty. Children use boots instead of shoes so there's more room for treats.

Christmas (pp. 56–57) This family holiday is celebrated around the world. It is a Christian holiday to mark the birth of Jesus Christ. It is celebrated by going to church, singing traditional Christmas carols, decorating trees, family feasting, and gift giving. Cookies, stollen, and fruit cakes are among the goodies eaten at this holiday family celebration. [Optional: Give children samples.]

Kwanzaa Kwanzaa is a holiday of shared harvest, shared memories, and shared beliefs. During this season, African American children often wear brightly colored designs that reflect African art. The holiday period is December 26 to January 1. It's a period of family celebration and reflection. Relatives enjoy time together, eat special foods, exchange gifts, and so on. The holiday centers around the seven principles of black culture: (1) unity—we help each other; (2) self-determination—we decide things for ourselves; (3) collective work and responsibility—we work together to make life better; (4) cooperative economics—we build and support our own businesses; (5) purpose—we want to restore our people to their traditional greatness; (6) creativity—we use our minds and hands to make things; and (7) faith—we believe in ourselves, our ancestors, our future. Each day of Kwanzaa is dedicated to one of the seven principles.

Optional [*Powwow Summer* by Marcie R. Rendon is an interesting book with beautiful photographs. It describes Native Americans celebrating the circle of life with ceremonies of singing and dancing around a drum. Today these ceremonies are called powwows, and one is held somewhere almost every weekend all summer. The book introduces the reader to the Downwind family, who goes on the powwow trail with its children every summer.]

Activity

To summarize the lesson, ask the students to close their eyes and think about one new thing they learned about family celebrations. Have them signal with "thumbs up" when they are ready to share. Encourage students to expand on previous peer responses or provide an idea shared for the first time rather than just repeating earlier statements.

Anticipated responses include families everywhere celebrate; celebrations bring families together; family beliefs determine how they celebrate; not all families of a given culture celebrate the same way; birthday is almost a universal day for celebration (but there are places in the world where people do not think about time in the same way we do and therefore individuals may not know their exact date of birth).

Summarize

- Families celebrate around the world.
- Families decide what and how to celebrate.
- Not all families from the same culture celebrate in the same ways.
- Families share languages, traditions, customs, and values. Often these are made visible to others through celebrations.
- Celebrations tend to bind people together.

Assessment

Provide each student with a sheet of paper numbered 1–10. Ask each student to place a + by the number if the statement is correct and a – if it is incorrect.

  –   1. People everywhere celebrate their birthdays in the same way.

  –   2. Everybody celebrates his or her birthday.

  +   3. Most children around the world wear clothes much like ours most of the time.

  +   4. Sometimes children—and even adults—wear special clothes for special holiday celebrations.

  –   5. Muslim children, even in America, might celebrate Ramadan by praying and feasting from sunrise to sunset.

  –   6. All Japanese boys everywhere celebrate Children's Day.

  +   7. Mother's Day is celebrated in many cultures. Flowers, candy, gifts, and special treatment of mothers are usually a part of that special day.

- 8. If you lived in China you would be forced to celebrate Chinese New Year.
+ 9. People in many parts of the world celebrate Christmas.
+ 10. Hanukkah is an eight-day holiday celebrated by Jewish people.

Home Assignment

Ask each family (in advance) to be thinking about a favorite celebration. Ask each family to identify one tradition or custom it would like the child to share with classmates. Encourage the family to send photos, artifacts, or food to add meaning and interest to the presentation.

Dear Parents,

We have been learning about family celebrations across the globe as a means of providing a sense of connectedness/specialness. Please discuss with your child ways in which your family celebrates. Prepare your child to share one tradition or custom that your family enjoys as a part of celebrating. Photos, artifacts, or a food item will be welcomed. We will use the responses during our next class discussion. Thank you!

Sincerely,

FIGURE 10   Model Letter to Parents

Lesson 7

. . . .

Our Family Ancestors: Immigrants to the New World

Resources
- Globe
- Photo album
- Photograph representing ancestors
- Graphic depicting ancestry
- Word cards: ancestors, immigrant, generation, family customs
- Question cards: Why did people immigrate to America? How were their lives different from ours? Why did people from the same country tend to settle close together? What did you learn about your teacher's ancestors?
- Time line
- Our Family Ancestors: Parent Interview Information Sheet (Figure 12)

Children's Literature
Maestro, B. (1996). *Coming to America, the Story of Immigration*. New York: Scholastic.

General Purposes and Goals
To help students: (1) understand and appreciate the contributions of their ancestors; (2) realize that some of their customs and traditions probably originated with their ancestors; (3) realize that their ancestors immigrated to America from other parts of the world; and (4) understand and appreciate how life for their ancestors was very different from that of their immediate family.

Main Ideas to Develop
- Ancestors are all the people in your family, starting with your parents, who were born before you. These relationships are often shown on a graphic known as a *family tree.*
- All families have ancestors represented around the globe.
- Immigrants are people who come to a new land to make their home.
- Life for our ancestors was very different from ours.
- Often our family customs and traditions originated with our ancestors who immigrated to America from other parts of the world.

Teaching Tips from Barbara

I sent the home assignment to the students' families several days before this unit so that I was sure to have the information to use with the lesson. Then I started the lesson by pointing out and marking on a world map where my ancestors were from. At the end of the lesson, I added stickers to the map that showed where my students' ancestors were from.

Starting the Lesson

Share the results of the home assignment. Begin the lesson by sharing old photos of one or more of your ancestors. Ask the students what questions come to mind when looking at the photos. Responses might include Who is it? When did this person live? Where did this person live? Why is this photo in our album? Introduce the word *ancestor* and explain that it means a family member who lived in the past.

Introduce the graphic (family tree) depicting your family, illustrating how you are related to your ancestors. Have students locate the individual whose photograph you have shown (e.g., great-grandfather). For the purpose of this lesson, focus on one or two individuals and briefly explain your relationship to the others.

Great-grandmother —
Great-grandfather — Grandmother

Great-grandmother —
Great-grandfather — Grandfather

Mother

You, the child

Great-grandmother —
Great-grandfather — Grandmother

Great-grandmother —
Great-grandfather — Grandfather

Father

Identify the ancestor and indicate where she or he lived by locating it on the globe. Explain how most ancestors who immigrated long ago came to the United States by boat, crossing the ocean and arriving after many weeks—possibly months—to begin a new life in a new land (Note: This took place long ago—after the Pilgrims arrived. Point out the period on the time line.) Explain that most of the recent ancestors of American children were born here, but some came by ship or plane from across the oceans or by car or on foot from Canada or Mexico.

Suggested Lesson Discussion

America is a nation of immigrants—people who come to a new land to make their home. All Americans are related to immigrants or are immigrants themselves. [Introduce the book *Coming to America, the Story of Im-*

migration by Betsy Maestro. Read the section that highlights early immigrants and the challenges they experienced. Following are key points from the book to emphasize.]

Long, long ago, there were no inhabitants in the Americas. During the Ice Age, people crossed the land bridge from Asia to Alaska in search of food. As the years passed, descendants of these early hunters spread out all over North and South America. While some continued to roam the open lands, others settled in small villages and later built cities. These were the people who were here when Columbus arrived. He called them Native Americans because he thought he had sailed to India. Today they are called Native Americans or American Native Americans. After Christopher Columbus crossed the Atlantic Ocean, other explorers came in search of land and riches for their countries, and in time settlers followed the explorers' routes and came to make new homes in America. They hoped for freedom and for opportunities to enjoy better lives. Besides these immigrants who chose to come to America, many other people were brought here against their will and forced into slavery.

By about 1700, thousands of people had arrived. People who came from the same country usually stayed together because they spoke the same language and tended to share the same values. Many gained freedom and a better life, but many others, including the Native Americans and millions of Africans, lost both.

With the influx of newcomers to America, the United States government in 1892 opened an immigration center on Ellis Island, near New York City. The purpose was to control the number of newcomers to America and make sure they were in good health, would work hard, and would stay out of trouble—that is, be good citizens in their new homeland.

[Return to your explanation of where your ancestor settled. Use a U.S. map to point out the location. Describe what he or she did for work, and what his or her spouse did. Explain family life: transportation, communication, recreation, and so on. Describe one or more family traditions that have been passed on from one generation to another. Use the graphic to review terms such as *ancestor* and *generation,* and show the "connections" to your immediate family. If the custom or tradition has been modified with each new generation, use the graphic, pictures, and/or dramatic explanation to point out the changes that have occurred over time.]

[Pique the students' interests by posing these questions: I wonder how many countries are represented in the classroom? Where do you suppose your ancestors are from? What did they do for work when they came to America? How were their lives different from ours? What customs or traditions do you enjoy based on your ancestry? Tell the students that they will have the opportunity to get answers to these questions through their home assignment.]

Activity

To summarize the lesson, have the class create two group journal entries: "Coming to America" and "Our Teacher's Ancestors," using an open-ended sentence format.

COMING TO AMERICA

During the Ice Age people <u>crossed the land bridge to America in search of food</u>.

As years went by <u>descendants of the early hunters spread out across America</u>.

After Christopher Columbus crossed the Atlantic Ocean, other explorers came in search of <u>land and riches</u>.

Many people from many countries came in search of <u>freedom</u>.

Many people, however, didn't come to America by choice. In fact, there were people from <u>Africa</u> who were forced into slavery.

People continued to come to America and finally in 1892 the United States government opened Ellis Island as a center for immigration

OUR TEACHER'S ANCESTORS

Our teacher's ancestors settled in _____. They came from _____. They did _____ for work. One of the special family traditions that they shared with their relatives and continue to practice is _____.

Summarize

- All of us have ancestors who immigrated to America from other places.
- Immigrants are people who came to a new land to make their home.
- Life for our ancestors was very different from ours today.
- Often our family customs and traditions originated with our ancestors.

Assessment

Ask each student to select a partner. Hold up word cards and have pairs talk about the concept or question. Include for the pair assessment the following concepts and questions: ancestor; immigrant; generation; family customs; Why did people immigrate to America?; How were their lives different from ours?; Why did people from the same country tend to settle close together?; and What did you learn about your teacher's ancestors? Randomly select students to share their responses.

Home Assignment

Have students interview family members to learn about their ancestry after they have read the group journal entries "Coming to America" and "Our Teacher's Ancestors." Send home copies of Figure 12 to help students conduct their interviews.

Dear Parents,

We have been learning about family ancestors and the influence they often have on our lives. I have asked your child to read our class journal entry that describes my ancestors.

Please allow your child to interview you about your family ancestors. A Parent Interview Information Sheet is enclosed. We will use the responses during our next class discussion. We would also like to encourage you and your child to make a family tree—at least a partial one representing one parent's ancestors. Talk about the special things your child has learned from individuals represented on the family tree. Describe a family custom or tradition that has been passed down from one generation to another that you enjoy either regularly or on special occasions. Prepare your child to share it with his or her peers during social studies class. Thank you!

Sincerely,

FIGURE 11 Model Letter to Parents

Questions to Parents

1. What country (countries) represent your ancestry? _____

_____

2. Identify at least one immigrant ancestor (e.g., father's grandfather).

_____ What do you know about his or her past (e.g.,

Where did he or she grow up?)? _____

_____.

3. What did he or she do when he or she came to America? _____

_____.

4. Where did he or she settle? _____

5. Why did he or she settle there? _____

_____

6. What did he or she do for work? _____

7. What did the family do for recreation? _____

8. How was his or her family life different from yours? _____

_____

_____

_____

FIGURE 12   Our Family Ancestors: Parent Interview Information Sheet
© 2002 by Janet Alleman and Jere Brophy from *Social Studies Excursions, K–3: Book Two*. Portsmouth, NH: Heinemann.

Lesson 8

. . . .

Recent Immigrants to America and Their Family Practices

Resources
- Pictures of recent immigrant families to the United States
- Globe
- Photos, pictures, artifacts representing a recent immigrant's family story
- Storyboard
- Family or community representative to share the recent immigrant's story
- Table 3: Family Comparisons Chart (April's Family and My Family)

Children's Literature
Kuklin, S. (1992). *How My Family Lives in America*. New York: Bradbury.

General Comments
This lesson is especially appropriate for classrooms that have children whose parents did not grow up in America and still have a lot of connections to their homeland (or, better yet, children who themselves have only recently arrived in America). This learning opportunity will recognize families who practice many customs, traditions, and perhaps even the language of their homeland.

General Purposes or Goals
To: (1) help students understand and appreciate the lifestyles of recent immigrants to America; (2) provide students with the opportunity to learn firsthand from one or more of their classmates and their families about the traditions, customs, and perhaps language that they brought to America and continue to practice at home.

Main Ideas to Develop
- Some families still have relatives who live in other countries.
- Many children your age have at least one parent who did not grow up in the United States.
- Often the traditions, even the language, that are remembered from a parent's childhood in another place are kept alive in America because of recent immigration.

Teaching Tips from Barbara
For this lesson I used a Venn diagram to compare April's family life to my family life. My students use them frequently in math and literature

lessons. After starting with a character in a book and then my life, I asked students who are recent immigrants or are children of recent immigrants to add their thoughts. Each time I've taught this lesson, I've had a few students that fit the description.

Starting the Lesson

Discuss the results of the home assignment. Then explain to the class that this lesson is especially relevant for students who have recently welcomed a child from another part of the world into their classroom or a child who has at least one parent who did not grow up in the United States. If such individuals exist in your classroom, draw on them and their families as primary resources for this lesson.

Other options are to use children's literature, or photos, pictures, and a storyboard, to introduce and describe one or more recent immigrant families and their family practices. An excellent source is *How My Family Lives in America* by Susan Kuklin. The families represented are from Senegal, Puerto Rico, and China. Their stories emphasize the everyday ways in which heritage is transmitted: stories, songs, games, language, and special occasions. They show the importance of choice and adaptation in family and cultural identity.

Suggested Lesson Discussion

[The following is a sample vignette for the storyboard or puppet presentation. This information was drawn heavily from the final section of *How My Family Lives in America*.] My name in America is April. I also have a Chinese name, Chin (Ching), which means "orchid." Both my parents were born in Taiwan, off the coast of mainland China. My father came here to go to school in California and my mother came later with her family. Because my brothers and sisters and I were all born in America, we are called Chinese Americans. We continue to speak some Chinese. At home we also practice our Chinese writing. [Show pictures of her father and mother and the characters that represent those words. Explain that Chinese words aren't made with letters, rather with their own special marks.] On Mondays through Fridays, I go to a public school and on Saturday I go to a Chinese school to practice reading and writing in Chinese.

At the Chinese school I enjoy eating cold sesame noodles. I eat them with a fork, but my grandmother's parents in Taiwan eat them with chopsticks. I also enjoy eating American foods with my family. One of my favorites is pizza.

At night I have homework to do. After my homework is finished, I often watch television and sometimes munch on french fries from nearby fast-food restaurants. My very favorite after-homework activity is a family game called chi chiao bang (chee chow bang). In America it is sometimes called tangram. To play, you move seven different shapes to build a new shape. I think it is lots of fun, even though it is very difficult. It's a game passed down to my family by my great-grandparents. I enjoy both the Chinese traditions that my father and mother brought with them to America and my American ways/habits (American school, television, french fries, pizza, etc.). I realize that many other children my age have at least one parent who did not grow up in the United States. In other words, they are recent immigrants to America. I am glad to enjoy both Chinese and American ways.

Activity

Have each student think about how his or her family is similar to April's family and how it is different. Have each prepare a comparison chart, using simple words or phrases (see Table 3). Encourage students to use words posted around the room as prompts for spellings.

TABLE 3   Family Comparisons Chart

APRIL'S FAMILY	MY FAMILY
Her parents are recent immigrants to America. They were born in Taiwan.	My parents were both born and raised in the United States.
Two languages (Chinese and English) are spoken in her home.	Only English is spoken in my home, unless some family member is learning another language.
April and her family enjoy foods from both Taiwan and America.	We tend to eat foods from America. Once in a while we will go to an ethnic restaurant to enjoy food from another country.

Summarize

- Many children your age have at least one parent who did not grow up in the United States.
- Often the traditions, even the language, are remembered from a parent's childhood in another place, and are kept alive in America.
- A tradition is something that is done in a certain way for many years.
- Many families choose to continue to practice certain customs and traditions from their ancestors.

Assessment

Have each student close his or her eyes and think about one important thing that he or she has learned during the lesson. Have them signal with "thumbs up" when they're ready to share with the class.

Home Assignment

Encourage each student to share his or her comparison chart focusing on April's family and his or her family. Then ask family members to talk about and list the things they have learned from recent immigrant families that live in their neighborhood or perhaps attend their place of worship or work where they do. Have students bring the lists to class for group sharing.

Dear Parents,

We have been learning about recent immigrants to America and their family practices. Encourage your child to share what she or he learned about April, whose parents recently immigrated to America from Taiwan. Then as a family talk about and list the things you have learned from recent immigrant families that live in your neighborhood (or families you have met through social organizations or through your work). We will use your responses in our next class discussion. Thank you!

Sincerely,

Figure 13   Model Letter to Parents

Lesson 9

Families Teach and Learn

Resources
- Photos, pictures, artifacts that illustrate types of teaching and learning that usually occur in the home
- Figure 15: Families Teach and Learn Chart
- Email address of another teacher somewhere in the world
- Computer

Children's Literature
Leedy, L. (1998). *Who's Who in My Family*. New York: Holiday House, Inc.

Monk, I. (2001). *Family*. Minneapolis: Carolrhoda Books, Inc.

Senisi, E. (1998). *For My Family, Love, Allie*. Morton Grove, IL: Albert Whitman & Co.

General Comments
This lesson will underscore the power of the family as a resource for teaching and learning. Students will come to realize that families everywhere teach their members a range of skills as well as knowledge about their heritage.

General Purposes and Goals
To help students: (1) understand and appreciate what they can be taught by members of their family; (2) appreciate and apply what they learn from members of their family; (3) experience feelings of self-efficacy/empowerment as a result of what they learn from their families; and (4) realize that families everywhere are a valuable resource for learning.

Main Ideas to Develop
- Members of groups learn the social behavior of their groups.
- Family members teach one another many things: how to behave; cooking skills; habits such as brushing your teeth, washing regularly, and dressing neatly; how to play certain games; how to fix things; how to do certain things such as play a piano, sew, and count; and so on.
- Family members can teach younger members about their family history, ancestors, and heritage.
- Family reunions are times for families to get together. Often family members share stories about the past. These occasions are great learning opportunities for younger members.
- Families all over the world are great resources for learning about family life.

Teaching Tips from Barbara

I began this lesson working with the family trees of my students and myself. Many of my students find it difficult to understand the relationships between the people in their families. For example, your aunt is also your parent's sister and your grandparent's daughter. I sent Figure 15 home as a home assignment. It's very straightforward and simple to fill in.

Starting the Lesson

Discuss the home assignment from the previous lesson. Then, ask students to silently study the display of pictures that represent types of teaching and learning that usually occur in the home. Ask students to think about the kinds of teaching and learning taking place in the pictures. Who seems to be doing the teaching? The learning? Why? Then elicit examples of the types of teaching and learning that the students have experienced at home. Encourage them to name types that are not illustrated in the pictures. List them on the white board.

Suggested Lesson Discussion

[Begin describing to the class the kinds of teaching and learning that went on in your home when you were a child. Even today as an adult, you learn from your parents and from other family members as well as from many other sources, and they learn from you. Use the chart in Figure 15 to guide your explanation. Incorporate photographs, pictures, artifacts, and vignettes into the explanation to the class about what you have learned from your family.]

Family members teach one another many things: how to eat; how to behave; habits such as always washing your hands before eating, avoiding coughing in anyone's face, and being quiet when other people in the house are trying to sleep; how to play certain games; how to do certain things such as ride a bicycle, play basketball, and sew; and knowledge about their history and their heritage.

Optional   [This is a place where you might decide to focus on kinship relations—connections among family members. You can illustrate by describing your family tree. Explain that you learned about your relatives from your parents. A children's book titled *Who's Who in My Family* by Loreen Leedy provides an authentic explanation, although it includes fanciful illustrations that we recommend avoiding during the introduction of a new big idea.]

Who's Who in My Family is a story about the students in Ms. Fox's class who make family trees. They learn how their aunts, uncles, grandparents, and cousins are related to them. They also learn the meanings of the words *stepbrother, stepsister,* and *stepparent.*

It's fun to discover facts about past and present relatives. You can collect this information about your family, then share it by making a family tree. A family tree is a chart that lists your ancestors and gives information about them. Most family trees include direct-line relatives —parents, grandparents, and great-grandparents.

Family trees usually include the following information for each person: full name (last name first), date and place of birth

Optional   This lesson is also the place were you might elect to talk about family reunions—get-togethers that often are filled with learning opportunities for the younger members. They hear stories about their family members and often enjoy special foods that certain family members are recognized for.

An excellent book by Ellen B. Senisi titled *For My Family, Love, Allie* sets the stage for a family reunion and the preparations surrounding it. Allie, the young girl in the story, finds a way to share a gift she makes for other family members. Visuals used by the author also convey the message that some families have people of more than one race.

Activity

Explain to the students that families everywhere teach and learn. Introduce the term *pen pal* and inform the students that they will have the opportunity to share what they learned about their teacher's family and what they learn from their families with a class in _____. Then they will ask the students in that class to share information about their teacher's family as well as their families. Arrange for an email exchange. Some classes may be able to extend the experience to individual students. The class will write an informal letter to be transferred via email to their pen pal class. The final paragraph will include a set of questions they want answered.

Activity

Distribute copies of Figure 15: Families Teach and Learn Chart to each table of students. Explain that they are to recall their teacher's "story" about what she or he has learned from his or her family. Have them use the categories to recall all the ways their teacher's family served as a resource. Use the completed chart to underscore the main ideas developed during the lesson.

Summarize

- Family members teach one another many things, including how to behave, skills, habits, how to play certain games, how to do certain things, and knowledge about their history and heritage.
- Family reunions are times for families to get together and share stories about the past.

- Families all over the world are great resources for learning about family life.

Assessment

Have each student select two items from the completed Families Teach and Learn Chart about his or her teacher that are the same as two things he or she learned from his or her family. Have individuals write two short paragraphs explaining more about them. For example: "Healthful Habits—learned to brush my teeth three times a day and if possible after each meal. My dentist says I won't have so many cavities if I take care of my teeth. My mother lets me pick the toothpaste because some kinds taste sort of bad." Have them share the responses with the class.

Encourage students to share with their families what they have discussed in this lesson, especially as it relates to their teacher. Also, encourage them to share the paragraphs they wrote about themselves and the things they have learned that are similar to their teacher's "story." Send home blank copies of Figure 15 for families to complete. Have them underscore the question at the bottom: What new thing do you want to learn from your family?

Dear Parents,

We have been discussing family members as teachers of many things. I have enclosed a chart illustrating several categories of activities that individuals learn from parents, grandparents, brothers, sisters, and other family members. Your child has learned about my family and what it taught me. Now, I would like you as a family to complete the chart. Make sure you discuss the question at the bottom of the sheet. We will use your response during our next class session. Thank you!

Sincerely,

Figure 14   Model Letter to Parents

BEHAVIOR	HEALTHFUL HABITS	HOW TO MAKE THINGS	HOW TO FIX THINGS	HOW TO DO THINGS	INFORMATION ABOUT MY FAMILY
1.	1.	1.	1.	1.	1.
2.	2.	2.	2.	2.	2.
3.	3.	3.	3.	3.	3.

What new things do I want to learn from my family? _____

_____

_____

_____

_____

_____

_____

_____

FIGURE 15 Families Teach and Learn

Lesson 10

. . . .

Family Rules and Responsibilities

Resources
- Word cards: Spoken Rules, Unspoken Rules
- Bulletin board: "Family Rules and Responsibilities"
- Pictures depicting rules
- Word cards and pictures and photos identifying types of rules to consider: space, time, possessions, work, family customs
- Pictures and photos illustrating family responsibilities
- Family Panel (parents to discuss family rules)
- Figure 17: Types of Family Rules Chart
- Figure 18: Family Responsibilities
- Baseball questions (ranging from easy to very hard) relating to family rules and responsibilities

Children's Literature
Berry, J. (1987). *Every Kid's Guide to Family Rules and Responsibilities*. Chicago: Children's Press.

General Comments
This lesson examines family rules and responsibilities. It identifies spoken and unspoken rules that can serve as guidelines for how to act and what to do. The lesson underscores the idea that every family is different, so each family needs to make its own rules. Categories for consideration include rules about space, time, possessions, work, play, habits, and customs. The need for consequences will also be examined.

General Purposes and Goals
To help students understand and appreciate: (1) the importance of family rules and responsibilities; and (2) likenesses and differences that exist among families regarding their rules and responsibilities.

Main Ideas to Develop
- Rules are guidelines that tell people how to act and what to do.
- Spoken rules are talked about and agreed upon by people who must follow them.
- Unspoken rules are not talked about, but the people who must follow them usually know that they exist.
- Every family is different and needs to make its own rules.
- Categories to consider include space, time, possessions, work, play, habits, and customs.

Teaching Tips from Barbara

I sent home a note asking students to brainstorm and list several family rules. I put each rule on an index card and then for the class lesson, we sorted the rules according to the categories. I created a poster for each category. We added other new rules to the posters for each category, especially categories without many rules.

Starting the Lesson

Begin the lesson by having the children share the results of their homework assignment. Then, lead into a discussion about the importance of rules at school and in the classroom and why we need them to tell us how to act and what to do.

Suggested Lesson Discussion

Just as we have rules at school, we need rules at home. In both places, there is more than one person—more than yourself. We need to think about others. Not all families have the same rules because families are different. The family members are different ages, have different beliefs, have different work schedules, live in different kinds of places, remember and practice different behaviors from their upbringing, and so on. Whatever the rules and responsibilities of your family, you need to know what they are and what the consequences will be if you don't follow them.

[Read the book *Every Kid's Guide to Family Rules and Responsibilities,* underscoring the following key points.] There are two kinds of rules: The first are spoken rules that are talked about by the people who must follow them. [You might begin explaining rules in your household. For example, "A spoken rule in our family when I was growing up was 'You must be in bed by 8:30 on a school night.' Another was 'No television until all homework is done.'"] What are spoken rules in your family? [Elicit responses from the students and write them on the white board under the label "Spoken Rules." Discuss the fact that not all families have the same rules.]

Unspoken rules are rules that are not always talked about, sometimes not even agreed upon. However, people who must follow them, such as family members, usually know that the rules exist. For example, if you came home from school and found a beautifully frosted cake on the kitchen counter, you'd know not to cut a big slice for yourself. Or, if you were playing ball in the backyard, you'd know not to play near the windows. [Elicit unspoken family rules from students. List them on the white board under the "Unspoken Rules" category.]

Spoken rules are usually better because they explain exactly what is and isn't acceptable behavior. Otherwise, you might unintentionally break a rule (e.g., "No one said I couldn't have a piece of cake." "No one told me I shouldn't play near the windows.").

Family members need to get together on a regular basis and talk to one another about spoken rules and discuss individual and group responsibilities. There are at least six categories of rules. [Use pictures and photos to illustrate the categories. Later, students will have an opportunity to add more pictures to the categories.] The categories are (1) rules about space (what areas in and around the home are OK to be in and what areas are off limits, what activities are appropriate in what areas, and when and where family members are allowed to go when they leave home); (2) rules about time (rules that tell family members when things happen, when things can and can't be done, and when things need to be finished); (3) rules about possessions (what each person owns, what owners can and cannot do with their belongings, how to borrow and return things, and what must be done in case the borrower loses the owner's things, abuses them, or breaks them); (4) rules about work (who is supposed to do certain tasks, what work needs to be done, when the work needs to be done); (5) rules about play (whom family members can play with, what can be played with, when play is appropriate, and locations where certain play can take place); and (6) rules about family habits and customs (what family members can and can't do when they are together, how customs and traditions will be celebrated, and how often family members can expect to follow the customs and traditions).

[After you have led an interactive class discussion and students have added examples to the categories, repeat the point that not all families have exactly the same rules because of differing circumstances.] Consequences may have to be imposed if rules are broken repeatedly. This may mean some sort of punishment such as canceling play time, a time-out, withholding allowance, and so on.

There are other family responsibilities besides following the rules. [Use pictures to illustrate family responsibilities]. Among them are earning the money to pay for family needs, shopping for family needs and wants, paying the family bills, taking care of small children and pets, preparing the meals, doing the laundry, organizing and cleaning the living quarters, taking care of the cars (washing them, getting gas, getting them serviced), taking care of things in the household that get broken, and looking out for one another. Because so many tasks need to be done to keep the family functioning, it's a good idea to find jobs that each person can do to encourage each person to contribute. When family members participate in positive ways, they feel empowered. [Encourage students to add pictures to illustrate the range of family member responsibilities.]

Sometimes family members shirk their responsibilities, so that other members have to do more than their share. Also, sometimes family members break the rules. In these instances, families experience problems or conflicts. These need to be addressed so that families can return to functioning properly. [Note: The next lesson will introduce students to strategies for managing conflict.]

Activity

Invite two or three parents to serve as a panel and talk about family rules in their homes. Give each student a copy of Figure 17. Ask each student to listen for examples that fit into each category and to place a button (or other specified object) in the appropriate box every time he or she hears an example. At the conclusion of the panel discussion, review with the students what they learned, examples of rules that panelists provided, and patterns that emerged among the panelists. Then as a class, list responsibilities that the panelists described, using copies of Figure 18.

Summarize

- Rules are guidelines that tell people how to act and what to do.
- Families, just like classrooms, need rules, and the people who make them up need to assume responsibilities.
- Families vary regarding their rules and responsibilities.

Assessment

Play Baseball: Prepare four levels of questions in advance. Develop lists of questions reflective of the goals and main ideas. Question difficulty should range from easy (base hit) to very hard (home run). Teams are identified and players decide if they want to try for a base hit, double, triple, or home run. Points are assigned according to level of difficulty. For example, a base hit = 1 point; a home run = 4 points. [Observe who selects what type of question. Keep a record of correct responses.] Sample questions:

1. What is an example of a spoken rule?
2. What is an example of an unspoken rule?
3. Why do families need rules?
4. When do family members need to be responsible?
5. What kinds of rules do families need to consider?
6. What is one rule about space that a family might have? About possessions? About time?
7. Why do families have different kinds of rules?
8. What is one rule your family has? Why?

Home Assignment

Have each student take home a blank copy of Figure 17 and the copy of Figure 18 that he or she filled out about the parent panelists. Encourage families to complete both and discuss why their family needs those specific rules and what are the consequences of not following the rules.

Dear Parents,

We have been learning about family rules and responsibilities. I have enclosed a chart illustrating several categories of family rules. As a family, list rules you have that fall into each category. Discuss why your family has them and the consequences of not following them. In red, add any rules that you think your family needs. Discuss why.

Then read the list of family responsibilities we learned about at school. Please discuss and list on the back of your sheet the responsibilities that family members in your household have. (Optional: Identify who is the responsible party for each of the tasks.) Your child may wish to draw pictures to illustrate each category. We will use your response during our next class session. Thank you!

Sincerely,

FIGURE 16   Model Letter to Parents

RULES ABOUT SPACE	RULES ABOUT TIME	RULES ABOUT POSSESSIONS	RULES ABOUT WORK	RULES ABOUT PLAY	RULES ABOUT FAMILY HABITS

FIGURE 17   Types of Family Rules

Family members have many responsibilities. Among them are the following family rules: going to school; earning money; shopping; and so on.

Our class developed this list after listening to our family member panelists.

1.

2.

3.

4.

5.

6.

7.

8.

9.

10.

11.

12.

13.

14.

15.

16.

17.

18.

19.

20.

21.

22.

23.

24.

FIGURE 18   Family Responsibilities
© 2002 by Janet Alleman and Jere Brophy from *Social Studies Excursions, K–3: Book Two.* Portsmouth, NH: Heinemann.

Lesson 11

· ·

Strategies That Enhance Family Life

Resources

- Chart displaying guidelines for a class meeting
- Chart displaying guidelines for a family meeting
- Rules for problem-solving triad
- Examples of telephone message pads, charts, "to do" lists, daily calendars, and so on that can be used for organizing, recording, and communicating family matters
- Optional: upper-grade peer mentors to serve as resources for this lesson

Children's Literature

Berry, J. (1987) *Every Kid's Guide to Family Rules and Responsibilities.* Chicago: Children's Press.

General Comments

The essence of this lesson is exposure to tools that enhance family functioning. Students will have simulated opportunities to use the strategies and they will be encouraged through their home assignment to share them with their families.

General Purposes or Goals

To: (1) help students understand and apply the school class meeting model to family matters; (2) introduce students to strategies for managing conflict; (3) introduce students to techniques for organizing and keeping track of family matters (e.g., chores, errands, special holidays, school calendar of events, school lunch menus, correspondence from school, etc.); and (4) encourage students to apply the strategies learned at school to enhance family life in their individual home situations.

Main Ideas to Develop

- A family meeting is a get-together for family members to help them discuss their rules, problems, future recreational activities, and other issues.
- Families need strategies such as a problem-solving triad to help them manage conflict.
- There are many techniques for organizing and communicating family matters.

Teaching Tips from Barbara

I had three kids work with me ahead of time to practice a family meeting. Then, in class, we performed the role-play and then listed the steps to follow as we reviewed the family meeting. Next, I picked another group of students to repeat the same role-play. This time we stopped at each step along the way to talk about the steps. At the end of the lesson, I sent home a sheet explaining the techniques and strategies. That way, families will be sure to discuss the strategies and choose one to try. I also had each student return a sheet explaining the strategy his or her family tried.

Starting the Lesson

Begin the lesson by having the students share the results of their home assignment. Then explain that a very good approach for discussing family rules and other family matters is the family meeting.

Suggested Lesson Discussion

A family meeting works like the classroom meeting but on family matters. Similar guidelines apply. [Briefly review with the class the guidelines used for class meetings. Then post the guidelines for a family meeting, as they are being discussed.] Meetings should be attended by all who reside in the household; distractions need to be avoided; every meeting needs to have an agenda (family members list the subjects they want to have addressed at the meeting); family members need to agree when the meeting will start and when it will end; every meeting needs to be led by a chairperson; the meetings need to be conducted in an orderly fashion; and the decisions that are made need to be approved by the parent(s) who lives in the household. [Discuss the similarities between a class meeting and a family meeting.]

[Role-play conducting a successful family meeting. You should act as the chairperson.] One of the uses of family meeting time is teaching its members strategies for managing conflict.

[Model the format and rules for using the problem-solving triad. Explain that one of its key benefits is to get lots of ideas (potential solutions) out in a hurry. The object is to select one and try to implement it.] The model works best with three people (person with the problem and two others).

RULES FOR PROBLEM-SOLVING TRIAD

Step 1: Person with the problem explains the problem. She or he is the only one that talks. The others listen. (1 minute)

Step 2: The two listeners clarify the problem by asking questions. (1 minute)

Step 3: The person with the problem listens and is not allowed to speak as the other two brainstorm—giving as many possibilities as they can for solving the problem. (2 minutes)

Step 4: Pause—Person with the problem thinks about all the possibilities for solving it. No one is allowed to talk. (1 minute)

Step 5: Person with problem explains how she or he will try to solve the problem, using one of the ideas suggested during brainstorming. (1 minute)

[Note: Time allocations can be changed. Just make sure this occurs at the beginning.]

[A sample scenario is: Dishes have been piling up in the sink for several days. Mother, whose job it is to do the dishes this week, according to the family job schedule, was called out of town unexpectedly. Beth, the middle schooler, is really mad because she's supposed to set the table and has no silverware available. It's all dirty. John, the second grader, says, "Dishes aren't my job." Dad says, "I'm not doing them. I had to work late and I'm exhausted." Beth says, "Let's try to solve this using the problem-solving triad." Role-play and debrief this situation.]

[Discuss the solution as well as the strategy. Send home a copy of the rules for the problem-solving triad for families to review, explaining that you use it to solve classroom problems and it works equally well with family problems. It's one strategy for managing conflict.]

It is important to have strategies for solving problems. It is also important to have techniques for organizing and communicating family matters. [Show and describe examples of a family chore chart, errand chart, technique for recording telephone messages for other family members, routine checklist or "to do" list, daily/weekly calendar/planner, etc.]

Families should have designated places to put important papers, messages, correspondence from school, and so on. Using problem-solving and organizational strategies helps your family function more effectively, accomplish more, feel more comfortable and relaxed, and have more time for recreation.

Activity

Have each student select one thing a family can do to function more effectively (e.g., family meeting, problem-solving triad, job chart, daily calendar) and then have upper-grade mentors (who have been in the class during the lesson) pair up with students and write one paragraph describing the idea. Have students share the responses with the class.

Summarize

- Family meetings are a great model for conducting family business.

- Problem-solving strategies are useful tools for managing family conflicts.
- Organizing and communicating family matters (e.g., school calendar, family chores, telephone messages, etc.) can make for family harmony and productivity.

Assessment

Have students pair up and role-play one thing a family can do to function more effectively (in preparation for discussing it with their families at home).

Home Assignment

Encourage each student to discuss with family members the paragraphs she or he wrote with the assistance of the upper-grade mentors.

Dear Parents,

We have been learning about strategies that enhance family life. Please read the paragraph describing something that a family might do to function more effectively. We use these techniques at school to ensure that our classroom is harmonious and productive. Talk about the strategies you use at home for the same purposes. If you are seeking additional ideas, your child may have some suggestions. Thank you!

Sincerely,

FIGURE 19   MODEL LETTER TO PARENTS

Lesson 12

Family Assistance

Resources
- Brochures that describe local services (e.g., library, fire department, postal service, Ronald McDonald House, Red Cross, etc.)
- Map of local community
- Paper symbols and pins for marking local sites on the map
- Photos of local services "visited"

General Comments
This lesson will provide students with a realization that family life is supported by government agencies as well as independent organizations. Services such as fire protection, mail delivery, road repair, and library facilities are available as a result of taxes families pay to the government. Some of the other agencies that help families in crisis are the Red Cross, Ronald McDonald House, Habitat for Humanity, and Salvation Army.

General Purposes or Goals
To: (1) help students develop an understanding of and appreciation for the kinds of support that are available to families in their local community; and (2) provide students with an opportunity to become familiar with one or more local organizations that assist families in crisis.

Main Ideas to Develop
- Governmental agencies help families meet some of their needs (e.g., fire protection, postal service, welfare, public library). Monies to support these agencies come from taxes people pay.
- Many agencies and locally supported groups are available to help families during crises (Red Cross, Ronald McDonald House, etc.).

Teaching Tips from Barbara
I started with a map of our neighborhood. Then we "took a trip" around the neighborhood, marking several places that provide assistance to families. After a few examples, the students were able to name several more places themselves. Students then worked in pairs to write about the places on the map. The sections were compiled and made into a book including a table of contents. The book was kept for students to share at the Family Night.

Starting the Lesson
Discuss the results of the home assignment. Then explain to the class that today you are going to take an imaginary trip around your local community.

Suggested Lesson Discussion

We are going to visit some special places—places that help families who have certain kinds of needs. Some of these needs occur regularly (e.g., having roads in good repair, mail delivery, public library), and some occur only under special circumstances (e.g., assistance from fire department). We will also visit places that assist families in crisis, such as the Red Cross and Ronald McDonald House. [The services available in your local area will dictate your selection. You might consider having a representative of one of the organizations serve as a presenter to the class. Remember, the emphasis is on the services available to families.]

[The following content is intended to be resource material. The services you include and the sequence in which you address them will be based on your particular circumstances.]

We will begin our imaginary trip by driving or walking from our school to the _____. [Use symbols and words. Attach them to the local map with pins.]

Fire Department   This organization provides families with help when a fire occurs on their property or when there's an emergency and an ambulance is needed. People who work there are highly trained and always ready. There are people on duty twenty-four hours a day. They are paid for from some of the tax money that your families pay to the government.

Police Department   This organization is also supported by the taxes your family pays to the government. The police officers are hired to help keep the families in the community safe.

U.S. Postal Service   This organization is responsible for making sure that the mail gets to and from your homes. The people who work here are paid with money collected from the sale of stamps and also with some of the money that your families pay in taxes to the government.

Public Library   Some tax money is used to help buy books and computers for the library. Additionally, families pay a small fee to secure library cards so the library workers will get paid, the library can be heated, and so on. This service is one of choice. Families who use it can borrow lots of books regularly for little or no money.

Many other services are available in our community, some financed through taxes and some paid for directly by your families.

Some services that we will visit today on our imaginary trip are available to families in crisis (e.g., a family whose house burns and who is left without clothes or a place to sleep; a family whose child becomes very ill and needs to stay near the hospital, etc.).

Red Cross   This organization is supported by grants and donations. Families who have extra money or household goods that they don't need often give them to the Red Cross so that when a family calls in crisis, money and goods are available to help. The Red Cross also receives donations of blood, so if a family member is in a bad accident and needs blood, the family can call the Red Cross. There's a blood bank at the hospital to take care of the problem.

Salvation Army   This organization, much like the Red Cross, is supported by grants and donations. Families who have extra money, clothes that no longer fit, or other unwanted items can donate to this organization. Around the holidays in malls and on street corners, volunteers with kettles and ringing bells work to raise money for this organization, so when a family is in crisis because of job loss, flood, fire, or some other dilemma it can call the Salvation Army. It can also visit the Salvation Army Store, where donated clothing can be bought at low prices.

Ronald McDonald House   [Note to teachers: This project in our local community is briefly described as an example of local support for families with sick children. Use examples of high interest in your local community.] A Ronald McDonald House is currently being built at this site. It will be a seven-bedroom house near a local hospital. This house will provide inexpensive overnight lodging close to a hospital in an emotionally supportive environment. It will have a full-time, live-in, paid house manager, but all the other workers will be volunteers. The house will be paid for by donations. Children can contribute. In fact, an interesting project that your class might consider is collecting soda pop cans. These are collected and sold to a scrap dealer, who in turn gives us dollars that we can contribute to the Ronald McDonald House.

Local Church   Local churches in the community provide social services to individuals and families. People do not have to be members to receive aid. Members of the churches donate time, money, and goods to help others. Some local churches serve as homeless shelters; some provide hot meals for individuals in need.

Activity

Conclude the imaginary field trip with a nutritious snack in the imaginary park across from the last stop. Using the map and the symbols, review where you went and what you learned.

Optional   In the teacher's snack pack, have a list of questions that focus on the goals. Ask the questions at the appropriate site and seek "thumbs up" as a signal that students are prepared with a response.

SAMPLE QUESTIONS FOR "QUIZ IN THE PARK"

1. What types of assistance can the police department provide our family?
2. How can we get that kind of help?
3. How do the police officers get paid?
4. Why should my family be concerned with the fire department? When would it ever need that department?
5. Why is the Ronald McDonald House important?
6. Why should my family know about the Red Cross?
7. How can my family help the Red Cross? Why might it want to do that?
8. What does the Salvation Army offer to families?

Summarize

- Every community has a variety of services that assist individuals and families.
- Governmental services are provided through taxes that families pay.
- There are agencies and locally supported groups available to help people in crisis.

Assessment

As an integrated social studies and literacy authentic assessment, the class could prepare a brochure describing places in the local community that provide services for families in need. Make sure that a local map with the sites identified is included. The students could share their "product" with their families and other members of the community. They could also be prepared to share it with new students who move into the community and their families as part of the orientation package.

Home Assignment

Have students share their brochure with family members. Have them review the map of family assistance sites. Ask family members to locate an additional place on the map where families can go to get assistance. Have them mark the site on the map, include the address and phone number, and talk about the type of assistance the family can receive there. Be sure the students return the homework for group sharing at the next class session.

Dear Parent,

We have been learning about agencies that help families meet some of their needs. As a class project, we prepared a brochure describing places in our local community that provide services. Please review the brochure, including the map. Locate and mark one additional place on the map where families can go to get assistance. Include the address and telephone number and talk about the type of assistance a family can receive there. We will discuss your response during our next class session. Thank you!

Sincerely,

Figure 20   Model Letter to Parents

Lesson 13

Family Support

Resources
- Fine arts school resource personnel
- Pictures of artists, athletes, or other individuals that you emphasize during the lesson
- Prints illustrating the work of Grandma Moses, Pablo Picasso, and/or Carmen Garza
- Cassette tape or CD of Mozart's music
- Tape of "I Have a Dream" speech by Martin Luther King Jr. (optional)
- Photos of local individuals who have "unusual" stories that illustrate family support that they have received in order to pursue dreams at a very young age

Children's Literature
Garza, C. (1990). *Family Pictures*. San Francisco: Children's Book Press.

Lepscky, I. (1982). *Amadeus Mozart*. Hauppauge, NY: Barrons.

Lepscky, I. (1984). *Pablo Picasso*. New York: Trumpet Club.

Mattern, J. (1982). *Young Martin Luther King, Jr. "I Have a Dream."* Mahwah, NJ: Troll Associates.

Rachlin, A. (1992). *Famous Children: Mozart*. Hauppauge, NY: Barrons.

General Comments
This lesson features unique family situations in which enormous support and early recognition of talent resulted in gifts to others. The lesson will introduce Mozart, Martin Luther King Jr., Garza, Picasso, and Grandma Moses. You might select from this list or use others, depending on the class composition. The fine arts consultants in the school district can suggest a range of resources.

General Purposes or Goals
To: (1) help students understand and appreciate the importance of family support; (2) introduce students to examples of family members whose talents were recognized early and because of family support became artists, political leaders, or other important figures whose contributions we continue to appreciate today; and (3) pique students' interest in thinking about their own talents and hobbies.

Main Ideas to Develop

- Families can support one another in a variety of ways (e.g., encouraging members with unusual talents and providing special assistance).
- Families can help their members develop interests, hobbies, and talents that will enrich their lives.
- In some cases, interests/hobbies/talents become careers. In other cases, they add quality of life to leisure time.

Teaching Tips from Barbara

To help make this lesson more meaningful to my students, I included two athletes from our area who have become successful due in part to family support. However, I also made it a point to feature famous folks from several different fields including music, the arts, and leadership. As a start to the journal writing, I had students draw self-portraits depicting themselves successfully doing a job in an area they enjoy. Then it was easier for them to write a journal entry with the open-ended starters.

Starting the Lesson

Share and discuss the results from the home assignment. Then begin by showing examples of art prints and helping the students listen to music by Mozart or another child prodigy.

Suggested Lesson Discussion

One of the most important things families can provide to their members is support. [Elicit and list examples of family support that your students have experienced.] During this lesson you will be introduced to some famous artists and/or a political leader whose talents were recognized and supported when they were children and as a result, we all enjoy today.

[Have students listen to music by Mozart. Elicit from the class how his music makes them feel. Then introduce Amadeus Mozart by showing his picture or thumbing through the pages of one of the children's books about him.] His family recognized his talent and interest early. His father, an expert in music, decided to give him lessons even though he was very young. After a while, his father decided to let others know of his talented child. At age seven, when other children were attending school, Amadeus was traveling with his father and sister to all the royal palaces in Europe. He was admired by people everywhere he went. However, he grew tired of travel. Also, his father realized that he had creative qualities that couldn't be developed while he was performing so much—and away from home. So Amadeus and his father decided to return home so he could study. The entire family was happy with the decision. Mozart wrote some of the world's most beautiful music and became one of the greatest composers who ever lived.

Another famous artist is Carmen Garza. From the time she was a young girl, she dreamed of becoming an artist. She practiced drawing every day. She studied art in school and then became an artist. Her family supported her, inspired her, and encouraged her over the years. She is considered to be one of the major Mexican American painters in this country. *Family Pictures,* which contains prints of Carmen's beautiful paintings, is the story of her childhood in a traditional Mexican American community in south Texas [share the book with the students]. Her paintings of her family and community show everyday activities that remain vivid in memory: picking oranges for her grandmother, making tamales with the entire family, and swimming in the Gulf of Mexico.

Grandma Moses [show her picture], a famous painter, had a very different life story. She had a limited education as a young woman, and at age twelve began working on a neighbor's farm. However, she had an obvious interest in art and during her childhood her father provided her with drawing paper and encouraged her to pursue her talent. At first, she chose not to pursue her art interest and instead became the mother of ten children. It wasn't until she was very old and her sons and daughters were raised that she began painting pictures of families doing things together. [Show prints to illustrate the specialness of Moses' work—happy times among families.]

[Use other examples provided by the fine arts coordinator or drawn from local resources that represent family support when members exhibit an unusual interest or talent.] A recent example in a local newspaper described a third grader who is the author of his own cookbook and spent the summer at one of the largest culinary schools in the world. When most children were watching *Sesame Street*, this boy was tuning into TV cooking shows. He was only two years old when he declared, "I want to be a chef." His parents, recognizing his exceptionally high interest, have supported him with their time and money. Students such as yourselves can work on hobbies and pursue your interests starting now. Often these hobbies and interests will remain lifelong pleasures, and for many they will develop into careers.

[Explore with the class your students' individual interests. List them. Invite local community members to serve as mentors to youngsters who wish to pursue their interests or learn special skills. Underscore the satisfaction an individual experiences when engaging in activities that he or she is especially good at and/or enjoys.]

Family support as well as support from other adults such as your teachers, friends, and neighbors help us to reach our dreams. [Return to the music of Mozart. Have each student draw a picture of a hobby, interest, or talent that she or he would like to pursue and be prepared to discuss the special kinds of support that are needed. Have students share the responses with the class.]

Optional   Martin Luther King Jr. was a great American who is known for his work for civil rights. He was born in Atlanta, Georgia in 1929—before most of your grandparents. When he was a little younger than you—age six—his friends' mother told him he could no longer play with her sons because his skin was a different color. He was very upset and ran home crying. His mother tried to console him and help him understand that there were some laws that treated people unfairly (e.g., different schools, segregated restaurants, segregated buses, etc.). These laws really bothered Martin and at a very young age he decided that one day he'd do something to change them. He studied very hard and finished high school when he was only fifteen. Then he went to Morehouse College, where he decided to become a minister.

Shortly after he took over his first ministry, a black woman named Rosa Parks was riding a bus home from work. The bus driver told her to give up her seat to a white man. She refused and was taken to jail. From that day on, Martin helped lead protests to change the laws. He won a peace prize for his efforts for peace and freedom. His most famous speech was "I Have a Dream." He dreamed that someday all Americans would be treated equally.

His parents and other family members supported his interest in working for freedom from the time that he was a little boy.

Optional   Pablo Picasso was a youngster who really wasn't understood by his family. He seemed to be very moody. He collected unusual things such as leaves, pebbles, peach pits, and cherry stalks, and he avoided all the wonderful toys he had been given.

Pablo realized very early in life that no two things are exactly alike—that nature never repeats itself. He kept that idea a secret and yet he cried and shouted when he broke a seashell, for example. His family tried to reassure him that there were others to replace it. He knew better.

Pablo had an incredible imagination and he was forever trying to change everyday reality into something else. One day, he used tomato sauce and made funny scrawls on the kitchen walls; on another day he ruined a living room wall by scratching it with a nail.

Pablo continued to pull all sorts of antics until his father, also an artist, came to realize that he was special. Once his father acknowledged Pablo's talent and encouraged him to paint, he became focused and produced some of the world's most original art. [Share the book *Pablo Picasso* by Ibi Lepscky.]

Activity

Table Talk—Reintroduce the individuals highlighted during the lesson: Mozart, Garza, and Grandma Moses, or others you have included. Ask each table to select one individual and talk about how his or her family provided support and why that support was so important. Then have them complete four additional open-ended statements. Encourage the students to use the word wall to assist with spelling.

Assessment

Have students complete the open-ended statements focusing on family support. Encourage the students to use the word wall to assist with spelling.

1. _____'s family provided support by
   _____.

2. Family support is important because _____
   _____.

3. My special interest, hobby, or talent is _____
   _____.

4. My family supports my special interest, hobby, or talent by
   _____.

5. As an adult, I'd like to use my special interest, hobby, or talent by
   _____.

Home Assignment

Encourage students to share their open-ended statements with family members, then discuss what the family can do right now to support the student's special interest, hobby, or talent.

> Dear Parent,
>
> We have been learning about famous people whose families provided unusual support when they were children. Please read your child's open-ended statements about what she or he has learned. Then discuss how you can support your child's special interest, hobby, or talent. Most will probably simply enjoy these interests as adults although some may follow them as their careers. Thank you!
>
> Sincerely,

FIGURE 21   Model Letter to Parents

Lesson 14

....

Family Living: A Celebration of Our Learning

Resources
- Table 4: Suggested Artifacts for Review
- Family Comment Form (Figure 22)

General Comments

For this lesson, students will have the opportunity to host an open house and share with parents, siblings, grandparents, aunts, uncles, and other relatives what they have learned during the unit. The class will decide on the most important things they learned about family life and what activities they want to engage in with their families.

General Purposes and Goals

To: (1) draw on prior knowledge, understanding, appreciation, and application conducted at home and at school to enhance meaningfulness; (2) revisit and reflect with family members on the big ideas developed about family living; and (3) engage in a family celebration with ethnic foods shared from the diverse family backgrounds.

Main Ideas to Develop
- A child defines *family* on the basis of personal experience.
- The family is an important social organization in society.
- Families come in all sizes.
- Families come in all ages. (Young families have young children. Middle-aged families often have teenage children, and older families often have grown-up children and grandchildren.)
- Most families are based on kinship—that is, the members belong to the family through birth, marriage, or adoption. However, some groups that are not based on kinship think of themselves as family because they share a home or feel ties of affection. For example, foster children and their foster parents are not related by adoption, birth, or marriage; however, they live together and consider themselves a family.
- Everyone you know lives in a family.
- There are many different kinds of families: nuclear, extended, adoptive, single-parent, blended, and foster.
- Families are more than groups of people. They consist of individuals who are related by birth or connected by a legal document such as a marriage certificate or adoption papers, and who share common values and provide love and support.

- Family members do not always live in the same home.
- A change is something that does not stay the same.
- Family members change (e.g., baby to teenager).
- Families change in size and composition.
- As families change, so do their needs. These changes may occur because of death, divorce, birth, marriage, adoption, and also on.
- Family life has undergone a variety of changes over time. Early families were dependent on the land—their immediate surroundings—whereas today, families depend on people and places across the globe.
- Long ago, families raised their own food, built their own houses, and made their own clothing out of the local resources available.
- Before people used machines or modern means of transportation, they had fewer choices about what they ate, what their homes were made of, and what they wore.
- There was less standardization and more individual creativity involved in meeting family needs in the past (e.g., homemade cake, knitted dress, etc.).
- With modern technology, multiple career options, local and global availability of resources, multiple recreational options, multiple social options, modern means of transportation and high-tech communication, modern family life has changed dramatically.
- Families often live far away from where their food or materials for their shelters are produced or where their clothes are manufactured.
- Climate and physical features influence family activities (e.g., recreation, available jobs, family decisions such as construction materials for shelters, local produce for eating, etc.).
- There are some places in the world where people still produce most of their own food, build their own houses out of materials produced locally, and make their own clothes. Usually, these places are found in developing parts of the world; however, some people, such as the Amish, choose this lifestyle based on their beliefs and values.
- Families share languages, customs, traditions, and values. Often these are made visible through planned activities on special days.
- Families across the globe participate in celebrations. Some are similar to our celebrations while others are very different.
- Celebrations tend to bind families—provide a sense of connectedness/wholeness/ specialness.
- Respecting diversity results from learning about it and experiencing it.
- Ancestors are all the people in your family, starting with your parents, who were born before you. These relationships are often shown on a graphic known as a family tree.

- All families have ancestors represented around the globe.
- Immigrants are people who come to a new land to make their home.
- Life for our ancestors was very different from ours.
- Often our family customs and traditions originated with our ancestors who immigrated to America from other parts of the world.
- Some families still have relatives who live in other countries.
- Many children your age have at least one parent who did not grow up in the United States.
- Often the traditions, even the language, that are remembered from a parent's childhood in another place are kept alive in America because of recent immigration.
- Members of groups learn the social behavior of their groups.
- Family members teach one another many things: how to behave; cooking skills; habits such as brushing your teeth, washing regularly, and dressing neatly; how to play certain games; how to fix things; how to do certain things such as play a piano, sew, and count; and so on.
- Family members can teach younger members about their family history, ancestors, and heritage.
- Family reunions are times for families to get together. Often family members share stories about the past. These occasions are great learning opportunities for younger members.
- Families all over the world are great resources for learning about family life.
- Rules are guidelines that tell people how to act and what to do.
- Spoken rules are talked about and agreed upon by people who must follow them.
- Unspoken rules are not talked about, but the people who must follow them usually know that they exist.
- Every family is different and needs to make its own rules.
- Categories to consider for rules include: space, time, possessions, work, play, habits, and customs.
- A family meeting is a get-together for family members to help them discuss their rules, problems, future recreational activities, and other issues.
- Families need strategies such as the problem-solving triad to help them manage conflict.
- There are many techniques for organizing and communicating family matters.
- Governmental agencies help families meet some of their needs (e.g., fire protection, postal service, welfare, public library). Monies to support these agencies come from taxes people pay.

- Many agencies and locally supported groups are available to help families during crises (Red Cross, Ronald McDonald House, etc.).
- Families can support one another in a variety of ways (e.g., encouraging members with unusual talents and providing special assistance).
- Families can help their members develop interests, hobbies, and talents that will enrich their lives.
- In some cases, interests/hobbies/talents become careers. In other cases, they add quality of life to leisure time.

Teaching Tips from Barbara

For this lesson, students review the material and information from the unit while preparing for the Family Night. You can review the posters and charts as you put them up for the Family Night. Students can create invitations to take home and also brainstorm a list of things to tell and show their families. As a group, have students watch as you demonstrate what a tour would look like. I also had my students practice introducing their family members to me.

Starting the Lesson

Elicit assistance from parents in setting up the ethnic food "sampling center." Having the foods labeled by name and country represented would be helpful. Incorporating some background about the foods and locating the countries represented could add a nice touch to the introductory remarks about the celebration.

Remind families that during this open house, the students will be showcasing what they have learned during the unit. Families will be guided by their children to various centers/exhibits set up to represent the unit. Family members are encouraged to engage in dialogue with their children and to add insights to their understanding.

Large-Group Discussion and Activity

At the conclusion of the event, encourage each student to take his or her Family Living booklet home, along with a Family Comment Form about the celebration for parents to complete and give to their child (see Figure 22).

Optional   Discuss the most exciting things that happened to you during your family celebration.

TABLE 4 Suggested Artifacts for Review

LESSON	SUGESTED ARTIFACTS
Lesson 1 What Is a Family?	• Bulletin board display of structures and functions
Lesson 2 Many Kinds of Families	• Family graph that tells the story of your class and the types of families represented and/or display of photos depicting kinds of families
Lesson 3 Families Change	• Collection of photos, pictures, and words showing family changes across time with additional blank cards available for changes families want to add
Lesson 4 Family Life Has Changed over Time	• Time line representing changes in family living over time
Lesson 5 Geographic Influences on Family Life	• Sample responses to students' assessment regarding geographic factors and how families are affected
Lesson 6 Family Celebrations	• Display of family traditions, customs, and games and ethnic food sampling center
Lesson 7 Our Family Ancestors: Immigrants to the New World	• Graphic depicting ancestry and book titled *Coming to America: The Story of Immigration*
Lesson 8 Recent Immigrants to America and Their Family Practices	• Book titled *How My Family Lives in America* and/or photos, pictures, and artifacts representing a recent immigrant's family story
Lesson 9 Families Teach and Learn	• Families Teach and Learn Chart (Figure 15)
Lesson 10 Family Rules and Responsibilities	• Types of Family Rules (Figure 17)
Lesson 11 Strategies That Enhance Family Life	• Family problem-solving triad
Lesson 12 Family Assistance	• Brochures, local map, and photographs representing local community services available
Lesson 13 Family Support	• Book and photo display expressing unusual stories that illustrate family support that children have recieved to pursue their dreams at a very young age

Dear _____,

The highlight of the celebration for us was _____

_____

_____

_____

_____

_____

_____

_____

_____.

We are especially proud of you because _____

_____

_____

_____

_____

_____

_____

_____

_____

_____.

Signed _____

FIGURE 22   Family Comment Form

Reflecting Back, Moving Forward

. . . .

How has my family changed over time? Can my understanding of these changes influence our family's thinking and considerations for what it might do differently? How can my ideas about our family's practices help in protecting the environment? Might my suggestions help our family be more environmentally sensitive and at the same time save money? Could my knowledge about the media's influences on people's decisions change some of my family's buying habits?

Self-efficacy is a sense of empowerment, of being able to make a difference using what has been learned. It is a state of mind that says, "I can do it! I can contribute. I can decide. I can figure it out." Our experiences with these units have involved not only children but their families. We have been gratified with their response to the home assignments. In our interviews with parents, one overarching theme was their reports of "I can" statements made by their children. We attribute this to four principles associated with self-efficacy that we threaded throughout the units.

1. The content should be emotionally and intellectually comfortable for students so as to provide good places to start. (All children have prior experience with cultural universals, so no student is disenfranchised because of culture, socioeconomic background, or achievement level.)

2. The content should have potential for immediate application out of school.

3. Home assignments should support students' transition from egocentrism to social engagement with family members and other children and adults.

4. The content and learning opportunities should develop students' awareness of their geographical and cultural contexts.

Communication seems, at least initially, to be quite abstract because students' prior knowledge is limited and what they do know is not organized and can be difficult to access. Once they got into it, however, the students were really quite intrigued—and interested in the changes that have taken place ever since their parents were their age. One father commented that his son got the impression that he was really old when he found out he only watched black-and-white TV when he was growing up.

Other parental comments:

- "My son couldn't wait to talk to our neighbors about careers in communication. After talking to the one that lives down the block about his PR job, he's convinced he'd like to have a job like that when he grows up. I reminded him that doing well in literacy will be important."

- "Our daughter has suddenly taken an interest in languages. She's hounding me about finding a camp or class she could enroll in over the summer."

- "Before this year, I've never thought about having children write editorials. The one the class wrote about 'what we can do to make sure special-needs kids feel welcome in our class' really impressed me. After our daughter read it to us, it really got us thinking about our new neighbor's son. We decided the first thing we needed to do was learn about his specialness, instead of avoiding the situation."

- "Our son's home assignment titled Accounting for Myself was tedious but powerful. The truth is that our whole family is becoming conscious of how we spend our time, and if TV is involved, carefully deciding what programs to watch."

- "Our daughter has taken an interest in commercials. I was half-heartedly watching when she suddenly blurted out, 'Is that cereal really that good for you? It's probably more expensive because it's being advertised on TV. They're using the bandwagon technique to get us to buy it!' Wow, I guess I'd better go back to second grade."

- "Our son couldn't wait to rummage around the house looking for maps. I was impressed when he found the blueprints to our house and proudly informed us, 'These are kind of a map.' Then, to top it off, he wanted to do map reading with us instead of watching his favorite television show."

Transportation seems, at least initially, to be a domain for adult decision making. However, students learned that their families make choices within limits defined by resources like money, time, and information, and they began to understand and appreciate the choices people could make, such as owning a car or depending on public transportation, and the trade-offs associated with each. Parents reported that their children were concerned about the choices they made, sometimes recommending that they could save a little money if they planned their errands better. Parents also reported that their children were fascinated with the multiplicity of careers associated with transportation. They developed new connections to neighbors, relatives, and parental friends who worked in the transportation industry and were anxious to use the interview schedule home assignment to interrogate anyone they observed who was connected to transportation.

One parent was taken aback after she heard the UPS truck pull up, the doorbell ring, and her son rush to the door. The next thing she knew, the UPS man was sitting on her sofa while her son conducted an interview. The congenial man in the brown uniform made her son's day! She mused over her son's interest in social studies and his passion for learning more.

Other parental reports included:

- "I must confess I was a bit perturbed when our daughter absolutely wouldn't go to bed until we drove to the airport to interview the car rental agent. She said that during the field trip to the airport, she spotted the car rental counters. While they weren't acknowledged, she secretly decided that she wanted to interview somebody that nobody else would think of. I was impressed with my daughter's poise—and the questions she asked the agent. Obviously, her teacher had her well prepared. The amazing part is that I learned something, too!"
- "As a parent volunteer on the field trip to the airport, I was simply shocked. The students all had their faces pasted to the windows during the entire ride. They were busily identifying transportation types, functions, etc. I was amazed at their level of engagement and their knowledge. They were discussing things I've never even thought of!"
- "We used to have lots of family squabbles on our weekend trips up north. Keeping the kids occupied while traveling in the car has always been a challenge. Suddenly, transportation is the social studies topic and it all changes. I'm amazed at how turned-on kids can get to the things that are part of their lives but they know little about—but have the capacity and want to learn!"
- "The assignments were thought-provoking. It's good for them to realize what we as families are confronted with issues associated with transportation. Maybe I shouldn't admit it, but I suddenly

felt a need to learn more about what's going on in their classroom. I can learn some things too."

The family living unit is filled with connections that children can
make to their own situations outside of school; however, sensitivity to privacy matters is important. We have observed that when the teacher
openly shares her own personal stories, artifacts, and memorabilia and encourages her students to share her life with their families, a sense of "we
are all in this together" emerges and most inhibitions evaporate. This was
obvious on Family Night, our culminating activity for the unit. One parent confessed, "I wasn't sure about that lesson about family structures, but
I soon figured out it was no big deal. After all, even the school principal
explained to the class how her family evolved from a nuclear family to a
divorced single-parent family and now is a blended family because she and
her new husband have a new baby and she has a grown daughter by a previous marriage."

Other parental comments included:

- "My son insisted he's from two kinds of families. I was puzzled.
  He explained that most of the time he lives with me and that
  counts as a single-parent family. However, when I went to California and he stayed with his dad and his new wife and her son,
  he was living in a blended family. At first I was hesitant about the
  whole thing. Then I realized that to him it is simply the way
  things are. Seeing the class graph about many kinds of families
  was reassuring."

- "When our son started asking us about geographic influences, I
  was stumped. The interview guide really helped us. After we got
  going, we found our list was endless. What a great way to begin
  connecting to geography. I never saw that subject's connection to
  my life before. Wow!"

- "History was never my favorite subject. I wish I would have connected with my family when I was my daughter's age. We had so
  much fun talking about how life has changed. My mother lives
  across town, so we drove over to get her input, too. Our daughter
  couldn't believe the contrasts in available toys and entertainment,
  for example. If her interest in history continues, I might consider
  some of the American Girl products. Of course, we'll start with
  books."

- "Rules have always been a somewhat difficult topic in our household. Part of it stems from my son's shared-custody situation. After my son and I did the survey, I asked him to do it with his dad.

Wow! They added in red some rules that they need! Maybe my son and his father are beginning to realize that rules are guidelines to tell people how to act and what to do."

Parents appreciated advance communication about completion dates for home assignments as well as specific directions about expected amounts of input. (One student told his parents that he had to interview at least a dozen people who had careers associated with communication.) A few parents also voiced a desire for more material about the units in general, including the main ideas and the rationales underlying the home assignments to help guide them in expanding their discussions with their children.

Personal efficacy, family impact, and meaningful understandings have been the hallmarks of our experiences with the units. We encourage you to frequently revisit the big ideas drawn from the units to help your students explain life experiences and develop habits of thoughtful conversations about the world around them. Provide parents with the lists of big ideas and provocative questions so they too may experience the luxury of helping their children make connections between book learning and real life, for example, by applying what they learned in school to a television program, retrieving data from the Internet to enhance a lesson, or discussing "how things work" at home and in the community.

References

Chapter 1

Brophy, J., & Alleman, J. (1996). *Powerful Social Studies for Elementary Students*. Fort Worth: Harcourt Brace.

Egan, K. (1988). *Primary Understanding: Education in Early Childhood*. New York: Routledge.

Evans, R., & Saxe, D. (Eds.). (1996). *Handbook on Teaching Social Issues*. Washington, DC: National Council for the Social Studies.

Good, T., & Brophy, J. (2000). *Looking in Classrooms* (8th ed.). New York: Longman.

Haas, M., & Laughlin, M. (Eds.). (1997). *Meeting the Standards: Social Studies Readings for K–6 Educators*. Washington, DC: National Council for the Social Studies.

Harris, D., & Yocum, M. (1999). *Powerful and Authentic Social Studies: A Professional Development Program for Teachers*. Washington, DC: National Council for the Social Studies.

Hirsch, E.D., Jr. (1988). *Cultural Literacy: What Every American Needs to Know*. New York: Vintage.

Krey, D. (1998). *Children's Literature in Social Studies: Teaching to the Standards*. (Bulletin No. 95). Waldorf, MD: National Council for the Social Studies.

Larkins, A., Hawkins, M., & Gilmore, A. (1987). Trivial and Noninformative Content of Elementary Social Studies: A Review of Primary Texts in Four Series. *Theory and Research in Social Education, 15,* 299–311.

National Council for the Social Studies. (1993). A Vision of Powerful Teaching and Learning in the Social Studies: Building Social Understanding and Civic Efficacy. *Social Education, 57,* 213–223. [Also included in the NCSS 1994 Bulletin on Curriculum Standards for Social Studies]

National Council for the Social Studies. (1994). *Curriculum Standards for Social Studies: Expectations of Excellence* (Bulletin No. 89). Washington, DC: Author.

Ravitch, D. (1987). Tot Sociology or What Happened to History in the Grade Schools. *American Scholar, 56,* 343–353.

Roth, K. (1996). Making Learners and Concepts Central: A Conceptual Change Approach to Learner-Centered, Fifth-Grade American History Planning and Teaching. In J. Brophy (Ed.), *Advances in Research on Teaching. Volume 6: Teaching and Learning History* (pp. 115–182). Greenwich, CT: JAI Press.

Chapter 2

Alleman, J., & Brophy, J. (1994). Taking Advantage of Out-of-School Opportunities for Meaningful Social Studies Learning. *Social Studies, 85,* 262–267.

Alleman, J., & Brophy, J. (1997). Elementary Social Studies: Instruments, Activities, and Standards. In G. Phye (Ed.), *Handbook of Classroom Assessment* (pp. 321–357). San Diego: Academic Press.

Alleman, J., & Brophy, J. (1999). The Changing Nature and Purpose of Assessment in the Social Studies Classroom. *Social Education, 65,* 334–337.

Brophy, J., & Alleman, J. (1991). Activities as Instructional Tools: A Framework for Analysis and Evaluation. *Educational Researcher, 20* (4), 9–23.